God and the Evil of Scarcity

GOD

AND THE EVIL OF

SCARCITY

Moral Foundations of Economic Agency

ALBINO BARRERA, O.P.

University of Notre Dame Press
Notre Dame, Indiana

Library of Congress Cataloging in-Publication Data

Barrera, Albino.
God and the evil of scarcity : moral foundations of economic agency /
Albino Barrera.
p. cm.
Includes bibliographical references and index.
ISBN 0-268-02192-9 (hardcover : alk. paper)
ISBN 0-268-02193-7 (pbk. : alk. paper)
1. Economics—Religious aspects—Christianity.
2. Economics—Moral and ethical aspects.
3. Scarcity. 4. Malthus, T. R. (Thomas Robert), 1766–1834.
I. Title.
BR115.E3B35 2005
261.8'5—dc22
2005019769

This book is printed on EcoBook paper.

In thanksgiving for my brother Delfin,

for his filial devotion and fraternal selflessness

CONTENTS

PART III
Scarcity and Profundity in Participation

CITATION CONVENTIONS

Works of Aquinas

De potentia   *On the Power of God*
Citations of *De potentia* give question and article. For example:
De potentia III, 7 = question 3, article 7

De veritate   *Truth*
Citations of *De veritate* give question and article. For example:
De veritate q.5, a.1, ad.9 = question 5, article 1, reply to the ninth objection

SCG   *Summa contra gentiles*
Citations of SCG give book, chapter, and paragraph number. For example: SCG III, 69, #16 = book III, chapter 69, paragraph number 16

ST   *Summa theologica*
Citations of ST give part, question, article, and part of article. For example: ST I, 44, a.1, reply = part I, question 44, article 1, reply; or ST I-II, 49, a.2, ad.3 = first part of Part II, question 49, article 2, reply to the third objection

See References for translations used.

Bible quotations are taken from the New International Version, www.bible gateway.com.

PREFACE

Why would an all-knowing, all-loving, all-powerful, and all-provident God permit a world of material scarcity? The Reverend Thomas Malthus, in his *Essay on the Principle of Population*, describes the human condition as an inexorable state of precarious subsistence because of the disparity between demographic growth and food production. In an effort to reconcile this dismal finding with his belief in a benevolent Creator, he concluded his much-celebrated work with a theodicy that regards want and poverty as instrumental in the formation of the mind. However, his theology was deemed unorthodox in its implications for soteriology, and his theodicy was dropped from all later editions of the book. William Paley and John Bird Sumner eventually reworked Malthus's question and argued for a probationary-state-of-life explanation of scarcity. Besides such early nineteenth-century scholarship, I am not aware of any other sustained analytical effort to address the puzzle of why economic privation is tolerated in divine providence. Theology, philosophy, and economics have still much more to offer on this issue.

Under an overarching framework of faith and reason, this book uses Aquinas's metaphysics of participation and Sacred Scripture's invitation to covenant fidelity and kingdom discipleship as analytical lenses with which to examine the teleology of scarcity. I maintain that the economic agency occasioned by scarcity serves as a venue for partaking in God's goodness, holiness, righteousness, and providence. Scarcity engenders greater depth in such participation in divine perfections and activity.

Chapter 1 summarizes and critiques Malthus's theodicy and briefly outlines its subsequent correction and reworking by Paley and Sumner. Part I draws upon the light of reason to show how economic life serves as a medium for sharing in God's providence. Using Aquinas's ontology, chapters 2 and 3, along with the three appendices, argue that economic agency is perfective as it receives and communicates God's goodness. Chapter 2 describes the nature of goodness and Aquinas's twofold order of the universe. Together, these form the conceptual framework for the philosophical segment of this study. Chapter 3 situates economic life within God's envisioned material sufficiency, which is contingent on free and intelligent secondary causality, a capacity that is specific and proper to humans alone. In light of the mode by which human beings receive and communicate the goodness of God, it argues that economic agency, as a rational activity, is perfective of the person. Scarcity evokes an even more intense participation in God's goodness through economic life. More technical examinations of the different types of scarcity, the nature of goodness, and the a priori metaphysical arguments for material sufficiency are available in the appendices.

Part II relies on the light of faith to evaluate the role of scarcity in God's initiatives on behalf of the human community. Using both the Hebrew Scripture and the New Testament, the four chapters of part II examine economic life as a venue for partaking in God's righteousness. Chapter 4 describes the manner by which God elicits Israel's participation in divine holiness and righteousness through the economic dimension of YHWH's in-breaking in human history. Such invitation is readily discerned in the Law's motive clauses that mark the nation as a distinctive contrast-society despite material similarities in its economic ordinances with those of its Near Eastern neighbors. Scarcity makes the observance of these statutes that much more difficult, and chapter 5 outlines Israel's struggles to live up to them and to expand them further in ways that are demanding but more in line with her covenant election as YHWH's Chosen People.

Using Pauline theology, chapter 6 examines the incarnational and instrumental nature of God's imparted righteousness. Incarnational righteousness communicates what Christ has won for us; instrumental righteousness manifests the Holy Spirit actualizing what Christ has made possible. This chapter outlines how a well-founded understanding of human righteousness must begin with the thoroughly Christological nature of both its juridic and ethical dimensions. Moral agency is not a tension of faith versus good works, but a seamless dynamic between them because both have Jesus Christ as their source, impetus, and object. Economic life, in response to scarcity, serves as a setting for growth in such Pauline righteousness. Chapter 7 appraises the incarnational and instrumental dimensions of economic agency in kingdom discipleship, that is, God's continual call for active participation by believers.

Part III pulls together the philosophical and theological arguments of the preceding two sections. Chapter 8 reexamines the nature of scarcity and summarizes its impact in generating greater profundity as humans partake of divine perfections and activity. The differences between this book's theodicy and those of the nineteenth-century Anglican theologians are outlined in chapter 9. Malthus, Paley, and Sumner viewed scarcity as essential to prodding human beings into activity and enterprise within the context of life seen as a state of probation. In contrast to these earlier theodicies, I maintain that scarcity provides an occasion for taking part in divine providence. The concluding chapter 10 recapitulates the case for material need in the wisdom of God's order of creation. The economic life precipitated by scarcity does not turn out to be that pedestrian after all but serves as an effective channel through which humans respond to God's initiatives and requite divine love.

Using both faith and reason to address the nature of scarcity, this study revolves around two complementary analytical cores: an ontology (part I) and biblical ethics (part II). The metaphysical (part I) and scriptural (part II) sections of this study stand on their own and could be read and understood without reference to the other. Integrating both parts, however, provides a better appreciation for the mutually reinforcing insights of a "faith seeking understanding" on this issue.

Written for theologians, philosophers, social scientists, and policymakers interested in the philosophical and theological foundations of political economy, this book offers five contributions to the literature. First, it advances an alternative account of scarcity in God's order of creation that addresses some of the shortcomings of the Paley-Sumner revision of Malthus's theodicy. Second, it examines the seeming incongruity of scarcity in God's providence through the prisms of both Aquinas's metaphysics and Sacred Scripture. To my knowledge, no one has approached this question from such perspectives. This is methodologically distinctive because most of the literature in philosophical or theological social ethics do not go so far as to lay out the ontological basis for their claims. A strength of this book lies in its employment of parallel metaphysical and biblical appraisals that strengthen each other's conclusions in resolving the puzzle of why an all-loving and all-provident God would permit a world of material scarcity. Third, in grappling with such a theodicy, this study presents foundational concepts essential to formulating a theology of economic agency. In fact, three chapters are devoted to analyzing economic agency in covenant election, in kingdom discipleship, and as a perfective secondary cause. Fourth, economists and philosophers are increasingly attentive to the ontological premises of their economic analyses and discourse (Maki 2001). By showing what natural theology has to offer in this regard, part I and the appendices contribute to this effort. Finally, in arguing that precarious subsistence living is not a natural, universal law (pace Malthus, Paley, and Sumner) and in highlighting the real causality and pivotal role of rational activity, this research articulates both metaphysical and scriptural warrants for activist ameliorative social policies. In particular, it outlines a conceptual justification for interpersonal transfers of economic resources. Chronic material deprivation is not the inevitable lot of human beings; rather, such a dismal condition reflects personal and collective failure in moral conduct. By contesting the policy implications of Malthusian theodicies, this analysis also serves to remind scholars and policymakers of the weighty practical ramifications of the theological and philosophical premises undergirding their approach to social ills. Note, for example, the negative impact of Malthus's principle of population on his era's thinking and attitudes toward poor relief (Waterman 1991a; 1983a). Such a seemingly abstruse question as to why a providential God permits a world of material scarcity has real life-and-death ripple effects.

My thanks to Norbert Lohfink, Walter Brueggemann, Luke Timothy Johnson, J. David Pleins, Ricardo Crespo, Ernest Bartell, Daniel Finn, Stephen Ryan, and Terry Keegan for their encouragement and their critical assessment of different sections of the book. I am unable to incorporate all their excellent suggestions but have tried to accommodate as many as I could given the space constraint. Needless to say, any errors that remain are solely my responsibility. The anonymous referees offered numerous incisive observations and recommendations that greatly improved the manuscript. Barbara Hanrahan, Jeff Gainey, Matt Dowd and the staff of the University of Notre Dame Press have been wonderful, helpful, patient, and efficient throughout the editing and production process. Carol Moran provided excellent proofreading assistance. I owe a deep debt of gratitude to all these good and generous people.

God could have willed into existence an order of creation characterized by a "sustenance without care" (*Kiddushin* 4:14; Danby 1933, 329) where people could easily satisfy their requisite material needs without undue hardship and, more important, without the factious competition attendant to apportioning the limited supplies of the goods of the earth. Moreover, provisioned with all the necessary material means to flourish in life, people could have been freed to devote themselves to the larger questions and more consequential matters of life. Instead of being preoccupied with the prosaic task of eking out a livelihood, humankind could have applied itself full-time to love of God and neighbor. As it is, however, economic life throughout history has been an all-exhausting enterprise, a source of division, an occasion for mutual exploitation, and often even the object of idolatry.

Grappling with the question of why a benevolent God permits a world of material want is, in effect, a struggle to decipher and understand the divine plan undergirding the order of creation. However, it also turns out to be an opportunity to get a better glimpse of the plan's Architect. In other words, discerning God's envisioned economic order reveals much about divine will and personal attributes. In trying to make sense of material exiguity within divine providence, this study has uncovered the paradox of how God proffers within such scarcity a plenitude of gifts: (1) a sacramental instrumentality in effecting divine providence in the lives of those who have yet to partake fully of God's life and (2) a manifold participation in divine goodness, righteousness, holiness, and governance. Indeed, scarcity becomes the occasion for God to provide for us through each other. Far from revealing a tight-fisted, parsimonious Creator, scarcity has turned out to be a testament to a God who never seems to tire of showering humans with unmerited divine benefactions and initiatives, one after another. There appears to be no end to the goodness of God.

CHAPTER 1

MALTHUSIAN THEODICY REVISITED

ESSAY ON POPULATION

In his *Essay on the Principle of Population,* the Reverend Thomas Robert Malthus disagrees with his contemporaries' optimism over human perfectibility.[1] Malthus argues that the human condition is one of subsistence living in which food production, growing arithmetically, cannot keep pace with a population base that increases geometrically. Given the propensity of people to procreate, improvements in wages or standards of living are merely temporary since families whittle away such gains by having more children. Thus, the long-run steady state is one of survival wages; anything above this leads to population growth which in turn depresses earnings back to bare sustenance, while anything below this equilibrium income spells physical death. Malthus discusses the checks, both negative (delayed marriages or abstinence) and positive (misery or death), on such population growth. At the root of these requisite restraints is the limited food-bearing capacity of the earth. The prognosis for such a steady-state equilibrium is extremely pessimistic: a state of vice, deep distress, and precarious subsistence with little or no surplus.[2] Thus, Carlyle (1888–89, 7:84) describes economics as the "dismal science."

In addition to its population dynamics, the *Essay* is also notable for its theodicy.[3] Malthus is not content with arguing for his principle of population. He goes beyond his demographic theory to address why a loving, beneficent Creator would allow such a state to persist. Malthus devotes the last two chapters of the first edition of his *Essay* to reconciling such a woeful economic condition with belief in a provident God.

Malthus maintains that an easy and straightforward rationalization is to specify scarcity as God's way of testing human beings, a state-of-trial theodicy. However, he finds this account problematic because it implies a lack of foreknowledge on the part of God ([1798] 1960, 127). Instead, Malthus proposes a formation-of-the-mind explanation.

Malthus's anthropology is unflattering. For him, people are by nature indolent and need to be prodded into action. Thus, scarcity is necessary because, left on their own, humans are inclined to rest and lassitude.

> The first great awakeners of the mind seem to be the wants of the body. They are the first stimulants that rouse the brain of infant man into sentient activity, and such seems to be the sluggishness of original matter. . . . The savage would slumber for ever under his tree unless he were roused from his torpor by the cravings of hunger or the pinching of cold, and the exertions that he makes to avoid these evils, by procuring food, and building himself a covering, are the exercises which form and keep in motion his faculties, which otherwise would sink into listless inactivity. ([1798] 1960, 128–29)

> [C]onsider man as he really is, inert, sluggish, and averse from labour, unless compelled by necessity. (131)

Using natural theology, Malthus argues that God created a world of scarcity to provide people with reason and incentive to apply themselves in work and striving. It is only through such enterprise that the mind is fully constituted. Malthus justifies the phenomenon of scarcity as the impetus for the "formation of the mind."

> [C]onsider the world and this life as the mighty process of God, not for the trial, but for the creation and formation of mind, a process necessary

to awaken inert, chaotic matter into spirit, to sublimate the dust of the earth into soul, to elicit an ethereal spark from the clod of clay. ([1798] 1960, 127–28)

Malthus's theology in these last two chapters was severely criticized for its heterodox assumptions and implications.[4] There are numerous theological problems in Malthus's theodicy,[5] of which I will discuss nine. First, his views on original sin have significant ramifications for the nature of divine creation. Malthus writes, "The original sin of man is the torpor and corruption of the chaotic matter in which he may be said to be born" ([1798] 1960, 127–28). An immediate consequence of this is that original sin is embedded within God's creation itself as part of human nature. This goes against the more common Christian understanding that there is only one principle of life, the principle of goodness. All of creation is good because God's creative act is entirely good. To implant original sin within the person by design and to rectify it as the mind forms is to juxtapose evil and goodness in the natural state of the person, a view that brings back Manichean and Albigensian dualism.[6] Thus, Malthus's notion of original sin has wide-ranging significance not only for the nature of divine creation, but also for the notion of evil as a mere privation of the good[7] (Augustine 1953).

Alternatively, to avoid changing the definition of evil, one could choose to describe material scarcity, want, and destitution as "good" because of their functional role in God's governance of creation.

Malthus chose solely to "reason up to nature's God" and so was betrayed into a non-solution of the problem of evil. *For in his system everything that is commonly thought of and experienced as "evil" has to be regarded as a necessary part of the providence of God, and hence is not really an "evil" at all, but a "good."* (Waterman 1983a, 201; emphasis added)

This approach, unfortunately, gives rise to other unanswered questions. For example, one would have to account for why material destitution and its accompanying hardships, ill health, and physical death are good to begin with and should not be considered as natural or moral evil. Moreover, why would God choose these as part of the design of the universe? Thus, as Waterman correctly holds, we have not addressed the issue of scarcity at all but have merely redefined it as a good.

Second, there are problems associated with Malthus's anthropology. His assumption regarding the natural state of humans presents an entirely new set of issues. The human mind is in sore need of formation and growth, the very reason why people have to be awakened from their "torpor." Humans (the mind in particular) are presumed to be grossly incomplete at their moment of creation. Waterman (1983a, 200) observes a logical inconsistency in Malthus's reasoning. Evil must first be perceived by the mind if evil is to discharge its function of stirring humans to action. However, the mind itself develops only through the evil that is perceived. There is a circularity in reasoning where the efficacy of evil depends on the prior existence of the mind that in its own turn is itself dependent on the prodding of evil. Furthermore, how can an inert and sluggish person be said to be created in the image and likeness of God (Waterman 1983a, 202–3)?

Third, Malthus's notion of original sin means there is no fall to speak of. Such a view of original sin leaves no room for authentic human freedom. It is not human choice that forfeits original justice since there is no original justice to lose in the first place. In effect, it is divine providence that imposes original sin given its choice of the "sluggish original clay" used in creating humans. The absence of freedom in bringing about original sin absolves human beings of responsibility for such a state. Neither can they be held to account for the ongoing damaging effects of original sin, in particular, further sinful acts. Divine providence, after all, is imperfect and flawed in its original design.

Fourth, Malthus's view of original sin has serious implications for soteriology, the branch of theology that deals with the redemption effected by Jesus Christ. There is no point in talking of salvation as a "restoration" or "recreation" of the human person since Malthus's "growth-of-mind" theodicy presumes a person that is still in-process. There is nothing to be restored, recreated, or transformed to begin with. Moreover, there is no need for forgiveness and redemption. Since torpor, sluggishness, and inactivity are the evils that need to be corrected, humans are fully capable of saving themselves literally through dint of their own work and effort.[8] There is no need for the saving act of Jesus Christ because humans can be "startled" out of their slumber in original sin simply by experiencing want and destitution. As LeMahieu (1979, 470) remarks, "sluggishness is not depravity," and there is no room for Jesus Christ because humans need to be saved from laziness rather than sin. Scarcity and its appurtenant pain are sufficient in effectively spurring humans into action. There is no need for Jesus to die on the Cross. Thus, it is not surprising that there is not even a mention of Jesus Christ in Malthus's entire *Essay*. "Christ is entirely redundant in his soteriology" (Waterman 1983a, 202).

Fifth, there is an unusual role reversal between good and evil. Malthus asserts, "It is highly probable, that moral evil is *absolutely necessary* to the production of moral excellence" ([1798] 1960, 136; emphasis added). Moral evil cannot be a necessary condition for moral excellence, although the former can admittedly occasion a more penetrating experience of the latter. To make moral excellence contingent on evil is to reverse the long-standing juxtaposition of good and evil in Christian theology. Augustine (1953) defines evil as a mere privation of the good. Thus, evil is merely parasitic on the good. Goodness is the primary experience, the absence of which gives rise to evil. Not in the case of Malthus, who makes evil a necessary condition for growth in goodness. If moral evil were the necessary "rite of passage" for moral excellence, then it is moral excellence that is parasitic on moral evil. Furthermore, this also means that moral evil is antecedent to moral excellence. This has unusual consequences for the dynamics of spiritual theology because sin becomes the unavoidable pathway to holiness; there is need to sin first in order to reach the heights of the spiritual life. It also has significant consequences for Christian cosmology's claim of goodness as the sole principle behind God's creative act. Goodness can be neither the exclusive nor even the primary principle of creation since it is itself "absolutely" dependent on evil for its own growth and development. According to Malthus, as a critic puts it,

> Men did not fall from Grace; they rose from the living death of inaction. . . . *The evils that stirred men to activity provided them with an identity, direction, and purpose wholly missing in the "natural" state.* (LeMahieu 1979, 472; emphasis added)

Observe the ironic implication. Evil is the proximate venue and primary cause for bringing about the good (formation of the mind).

Unlike Christian thought in which salvation is effected by grace, Malthusian theology employs evil (want and destitution) as the principal determinant of the new creation. LeMahieu highlights this odd implication in Malthusian thinking:

> Evil was the Prime Mover of the human realm. It was consequently the force behind civilization. *Malthus confronted the potentially embarrassing*

problem of evil by transforming it into a theory of incentive. (1979, 469; emphasis added)

To further illustrate why the role of goodness and evil relative to each other is a consequential matter, consider LeMahieu's concluding paragraph characterizing Malthus's theodicy:

Evil was the *efficient cause* of human creativity and this creativity was the *final cause* of men's happiness, freedom, and greatness. Malthus's theology of scarcity buttressed a morality only vaguely suggested by Calvin. Here at last was the Protestant ethic and the spirit of capitalism. (1979, 474; emphasis added)

Notice the centrality of evil to the point of even being perceived as an efficient cause. Observe too how the formation of the mind as expressed in human creativity serves as *the* final cause in Malthusian thought. This is in sharp contrast, for example, to a Thomistic world in which moral agency is at the heart of an efficient causality that seeks its delight in the good and in which final causality goes beyond human development to find its ultimate rest in God as the Good.

Sixth, flowing from the aforesaid problem on the improper juxtaposition of good and evil is a difference pertaining to the nature of goodness.

A being with only good placed in view, may be justly said to be impelled by a blind necessity. The pursuit of good in this case can be no indication of virtuous propensities. (Malthus [1798] 1960, 136; emphasis added)

Consistent with his view that "moral evil is absolutely necessary to the production of moral excellence" (136), Malthus could be said to have a "compelled theory" of moral development. The person is induced to reach out for the good only after a first-hand encounter with the revulsion of evil. The person is thus "pushed" toward moral excellence by moral evil. Malthus reinforces the need for such a dialectic process in describing the value of contrasting experiences:

An ardent love and admiration of virtue seems to imply the existence of something opposite to it, and it seems highly probable that the same beauty of form and substance, the same perfection of character, could not be generated without the impressions of disapprobation which arise from the spectacle of moral evil. ([1798] 1960, 136)

For Malthus, a full appreciation of goodness comes about only through comparison. Outside of this dynamic, the pursuit of the good can occur only when "impelled by a blind necessity" (136).

In contrast, Aquinas views the *good* as fully capable of eliciting desire and action on its own. God is the Final Good. The perfection in God as Final Cause[9] is so ravishing as to be desirable on its own terms. It is a logical inconsistency for the alluring nature of God to be dependent on the prior experience of evil. Perfection and completeness confer goodness with a desirability all its own. There is no need to endure evil's gross imperfection and incompleteness first in order to imbue goodness with an agreeable charm. Goodness is able to achieve this by virtue of its own qualities. It has within itself an intrinsic power to attract. As it is, in Malthus's formulation, goodness stands out in an appealing mode only when placed side by side and differentiated with the repulsiveness of evil. Malthus's good is thus a "second-best" solution, merely a much better choice than the alternative available. The contrast between Malthus's and this book's theodicy in this regard can be viewed as the difference between a "compelled" and an "enticed" theory of goodness. In my theodicy, there is no need for evil to be the impetus for seeking that which is good because the end that attracts on its own is no less than God as Final Cause.

Seventh, Malthus dismisses the traditional Christian understanding of eternal punishment and judgment. He does not believe in eternal damnation and proposes that minds unresponsive to the stimulus of scarcity simply revert back and mix in again with the original clay from which they came.

[T]hose beings which come out of the creative process of the world in lovely and beautiful forms, should be crowned with immortality, while those which come out misshapen, those whose minds are not suited to a purer and a happier state of existence, should perish and be condemned to mix again with their original clay . . . [thereby] condemning to their original insensibility those beings that, by the operation of general laws, had not been formed with qualities suited to a purer state of happiness. (Malthus [1798] 1960, 140–41)

Such a view of divine judgment means that the gifts of existence and eternal life are not permanent; they are merely provisional. But creatures cannot revert back into non-existence or be "recycled" for the next batch of "original clay." In the first place, human beings are unique and created for their own sake (SCG III, 111). To consign them back to the original matter from which they came is to eradicate such uniqueness. Moreover, God never takes back whatever divine providence gives or does, including the gifts of existence and eternal life (*De potentia* V, 4). God is immutable and does not change.[10] There is neither change nor failure nor need for second "attempts" from God. For creatures to revert back into non-existence for their "misshapen" outcomes is to imply a lack of divine foreknowledge, ascribe temporality to God, and question divine omnipotence and perfection since God makes mistakes after all.[11] Reverting "misshapen" vessels back to the original mix of clay is essentially "annihilationism" (Waterman 1983a, 199–200).

Eighth, Malthus circumscribes divine omnipotence. His drawn-out process of mind-formation implies that God needs time to complete divine work.

> God is constantly occupied in forming mind out of matter and that the various impressions that man receives through life is the process for that purpose. (Malthus [1798] 1960, 128)

Moreover, as already mentioned, his idea of misshapen vessels reverting back to the original mix of clay implies that divine creation is subject to miscalculations (Waterman 1983a, 199–200, 202–3). Furthermore, he sees incompatibilities between divine omnipotence, on the one hand, and divine benevolence and omniscience, on the other. Malthus is caught in a web of inconsistencies as he grapples with reconciling these seemingly disparate divine qualities (Pullen 1981, 41–42). On the one hand, he argues that, given divine omnipotence, God could have created a fully formed tree but chose not to in order to provide humans with occasion for work and exertion. In a later passage, however, he delimits divine power by surmising that God too may be subject to certain set ways of doing things.

> And unless we wish to exalt the power of God at the expense of his goodness, ought we not to conclude that *even to the Great Creator, Almighty he is, a certain process may be necessary,* a certain time (or at least what appears to us as time) may be requisite, in order to form beings with those

exalted qualities of mind which will fit them for his high purposes? (Malthus [1798] 1960, 127; emphasis added)

Needless to say, Malthus binds God to such a necessary process in preparation for his thesis on the role of the principle of population in the formation of the human mind.

There is no need to circumscribe God's omnipotence to affirm divine beneficence or omniscience. For example, in Aquinas's twofold order of the universe, God has absolute power to design the foundational elements and dynamics of the natural world as God sees fit. After all, God has absolute existence[12] and therefore enjoys absolute freedom. God can say "I am what I will" or "I do what I will." Thus, God cannot be bound to anyone or any process since it is God who creates and sets these in place to begin with. Moreover, God cannot be restricted by any binding, immutable process because only God enjoys absolute existence and freedom. If God were obligated to conform to a particular operation, then such a process must have an existence independent of and, perhaps, even prior to God.

As we will see in part I, we can accommodate Malthus's concern (for God following a certain set process) by acknowledging that after creating the natural world, God chooses to let nature unfold and take its course according to its created mode of operation. For example, as seen in chapter 3, God permits the creation of new beings through secondary causes within the natural world. Consequently, God's omnipotence is not incompatible with the world evolving through human striving and effort since such secondary causality is part of God's governance. There is no need to hold God bound to a particular process as Malthus does.

Ninth, to accept Malthus's principle of population and its accompanying hardships as providential is in effect to say that misery and vice are constitutive of God's created order. Suffering, however, is not intrinsic to human nature but is merely accidental. God did not create humans to subject them to pain and suffering, even for a noble and greater end. Rather, God created humans with the immediate invitation to share in divine life and happiness. Suffering is incidental and consequent to the human failure to respond to such a proffered gift. There is a difference between saying that God *wills* suffering (as in the case of an embedded destitution in the natural order by divine design) and saying that God *permits* suffering (as in the case of scarcity as a consequence of moral failure). Economic suffering is an evil, a privation of the good, and it cannot be said to be integral to creation.

In summary, LeMahieu (1979) faults Malthus for changing the notion of original sin, for having no place for Jesus Christ, and for dismissing final judgment. Waterman (1983a, 202) enumerates a long list of unorthodox positions that places Malthus well outside the canons of the Church of England: the Pelagian and Manichean implications of his views; the lack of divine omnipotence; and the redundancy of the Incarnation, redemption, and revelation. Prominent theologians and friends from the Church of England persuaded Malthus to drop the offending chapters from the second edition (LeMahieu 1979, Pullen 1981, Waterman 1983a, 1983b, 1991a). Chapters 18 and 19 disappeared altogether from the five subsequent editions of the *Essay* published during his lifetime.[13]

Paley ([1802] 1972) and Sumner ([1816] 1850) eventually took up Malthus's original question of how a loving, provident God could permit a world of scarcity. However, instead of using Malthus's formation-of-the-mind theodicy, Paley and Sumner employ the more traditional state-of-probation approach in which evil serves an instrumental role in challenging humans to growth in virtues. Material want and its concomitant burdens rouse humans to further intellectual and moral development.

REFORMULATING MALTHUS'S THEODICY

William Paley

Like Malthus, Paley ([1802] 1972) employs natural theology to account for how scarcity befits the created order of a benevolent God. He uses the same conceptual framework as the last two chapters of the *Essay,* proposing that there is a predetermined order undergirding the world despite humans' experience of contingency. What may appear as chance to people is actually a measure of their ignorance given the much larger unseen reality that envelops humanity. This natural world is marked by diversity both in terms of creatures and of human circumstances. Material exiguity is a consequence of such diversity and chance in human affairs. Paley argues that such scarcity is functional in animating humans to effort and activity in preparation for a more permanent state of happiness in the future afterlife.

The core of Paley's theodicy is similar to that of Malthus: scarcity is a useful venue by which God induces humans to greater striving and exertion.

However, Paley avoids the theological errors that mar the last two chapters of the *Essay*. First, he does not delve into the matter of original sin, nor does he speculate on the ultimate fate of those who fail the process of trial and formation. Recall that Malthus paints himself into a corner because of these premises, particularly that on original sin. Paley arrives at the same conclusion without having to subscribe to these heterodox axioms. This only goes to show that Malthus's premises (on original sin as the torpor of the person or of final punishment as a reversal to original insensibility) are not critical at all for the goal of establishing the functional role of scarcity in the natural world. Furthermore, Paley takes a much broader approach by not limiting himself to intellectual formation, as Malthus does, and by simply staying within the traditional state-of-probation school. The latter is much more expansive in scope and can readily accommodate the former as a subset.

> [I]t is a state of moral probation. . . . It is not a state of unmixed happiness, or of happiness simply: it is not a state of designed misery, or of misery simply: it is not a state of retribution: it is not a state of punishment. . . . [It is] a condition calculated for the production, exercise, and improvement, of moral qualities, with a view to a future state, in which these qualities, after being so produced, exercised and improved, may, by a new and more favoring constitution of things, receive their reward or become their own. (Paley [1802] 1972, 386–87)

Moreover, Paley avoids the problem of circumscribing the omnipotence of God by simply acknowledging that God works just as easily through chance and contingency as with the constancy of laws. After all, chance and contingency are merely a measure of human ignorance within the much wider vision of divine providence.

John Bird Sumner

In an even more extended treatment of Malthus's original question, Sumner builds on Paley's reformulation of the last two chapters of the *Essay*'s first edition. Just like Malthus and Paley, Sumner ([1816] 1850) acknowledges a predetermined intelligible order of creation that reflects the wisdom of God. Variety and contingency are features of divine creation. Scarcity is viewed within a traditional state-of-discipline and school-of-virtue approach.

Life, therefore, is with great propriety described as a race in which a prize is to be contended for; as a season for sowing the seeds of a future and immortal harvest; as a journey, in which mankind are merely pilgrims; as a warfare, in which the combatants must arm themselves with all the virtues, and employ them with zealous courage and enduring patience, that they may be fitted to partake hereafter in the glories of an eternal triumph. (Sumner [1816] 1850, 184)

Just like Malthus and Paley, Sumner's starting point is an anthropology of sloth that needs constant nudging:

The only stimulus felt by him, is that of necessity. He is impelled by hunger to hunt for subsistence, and by cold to provide against the rigour of the seasons. When his stock of provision is laid in, his rude clothing prepared, and his cabin constructed, he relapses into indolence; for the wants of necessity are supplied, and the stimulus which urged him is removed. ([1816] 1850, 195)

Thus, with the exception of the theologically unorthodox views on original sin and final judgment, Sumner shares much of the same premises undergirding Malthus's theodicy and reaches the same conclusions. Embedded within the order of creation is a necessary principle of population with its ensuing hardships and misery. These are venues for industry and human accomplishments. Sumner goes farther than both Malthus and Paley in extending the collateral effects of the principle of population to include the necessity for private property ownership and for inequalities in wealth and social rankings. It is not surprising that Sumner is against ameliorative social policies and deems them to be counterproductive and against God's providential designs.

Critique

Paley and Sumner did much to provide an adequate, orthodox theology undergirding Malthus's theory of population. Nevertheless, their theodicies could still be improved. In particular, their exposition could be further strengthened with a more explicit and developed metaphysics. Such a foundation would have allowed a more sustained and in-depth examination of the nature of scarcity. For example, Paley does not delve into a cosmological explanation for the phenomenon of scarcity. All he does is to sweep it under the panoply of chance and contingency operative within an all-knowing divine providence (Paley [1802] 1972, 387). The disorder that follows in the wake of Malthus's principle of population should simply be accepted as part of an unfolding divine governance. Sumner is no different in his views regarding scarcity: material privation should simply be taken as a given.

Metaphysics is an essential starting point in examining scarcity because it is important to situate such a phenomenon within the nature and order of created goods. Moreover, created goods themselves have to be examined within the larger context of the whole order of the universe. Furthermore, one has to account for the conceptual linkages between the somatic nature of human beings, their competing claims over the same finite goods of the earth, and the nature of quantity as an accidental property of beings.

A theodicy of scarcity unavoidably gives rise to a particular manner of viewing social affairs. Observe how the misgivings of Malthus, Paley, and Sumner over remedial social policies flow from their conviction that the principle of population is a natural, universal law. Using metaphysics as a starting point of analysis has the added advantage of bringing to the fore the theory of reality undergirding the social ethics that inescapably accompanies any theodicy of scarcity. It also provides a fuller appreciation of the Christian understanding of evil as a mere privation of the good. In addition, while Paley and Sumner view the principle of population as conducive to growth in virtue, they do not explicitly develop the mechanisms linking scarcity and virtue. Using metaphysics, one can analyze the impact of scarcity on human beings in their mode of operations. Ontology helps us to comprehend why virtue formation can be part of a theodicy of scarcity.

Another area that could benefit from a more in-depth discussion afforded by a fully articulated metaphysics is the nature of scarcity as an evil. Paley does not commit himself to a clearly stated position on scarcity as an evil and to what extent it is a consequence of natural or moral evil. However, we can infer from his discussion of the salutary outcomes of scarcity that he most likely views it as primarily stemming from physical evil since he uses the beneficial effects of changing seasons as a lead-up to his thinking on the functional role of scarcity. The only explicit stand he takes is that scarcity is not a punishment for sin. Such would be incompatible with his position that the human condition is a state of probation rather than a state of retributive punishment.

Finally, just like Malthus, Paley reverses the role of good and evil. In concluding his theodicy, Paley writes:

> Now relative virtue presupposes, not only the existence of evil, without which it could have no object, no material to work upon, that evils be, apparently at least, *misfortunes;* that is, the effects of apparent chance. It may be in pursuance, therefore, and in furtherance of the same scheme of probation, that the evils of life are made so to present themselves. ([1802] 1972, 391–92; original emphasis)

His latter point on the role of evil in a state of probation is entirely consistent with the Christian understanding that God permits evil for the good it may occasion. However, the first claim is problematic because virtue and goodness are made contingent on the prior existence of evil. In fact, by his own description, evil provides the materials with which the person works to achieve virtue and goodness. This stance is similar to Malthus's ([1798] 1960, 136) view that evil is "absolutely" necessary for the good to be desired. Goodness is unable to elicit an act of the will by virtue of its own desirability; goodness requires contrast with evil before it is able to attract. Moreover, this also means that goodness is parasitic on evil, contrary to the traditional Christian view of evil as a mere privation of the good.

PARTICIPATIVE THEODICY

Malthus should be given credit for broaching the need for a theodicy of scarcity. Despite the Paley-Sumner reworking of his question, there are still untapped theological approaches within the Christian tradition that can be fruitfully employed in analyzing Malthus's original problem. In this book, I use two such frameworks to shed light on the place and role of scarcity in God's order of creation: Aristotelean-Thomistic metaphysics and Sacred Scripture.

In part I, I employ Aquinas's twofold order of the universe to lay out a metaphysics of scarcity and economic life. Within Aquinas's static and dynamic order of creation, humans participate not only in God's existence but also in divine governance and providence in a manner proper to their mode of being and operation: free and reasoned. This is particularly evident in the economic dimension of the created order.

Metaphysical arguments make the case for a divine creation that endows creatures with material sufficiency to attain their ends. However, this sufficiency is merely conditional. It is subject to the rational exercise of moral agency in rectifying shortfalls that arise from human finitude and defectibility and from the contingency intrinsic to economic processes. Such responsive activity is uniquely human and is perfective. Viewed in terms of Aquinas's metaphysics of participation, the allocative task in the wake of scarcity becomes an occasion not only for human participation in divine providence-governance but also for a more profound human sharing in God's excellence. The divine goodness proffered is a goodness received and then mirrored by rational beings in both its ontological and moral dimensions. Although it can impede human beings from reflecting the fullness of such divine goodness, scarcity can also be ennobling as a catalyst to the reasoned exercise of human freedom in both receiving and communicating that divine goodness.

In part II, I employ Sacred Scripture as a historico-religious, narrative examination of the problem of scarcity.[14] The theme of the fullness of God's gift of life (spiritual and material) runs throughout the Bible. I argue, however, that this offered plenitude is merely provisional; it is subject to the degree to which humans attend to the Covenant and the Kingdom. The Pentateuch's and the prophets' teachings on debt release, interest-free loans, land return, gleaning, tithing, and almsgiving reveal YHWH's expectations regarding sharing the finite fruits of the earth. Israel's experience and struggle with scarcity precipitate an even deeper appreciation and understanding of her covenant election. Drawing from the New Testament teachings on righteousness and economic life, I also assess the use of scarce material goods in the Kingdom of God. Whether as a condition of fidelity to the Covenant or as part of discipleship, how humans cope with the finitude of the gifts of the earth becomes a critical channel for their partaking of God's righteousness. Scarcity can give rise to manifold occasions of sin and strife; however, it can also engender a more profound human participation in God's initiatives on behalf of humanity.

RESEARCH QUESTION

What precisely is the nature of the evil that is the subject of this theodicy? Since human beings require material inputs for survival, basic health, and human flourishing, the inability to fill these material needs constitutes an evil. The classic formulation of this phenomenon is Malthus's principle of population in which demographic growth is constantly in tension with the earth's capacity to provision human needs so much so that people are reduced to a long-term steady state of subsistence living characterized by vice and misery. Thus, the human lot is one of uncertain survival with not much surplus, and perhaps, even of severe indigence for many. This is a situation in which demand (real needs and not merely superfluous wants) greatly exceeds available supplies, that is, according to the taxonomy described in appendix 1, a state of Malthusian scarcity.

As we see in part I, such Malthusian scarcity comes from various imperfections (including moral failure) in the social processes and creatures in God's order of creation. God as omniscient Creator foresees the chance, the contingency, and the chain of definite causes-effects that give rise to conditions of material exiguity. Moreover, God as sovereign, omnipotent Creator has complete dominion over creatures' natures and modes of operations and over the degree of their imperfections that are the root causes of material shortfalls. Why then did God, as omnipotent and omniscient Creator, not provision the natural world with bounteous supplies that would be more than sufficient to make up for foreseen material shortages that chance, contingency, and definite effects (from definite causes) precipitate? God could have easily spared humans from the dismal lot of Malthus's principle of population[15] through a simple recalibration of the earth's initial endowments or a readjustment of creaturely frailties in that moment of eternity when God willed the world into existence. God could have easily created a world more robust to the limiting formal imperfections (including moral evil) that give rise to material privation. God could have easily preserved humans from the evil—the vice and the misery—attendant to Malthusian scarcity. But God did not. Instead, God created a world of mere *conditional material sufficiency* characterized by limited provisions, with a restricted "room for error," and with little "cushion" as to put humans on a precarious knife-edge balance between meeting needs or falling into material privation that can often be severe and prolonged. Why does God allow material want in human experience?[16] That is the object of this study's theodicy.

PART I

Participation in God's Goodness

CHAPTER 2

COMMUNICATING THE GOODNESS OF GOD

The metaphysics of St. Thomas Aquinas is a proper starting point in assessing the nature of scarcity because human want is best understood in the context of the perfections proffered by God to creatures. Goodness is the essential backdrop to use in studying the phenomenon of economic scarcity[1] as an evil. After all, evil is a mere privation of the good (Augustine 1953). The good is that which perfects and completes us, and consequently, that which we find appealing. Existence is the starting point, that is, the primary goodness from which all other creaturely perfections follow.[2]

UNCREATED AND CREATED GOODNESS

God must have necessary existence. After all, it would go against the very definition of what it is to be God if God were to be dependent on something or someone else for existence. God would not be God at all if such were the case. God's existence must be absolute; to exist must be in the very nature of God itself.[3]

In contrast, all creatures, including humans, are merely contingent in their existence. As humans, we know that our existence is not necessary because we have experienced firsthand the impermanence of our perfections: we age, ultimately become enfeebled, get sick, die, and turn into dust. And yet the world will continue to exist without us, indeed even flourish, long after our physical death.

From where do we come if our existence is merely provisional? Conditional beings derive their existence only from necessary beings; contingent existence can only come from necessary existence. In other words, human existence is merely a participation in the absolute existence of God.

We can draw two inferences from this finding. First, participated existence is the gateway for all other possible created perfections. After all, creatures can enjoy the qualities they have only if they exist to begin with. The first goodness proffered by God to humans, or any creature for that matter, is the goodness of existence. Second, since creatures merely "borrow" their existence from God (the only being with necessary existence), it follows that all their other perfections also merely participate in the perfections of God. After all, it would be improbable and illogical for creatures who are unable to guarantee their own existence to be the ultimate source of their other perfections.

COMMUNICATING THE GOODNESS OF GOD

Effects mirror their causes (SCG III, 20, #5). We are able to say something (though not everything) about causes by observing and studying their effects. This dynamic applies to God and creatures as well. Since creaturely perfections are merely a participation in the perfections of God, the excellence of creatures provides a glimpse into the goodness of God.

God's perfections must be infinite, ineffable, and immeasurable if God is to be God at all. Absolute perfection is an attribute we would expect God to have. Four inferences can be drawn from this necessary supreme and boundless perfection. First, since creatures are merely contingent in their existence and in their other perfections, individual creatures can reflect (that is, communicate) only a very small part of the goodness of God. Second, given the immensity of divine perfections, there is need for an enormous variety of species characterized by differing grades of perfections if creatures are to convey jointly the richness of God's goodness, to the extent possible.[4] Third, despite such diversity, not even the entire ensemble of creatures (the universe as a whole) is able to disclose the fullness of divine goodness because of the infinity of God's perfections. In other words, every creature mirrors particular perfections in God, albeit as a poor and imperfect copy. Fourth, created goodness participates in uncreated goodness at many levels: from existence to all other possible creaturely qualities including perfective activities.

COMPLETE CREATED GOODNESS

Uncreated goodness (God) is complete and unchangeable; otherwise, God would not be God at all. God is not subject to further development and growth. The same, however, cannot be said of created goodness.[5] Take the case of human beings, for example. We are not born with an immediate and full use of our faculties of reason and will. In fact, it takes a lifetime of "learning by doing" to grow in the reasoned use of our freedom. It takes much effort and commitment to reach the peak of these rational powers that are unique to humans. And it is only in giving full vent to these intellectual gifts that we are able to approximate the fullness of what it is to be human.

Put in more technical terms, although existence is an important perfection we (and other creatures) already possess, that attribute does not represent the totality of all the goodness we can achieve; in fact, it is incomplete. Existence (as a goodness) requires further activity to attain the other perfections creatures are capable of possessing. Creatures build on their initial perfection (of existence) to reach for other necessary, albeit additional, perfections according to the mode of their being and operation. For human beings, their mode of being and operation is intelligent activity; it is through their reasoned use of freedom that humans acquire the requisite supplementary perfections that make them truly and fully human—growth in moral virtue and character. In other words,

complete created goodness = existence as perfection + perfections from creaturely activities

Created goodness can only be completed in activity. For example, given their unique powers of reason and will, human beings attain the fullness of the goodness possible to them only in the measure they allow their initial goodness of existence to blossom into moral excellence—the pinnacle of what human activity is capable of achieving given their mode of being and operation. Creaturely activity is a necessary, indeed, the only venue by which created goodness can be brought to its fruition.[6]

TWOFOLD ORDER OF THE UNIVERSE

Given the central role of activity for completing creaturely goodness, it is important to understand the larger milieu, dynamic, and trajectory within which all creaturely activities unfold, namely, the twofold order of the universe. There are three core features to this phenomenon.

First, God is the Final End to which all creatures tend. This premise can be logically derived from the preceding exposition on the nature of uncreated and created goodness. All creatures find their end in that which completes and perfects them. After all, by its nature, an "end" is that which consummates and fulfills. However, as already mentioned, all creaturely perfections (including existence) are only contingent, that is, a mere participation in the goodness of the Absolute Being (the only one that possesses necessary existence and from whom all perfections necessarily flow). Thus, the creaturely perfections that created beings seek and in which they find their end ultimately rest in God as the source of all perfections. Thus, God is the Final End of all creatures.

Second, since God is the Final End of all creatures, the activity of the universe as a whole (that is, the entire ensemble of creatures) is necessarily geared toward reaching out to God. In other words, the universe can only find its ultimate perfection and completion in God. This is called the external order of the universe.

Third, despite being a single entity, the universe nevertheless consists of a diversity of creatures with varying grades of perfections. This manifold variety in species and qualities is necessary in order to better reflect and communicate the goodness of God, to the extent possible. These disparate and distinct "parts" of the universe (including human beings) interact with each other in the course of their activities according to their mode of being and operation. It is through such mutual interaction and activity that creatures reach the fullness of their respective complete created goodness described earlier. At first glance, we might expect a dissonant cacophony of creaturely activities independent of each other, given the extensive range of species with differing grades of perfections. This, however, is not the case because creatures constitutive of the universe form an internal and intelligent order in which diverse beings are oriented toward each other in such a way as to bring the whole universe (and every constituent part) to its final end in God. In other words, there is a large and intrinsic social component to individual creaturely activities because they perform the double function of (1) effecting the complete created goodness of individual creatures even while (2) contributing toward the universe's attainment of its own final end in God. Activities are perfective both at the level of individual creatures and at the level of the universe as a whole. This dynamic is called the internal order of the universe. *Parts of the whole universe interact with each other for the sole purpose of bringing each other and the whole to their final end in God.*

The external and internal orders of the universe mutually serve and reinforce each other. The external order provides an end to which the internal order and its parts are oriented; the internal order moves the whole (universe) to its end in God. Thus, there is a twofold order in the universe (J. Wright 1957, 1967). It is within this larger backdrop that human activity takes place. It is within this larger setting that humans grow in the moral excellence that completes their created goodness. It is to this internal order that we now turn our attention given its central importance for human activity and perfection.

ECONOMIC SPHERE

Humans act to pursue and complete their created goodness according to the mode of their being and operation (intelligent activity) within the internal order of the universe. Furthermore, there is an unavoidable and large intrinsic social component to this unique rational activity. Humans, after all, are social beings.

Interpersonal activities are mediated through human partnerships and associations of differing sizes. Thus, the individual person contributes to and benefits from society through the nuclear family; the extended family of aunts, uncles, and cousins; the immediate neighborhood; the local community; attendance and membership in schools, churches, firms, unions, and professional groups; citizenship in the nation; and fellowship in the global family of nations. Moreover, humans pursue their activities and collaborate with each other not only in various communities of differing sizes, but also in the manifold spheres of life—religious, political, social, cultural, and economic. This study is interested primarily in the economic realm of the internal order of the universe.

Different spheres of life—political, economic, religious, and cultural—are governed by their own unique and specific rules, dynamics, and requirements. For example, we have the "laws" of supply and demand in economics in which unfilled or excessive demand leads to an increase in price, which in its own turn causes a corresponding drop in consumption. Despite these "laws" peculiar to the different facets of life, all spheres are nonetheless uniformly oriented toward and bound by the primary obligation of making their distinctive contributions to effecting both the internal and external orders of the universe. In the case of economic life, individual and collective economic activities (no matter how disparate) are ultimately meant to serve the goal of attaining God as Final End both for the self and for others (the end of the twofold order of the universe).

There is a necessary economic dimension to human flourishing and the attainment of that final end in God. After all, human beings are material and require food, clothing, shelter, and medical care if they are to survive and attain a modicum of basic health that allows them to function and grow. Moreover, the pursuit of intelligent activity, even of the most spiritual kind, for example, study and contemplation, requires material inputs as well, such as books and a proper education. Furthermore, humans are social beings and thrive only within communities. Economic life is communal by nature, and many goods and services can be produced and enjoyed only in collaboration with others. Thus, there are at least three identifiable proximate ends for the economic sphere by virtue of its role in the internal order of the universe. First, economic life is meant to furnish material provisions necessary for human flourishing. Second, it is an essential venue for growth in moral excellence through the personal effort and interpersonal cooperation required by economic activity. Third, it provides the setting within which humans are able to discharge their obligation of caring for the goods of the earth and each other through virtuous economic activity.

MATERIAL SUFFICIENCY BY DIVINE DESIGN

Any study of the nature of scarcity[7] in God's envisioned order of creation must take into account the aforesaid three proximate goals of the economic sphere at the service of that final end in God. The ease or difficulty with which human beings are able to attain these three proximate ends of economic life is largely dependent on the severity of the scarcity experienced. The degree to which this material scarcity is encountered, however, is in its own turn largely a function of how extravagantly God had endowed the earth to begin with. Plenitude in the gifts of the earth leads to a greater "room for error," ease in procuring the necessary material means for human flourishing, and less occasion for war and strife due to rival consumption and inordinate wealth accumulation. There is much at stake in the initial endowments and in the abundance (or lack thereof) embedded by God in the creation of the earth.

I submit that a case can be made for material sufficiency as part of God's envisioned order of creation. Seven arguments for such material sufficiency can be drawn from the divine attributes one would expect if God is to be God at all. First, God as Creator of the universe is the Architect of all creation.[8] Imperfections or deficiencies that impede the essential operations of the universe and its parts (such as destitution for human beings) would reflect imperfections or faulty planning on the part of their Creator. Since perfection is a necessary attribute of God, we would expect divine plans to be flawless. This necessarily includes adequate material provisions for the survival and sustenance of human beings and other creatures.

Second, besides a necessary perfection in divine planning for the universe, we would expect a similar perfection as God executes these plans.[9] This means that there can be no shortcomings in the divine governance of the world if God is to be truly God. This includes ensuring that creatures have the necessary means to discharge their activities properly according to the mode of their being and operation. For human beings, this includes access to requisite material inputs for physical survival, basic health, and growth.

Third, goodness is self-diffusive and seeks to share itself where there was no goodness before. God is necessarily self-sufficient and complete, not dependent on anything or anyone. Creatures do not add anything to God's perfection. Thus, human beings are created for their own sake as God's way of sharing divine goodness. It would be contrary to the perfect self-diffusiveness of divine goodness to impart its perfection in a grossly flawed fashion as would have been the case if the world had been created with insufficient material provisions by divine design.

Fourth, divine justice must be perfect in God. It would be an act of malice on the part of God to intentionally create human beings and then leave them by divine plan to wallow in destitution for want of material provisions. This would be evidence of an impairment in divine will.

Fifth, effects mirror their causes. Creatures merely participate in the perfections of God; they reflect various dimensions of divine qualities that are found in God in a supereminent manner. Generosity and provident foresight are among the virtues found in human beings. Thus, these qualities must be in God to an even greater degree. At the very least, this would include the divine provision of material goods for human sustenance. God, after all, must be the paradigm of liberality and prudence.

Sixth, creatures attain their complete goodness only through the additional perfections wrought by their respective activities. Human beings require material sustenance if they are to engage in the activities proper to their mode of being and operation. Thus, God must necessarily provide these material needs if God intends human beings to attain the fullness of the goodness accessible to them. It would have been a defect in God to knowingly create creatures and not provide the means necessary to achieve their complete goodness. Existence would have been a futile and sterile exercise on the part of creatures. God would have created creatures that are by design doomed to fail in reaching their intended final end.

Seventh, if human beings are to enjoy the power of real causality, it is necessary for them to have the necessary material inputs to sustain them according to their proper mode of being and operation. Otherwise, in the absence of such real causality, ours would have been a world in which God directly effects all activities in the universe without the use of creatures as intermediate causes (occasionalism).

In summary, if God is to be God at all, there can be no errors in divine providence or in divine governance. This means that God must have created the world with an adequate provision of material means necessary for creatures, including human beings, to attain their final end, each according to their proper mode of being and operation.[10]

CONDITIONALITY

The aforesaid a priori metaphysical arguments for a requisite material sufficiency in the world by divine design is not validated by empirical evidence. For most of human history, people have lived in precarious existence because of material want. In fact, it is only in the wake of the Industrial Revolution that we have been able to enjoy surplus and an overall improvement in standards of living across the world. Nevertheless, despite this signal achievement, most of the world's population still live in poverty (World Bank 2000).

This jarring disparity between the foregoing a priori metaphysical arguments and actual empirical evidence can only mean that the material sufficiency of God's envisioned order of creation must be merely conditional. And indeed, this conditionality is revealed in economic life through secondary causes. It is to such secondary causality that we now turn our attention in the next chapter.

CHAPTER 3

ECONOMIC AGENCY AS PERFECTIVE SECONDARY CAUSE

This chapter evaluates the role of economic life as a venue for partaking of God's goodness, appraises the impact of material scarcity on such participation, and argues that rational agency is central to the economic sphere's attainment of its proper order. It examines the nature of economic activity as a secondary cause and situates perfective economic agency within Aquinas's twofold order of the universe. Economic life is a channel for receiving and then communicating God's goodness.

ECONOMIC AGENCY AND SECONDARY CAUSALITY

Creation-providence-governance

Creation is an act that is uniquely God's because it is the conferral of existence to a nonbeing; as we have seen, only God has uncreated existence and all other beings merely participate in God's necessary existence.[1] Moreover, creation is an act that can be God's alone because it occurs "without either motion or time" (ST I, 104, a.1, ad.4).

Since it is not part of their essence to have to exist, creatures need to be sustained in continued existence (ST I, 104, a.1; I, 104, a.3). Thus, God's act of creation flows seamlessly into divine providence. Divine providence is a timeless divine plan that directs creatures to their end. Implementation of such a plan in time pertains to divine governance as God conserves (divine conservation) and brings creatures to their end through creaturely intermediaries (divine concurrence). Divine providence (order of intention) unfolds through divine governance (order of execution) as God works through created activity. Divine providence belongs to the eternal while divine governance pertains to the temporal (ST I, 22, a.1, ad.2). *God provides for creatures through other creatures using the very order of creation itself in a series of determinate causes and effects.* Thus, while God's providence for creatures, indeed every creature, is immediate and direct, its implementation in divine governance employs secondary causes in sustaining and bettering creatures (ST I, 22, a.3; I, 104, a.2, ad.1; I, 105). Thus, economic life is intelligible through the prism of secondary causality.

Nature of secondary causes

The act of existence is an effect that is proper to God alone as the First Cause; all other perfections are proper to secondary causes.[2] *Being as being* is properly attributed to the primary cause, and *being as effect* to the secondary causes; *the cause of being* is to the First Cause as *the cause of becoming* is to secondary causes (ST I, 104, a.1, reply).[3] Thus "is the activity of God determined and particularized by secondary agents" (Johann 1947, 25).[4]

Primary-secondary causality is a special case of the relationship within principal-instrumental causality. Take the case of a sculptor, his block of marble, and his chisel. The sculptor is the principal agent that brings about a statue from a block of marble using a chisel as an instrument. The artist's sculpting and the chisel's cutting at the marble form a causal unity in the term—the statue. Despite this causal unity, however, the perfection or formality of the ultimate effect (the statue) is attributed and proportioned to the principal agent alone (ST III, 62, a.1; Albertson 1954, 433). After all, the form of the statue derives from the idea conceived in the artist's mind and not in the chisel's form. This also highlights the distinctive feature of what makes an instrument to be an instrument: it produces an ultimate effect that exceeds its own nature. The outcome goes far beyond the capabilities of the native power of the instrument's form (Albertson 1954, 414, 415, 420). While the chisel has the capacity to cut and shape marble, it is beyond the chisel's nature or power to create by itself an intelligible form from a block of marble.

Unlike principal-instrumental causality in which the perfection of the ultimate effect is formally attributed and proportioned to the principal agent alone and not to the instrument, there are proper final effects imputed to both primary and secondary causes.[5] God's creation-providence unfolds through the secondary causality of creatures, and humans have a pivotal role in this dynamic. Human participation in such causality affirms the authenticity of human freedom. It ratifies freedom because the reasoned use of it is the unique quality that human beings bring to producing the effects that are proper to them alone. The rest of the chapter focuses on the effects that are proper to human beings as secondary causes in economic life.

ECONOMIC AGENCY AS PERFECTIVE

Economics is one of the many spheres in which the concrete embodiment of God's plan unfolds.[6] The order of creation, especially human affairs, can be viewed as a threefold movement of a goodness proffered, a goodness received, and a goodness communicated. Economic life is the terrain in which the material conditions of divine providence are actualized and sustained.

The order proper to the economic sphere merely serves as a means to the even larger goal of bringing human beings to their beatitude, their final end: knowing God to the extent possible and attaining that "ordination to God which terminates directly and immediately to the divine essence" (J. Wright 1957, 117–18; ST I-II, 3, a.8). Economic life satisfies the material conditions needed to achieve such beatitude directly (via the economic order) and indirectly (via the other spheres of life). It is also an occasion for the interior perfection of people—the immanent perfective nature of rational secondary causality.

The economic order is an unusually fertile ground for perfective human action because of the intrinsic difficulty of its requirements. Unlike other particular realms, economic life as a venue for the human communication of

God's goodness is exacting because it requires order among discordant wills, unceasing intelligent activity, and interpersonal resource transfers that are often sacrificial, especially in the face of scarcity.

Stewardship of the goods of the earth

Viewed in the broader Aristotelean sense of household management, economics is about the proper care of the goods of the earth as part of the order of creation. In terms of both existence and activity, every creature manifests a particular dimension of God's perfection. Thus, Aquinas asserts that the dynamics of the internal order of the universe require that parts act on each other to bring out the fullness of each other's reflection of God's goodness and to bear each other to their respective proximate ends. Material goods serve human needs even as human beings, in their own turn and as intelligent creatures of a higher perfection, care for the goods of the earth in order to bring such creatures of a lower perfection to a higher end.

Rational beings assist nonrational creatures in reaching the latter's proximate ends even as nonrational creatures, in their own turn, supply people's material needs.[7] Such an exchange allows beings of a lower perfection to participate in the excellence of the higher (J. Wright 1957, 104–7). In economic life this means that even as humans use the goods of the earth to fill their needs, they must utilize them in such a manner as to allow created goods to reflect the goodness of God.

Harmony with other rational beings

Human secondary causality in economic life is not limited to making the earth fruitful to fill human needs. Because of the intense cooperation needed in this sphere and because of the social nature of the person, human secondary causality is equally, if not more importantly, also about effecting goodness in interpersonal relationships.[8] Moreover, secondary agents produce effects proper to them through that power that is distinctive to them. In the case of humans, "proper goodness" and "proper mode of operation" pertain to the use of rational freedom, a big part of which involves social exchange.

Human beings find their peak perfection in serving as a catalyst for goodness not merely among lower creatures (the goods of the earth), but most especially among other rational beings (SCG III, 21, #6). After all, human perfection is directly proportional to the degree to which people are able to evoke or cause goodness in other creatures, especially moral excellence in rational beings.[9]

Requisite intelligent activity

Order in economic life means that all beings within this sphere are able to conduct their proper operations and achieve their proper ends. There is conformity to the divine plan to the extent that the divine goodness is communicated. The economic sphere is at the service of rational beings by providing: the material means for human survival and integral human development; a venue for human labor and creativity; an occasion for growth in moral excellence; an opportunity to participate in divine governance; and a channel for community building, harmony, and solidarity. Establishing such an order in relations in economic life is an exacting venture because of the multiplicity and complexity of relationships involved; it stretches rational activity to its limits. It is interdependent (because it requires collaborative intellectual activity), extensive (because of its externalities in affecting other facets in life), and intensive (because of the depth of the sacrifice it can require of economic agents). However, such taxing demands made of intellectual activity become occasions for individual and collective growth in perfection.

In describing the propriety of God sharing causality with creatures, Aquinas concludes that the degree of excellence to which creatures exercise such causality is proportioned to the degree of their similitude to God. This means that there is greater moment in the causality exercised by more perfect beings compared to less perfect beings. This also means that human beings have a greater measure of accountability and responsibility for the attainment of the twofold order of the universe (*De veritate* q.5, a.8, reply; SCG III, 64, #8). Much can be rightfully expected of human agency.

The centrality of human contribution in the economic sphere is well-illustrated in Malthus's principle of population. Recall that he predicts long-term subsistence living for people because of the gap between the geometric expansion of population and the arithmetic increase in food production. He assumes that these two growth rates are independent of each other; they are not, since population pressure precipitates technological innovations that allow food production to keep up with, and perhaps even exceed, population growth.[10] And, in fact, economic history has proven Malthus's dismal prognosis wrong because of human ingenuity in increasing the yields of the fruits of the earth. Two hundred years after his *Essay on Population*, not only is the global community able to support more people, but it is able to do so at an even higher average per capita income, the highest ever in human history. This signal accomplishment is largely due to the proper exercise of both speculative and practical reason by the only intelligent secondary causes—humans.

The economic order is a proper effect of human beings as secondary agents of divine governance. Only intelligent activity can effect the requisite harmony in relations among the manifold creatures found in the economic sphere. Since only human beings are capable of rational operations, they bear sole responsibility for the character of economic life. Only if such intelligent and free causality conforms to divine providence is this proper order attained.

Economic transfers as correctives

We expect a pivotal role for human agency in effecting the envisioned conditional material sufficiency in God's providence. As argued in the preceding chapter, there is an existential material sufficiency by design coming from a God of eminent goodness and flawless providence. However, humans face a variety of circumstances in the order of creation given the inherent multiplicity of creatures with their manifold grades of perfections.[11] Thus, individual human beings will experience different degrees of sufficiency in their material provisioning, with some enjoying superfluity even as others are in dire want and poverty. These variations in personal circumstances stem from moral evil and the contingency of social processes and outcomes. They can be rectified only through voluntary, intelligent activity. Divine providence provides material sufficiency for all (despite expected variations in their individual circumstances) through secondary causes. Since human beings are the only creatures endowed with free secondary causality, they are the only ones capable of deliberate, ameliorative action in providing material sufficiency for every person. Thus, from the point of view of distribution, human beings bear the full brunt of the conditionality embedded in the ontological material sufficiency described earlier.[12] The provision of the material means necessary for human survival and growth is a proximate end of economic life. It is a distinctive contribution of the economic sphere to the twofold order of the universe. After all, there is an unavoidable human need for material goods and services.

Moral evil, chance, and contingency—as causes of scarcity—highlight the importance of rational activity. *Such material shortfalls can be corrected, but only by actions that are by nature free. After all, operations that are oriented to predetermined outcomes by necessity cannot, by their nature, deviate from such outcomes. Only humans are capable of acting not by necessity but by choice.* This raises the stakes for human responsibility because the burden of adjusting for deviations from the envisioned conditional material sufficiency in the order of creation falls squarely on human agency.

The phenomena of rival consumption and limited supplies of material goods make economic transfers truly self-donative. This is consistent with the self-diffusive nature of goodness. Such sharing—founded on reason, deliberate choice, and selflessness—accentuates human beings' greatest similitude to God among all creatures.

A world of material sufficiency is provisional on the proper exercise of human reason and freedom. There is material sufficiency only if human beings live up to their role of bringing about the internal order called for as part of the dual order of the universe. The same human freedom that can impede the Creator's provision of material goods in sufficient quantities is also a freedom that can choose instead to be an instrument in effecting such material plenitude. Free and reasoned activity are the very means employed by God to provision the whole universe and its parts. In fact, the quality of God's provisioning as received by humans and other creatures is dependent on human cooperation.

Impact of scarcity

God's creative act is not random but is purposeful. Every facet of God's governance is designed to bring creatures to their highest end. Thus, the phenomenon of scarcity must have a role to play in divine providence. God permits a world of material want in order to imbue humans with even greater perfections. Creatures participate in God's goodness through their proper operation. For humans, this is through intelligence and freedom; scarcity demands much of these faculties.

The self-diffusiveness of goodness and the nature of economic life match each other very well. Just like God's goodness, there is a self-diffusive feature to creatures' participated goodness. It seeks out, appropriates, and then shares with others the goodness attained. Moreover, it is dynamic and creative in its reception and communication of that goodness and is necessarily outward in its orientation. Economic life matches these characteristics well because, by its nature, it requires much collaboration and mutual sharing due to the rival consumption of the finite quantities of the goods of the earth. Furthermore, it calls for continuous intelligent activity because of its inherent dynamic fluidity and contingency. Much deliberate effort is involved in seeking out, working for, and then sharing the good that is particular to the economic order. Relations are important because the reception and communication of God's goodness is mediated through the three-cornered relationship between God, the human person, and other rational beings. Indeed, economic agency is an avenue for participation in divine attributes and operation through secondary causality in divine governance. Unconditional material sufficiency (de facto inexhaustible material abundance) would have removed or dulled the efficacy of these venues for growth in perfection.

Material shortages make it that much more arduous for human beings to exercise their proper causality in the economic sphere. Scarcity can make secondary causality much more difficult by exacerbating the defectibility of personal and collective moral agency. The more severe the scarcity, the more urgent is the necessary sharing and the greater, too, is the likelihood for divisive competition and inordinate accumulation or hoarding. However, since humans are free and do not respond by necessity, they may use conditions of scarcity as stepping-stones toward even greater perfection, as in the case of redressing others' material destitution through self-sacrifice. Even as it engenders difficulties in attaining the order that is proper to the economic sphere, scarcity brings with it the possibility of an even more profound participation in God's goodness.[13]

Scarcity becomes an evil and, therefore, in need of an explanatory theodicy to the extent that it disrupts the particular order proper to economic life, thereby upsetting the twofold order of the universe itself. The order-disrupting impact of scarcity may well evoke free and reasoned compensatory action from rational creatures (as parts of the whole), keep the pursuit of the twofold order on track, and in the process, realize accidental perfections for themselves (humans) so essential to moving from ontological to moral goodness as we have seen in chapter 2. Of course, rational creatures may choose to do otherwise and exacerbate, rather than mitigate, the ill effects of scarcity. In either case, the scarcity of material goods defines the terrain of the economic life that has to be traversed, while human agency is the mode for actualizing the order proper to the economic sphere. Scarcity shapes the difficulty of the terrain in which accidental perfections are to be acquired and in which the pursuit of moral excellence is to take place. Scarcity, besides being a constraint, is itself a product of such activity. This is a self-reinforcing, self-feeding cycle that can lead to much good or ill.

Achieving the order that is proper to the economic sphere is no small task because its starting point of competing interests, contentious wills, and limited goods subject to rival consumption requires selflessness and mutual sharing. The nature of social dynamics in economic life demands much of human practical reason and will. A harmonious and efficacious collective secondary causality in the economic sphere is possible only with purposeful effort, the voluntary subordination of personal interests to that of the whole, and sizable resource transfers among individuals. Attaining the proper order in the economic sphere is intrinsically difficult, but it is precisely because of the exacting needs of such a terrain that personal and collective secondary causality becomes an ideal platform for growth in virtue and profound participation in divine attributes and activity.

COMMUNICATING AND PARTICIPATING IN DIVINE GOODNESS

We have come to the end of part I, and it is time to summarize the key arguments. Much preliminary work was needed before we could delve into a theodicy of economic scarcity. In the first place, we had to establish that God is indeed solely responsible for creatures and the order of creation. Second, we had to ascertain the nature of the goodness that is supposed to be subjected to privation whenever there is a dearth of material provisions. Then, we had to determine the nature of scarcity and the manner by which it mars the intended goodness as part of the order of creation. We have addressed these issues in the last two chapters and in the appendices.

Talking of a theodicy of scarcity makes sense only in the context of God as the paradigm and source of all perfections (God as Exemplary Cause), God as imparting such perfections (God as Efficient Cause), and God as the ultimate end of creatures (God as Final Cause). For if the deficiency of material goods does indeed hinder creatures from attaining the fullness of their derived perfections or from reaching their ultimate perfection, then the Creator bears responsibility for not ensuring an adequate supply of initial endowments of material goods for creatures to reach their intended end. After all, God as Creator is the ultimate provider for the order of creation since only

God has necessary existence. All other beings are contingent and merely participate in God for their existence and other perfections. God is both Formal and Efficient Cause.

The goodness that is subjected to privation whenever there is a lack of material goods necessary for human existence and development is also a participated goodness from God. This derived goodness finds its completion in God as Final Cause; it unfolds toward this ultimate end in the dual order of the universe whose parts help each other bring out the fullness of their similitude to God's goodness according to the nature of their being and the mode of their operation. Humans are unique among creatures because they attain God as end through knowledge and love. Through their intelligent activity, human beings interact with each other (and with nonrational creatures) in the manifold spheres of life. Rational creatures effect the requisite internal order of the universe in the measure they achieve the order proper to these spheres of life, including the economic realm. It is this particular order that is put directly at risk by material scarcity.

The world must have been created by God with material sufficiency for its conservation and the attainment of its end at the level both of the whole and of each individual human being. However, in the face of a long-standing human experience of want and destitution, it is clear that such material sufficiency is merely conditional. It is contingent on the degree to which the multiplicity of particular orders, especially the economic realm, achieves the envisioned internal order of the whole.

The weight of correcting economic disorders, Malthusian scarcity in particular, falls largely on human beings because they are the only free and intelligent secondary causes. All others merely act by necessity according to their nature and mode of operation. God wills a state of material sufficiency, rather than Malthusian scarcity, for human beings. However, actualizing such a state is dependent on human conduct. Aquinas describes this phenomenon well when he writes:

> Divine providence extends to men in two ways: first, in so far as men are provided for; second, in so far as they themselves become providers. . . . [M]en are provided for in different ways according to the different ways they have of providing for themselves. For, if they keep the right order in their own providence, God's providence in their regard will keep an ordering that is congruent with their human dignity. . . . However, if in

their own providence men do not keep that order which is congruent with their dignity as rational creatures, but provide after the manner of brute animals, then God's providence will dispose of them according to the order that belongs to brutes. . . . *God's providence governs the good in a higher way than it governs the evil. For, when the evil leave one order of providence, that is, by not doing the will of God, they fall into another order, an order in which the will of God is done to them.* (*De veritate* q.5, a.7; emphasis added)

Chronic material destitution is a condition that human beings bring upon themselves in deviating from God's providence.

The a priori warrants for an order of creation that provides material sufficiency to every human being, albeit conditional on personal and collective human response, have significant ramifications for moral conduct. These ontological arguments establish material sufficiency for every human being as an objective part of an order that is proper to the economic sphere. However, there is an inherent need within the order of creation for transfers of resources among human beings if material sufficiency is to be attained down to the level of the individual. This stems from the metaphysical requirement of a multiplicity in species and differing grades of perfections. These inherent variations, in addition to human finitude-defectibility and contingency in social and natural processes, mean that human beings will find themselves in a wide diversity of circumstances in which some enjoy a superfluity of goods even while others are at risk of death from severe material deprivation. Since "order is the proper effect of providence" (SCG III, 77, #5), the perfection of the twofold order requires that the abundance of others be used to alleviate the want of the destitute.

Economic transfers are central to attaining the conditional material sufficiency envisioned within the order of creation. Thus, people with some surplus provide for those who face material scarcity since only free secondary causes are able to make such remedial transfers. Such rational activity is an intrinsic part of God providing for human beings through each other. In more general terms,

God created all things immediately, but in creation itself He established an order among things, so that some depend on others, by which they are preserved in being, though He remains the principal cause of their preservation. (ST I, 104, a.2, ad.1)

The more noble or the more perfect the creature that is being assisted and preserved, the greater the moment attached to the secondary agents' acts of assistance and preservation. The demands on human agency are enormous because of the nature of the economic sphere. It is highly complex and technical and requires much from practical reasoning and moral conduct. It is highly dynamic and consequently in constant need of ameliorative adjustments and transfers. And it is subject to rival consumption and finite supplies, which make such economic transfers truly self-donative.

The possibilities afforded creatures by God are perfective of their recipients.[14] Part I argued that this is particularly true of economic agency whether it is in bringing about the fruitfulness of the earth as secondary causes in production, in providing order in relations among the disparate elements of the economic sphere, or in effecting self-sacrificial economic transfers to provide relief to those trapped in a state of Malthusian scarcity. The more severe the scarcity that has to be dealt with, the greater the perfective possibilities attached to the economic agency thus challenged.

In the order of creation, humans are rational in their secondary causality. This highlights their accountability for the internal order of the universe in general and for the economic order in particular. Humans can either obstruct or cooperate with divine providence and governance.[15] They are the only creatures capable of discerning, understanding, and then subscribing deliberately to God's intelligible plans. They have a tangible impact in the way other rational beings and the nonrational creatures of the earth are able to convey God's goodness. Since humans participate in the goodness of God, they too must mirror the inherent self-diffusiveness of such divine goodness. Their capacity for a real causality that is intelligent and free provides them with substantive means and venues for communicating such goodness. There are heavy obligations attendant to the goodness that has been received.

> [I]t is better that the good bestowed on someone should be common to many, than that it should be proper to one: since the common good is always considered more godlike than the good of one only. But the good of one becomes common to many, if it flows from the one to the other. (SCG III, 69, #13)

In the same way that there are varied ways and degrees by which creatures receive the goodness of God, the concomitant obligations that come with the divine goodness received also differ in their requirements. The heaviest claims fall on human beings because of their signal intellectual faculties. Consequently, they should in their own turn communicate the goodness of God through their rational activity. Economic life lends itself particularly well not only to such an endeavor of revealing God's goodness, but it also becomes a significant venue for the further reception of such goodness with even greater depth and profundity. Scarcity, which is the basis of economic life to begin with, makes this entire dynamic that much more demanding and sacrificial, but also that much more consequential and perfective.

PART II

Participation in God's Righteousness

CHAPTER 4

ECONOMIC AGENCY IN COVENANT ELECTION

Economic agency in covenant election is a participation in God's holiness, righteousness, and providence. This chapter advances this thesis by arguing (1) that there is an economic dimension to God's in-breaking in human history and (2) that God has used the consequent economic obligations from such intervention to elicit human participation in divine initiatives.[1]

ECONOMIC DIMENSION OF GOD'S IN-BREAKING

God's *sedeq* (righteousness) encompasses the maintenance of due order in the natural world and in human affairs (Achtemeier 1962b). Sacred Scripture is a chronicle of how God, in the course of establishing such due order, breaks into human history to draw a freely requited response to a generous invitation to a divine-human relationship. Historicity and sociality are two distinctive legacies of Israel to moral understanding (Ogletree 1983, 79–80). Such historicity imbues YHWH's relations with Israel with a concrete particularity within the medium afforded by the natural world and human nature. In other words, moral life evolves not in an abstract world of disembodied ideas but is grounded in the temporal, the material, and the worldly. Consequently, there is a constitutive economic dimension to God's in-breaking in human affairs. In the case of the Chosen People, this economic feature is highlighted (1) in the functional role of the Promised Land and (2) in YHWH's special concern for the poor.[2]

Land

Historicity brings in its wake a necessary economic element to God's in-breaking. In the case of Israel's engagement with YHWH, land serves as the pivotal venue in which this relationship unfolds. So important and central is the role of land in God's entry into human history that von Waldow (1974, 493) even goes so far as to suggest that land may be the more dominant and integral theme than the Covenant in the Hebrew Scripture. He observes that if its theology were to be summarized into a single proposition of faith, it could just as easily be "Israel and her Land."

C. Wright (1990, 4) concurs and notes that a theology of land clearly stands out as a constant refrain not only within the Pentateuch but throughout the Hebrew Scripture: the promise of land as central to God's covenant with Abraham; the redemption of that promise in Exodus; strictures for life on the land in the Covenant and the Law; punishment for failure to enter the land in the wilderness wanderings; appropriation and division of the land in Joshua; the early toil to survive and keep the land in Judges; the wars to secure the boundaries and peace on the land in the time of David and Solomon; the scandal of sins perpetrated on the land in the prophetic indictments; a despoiled land and its loss during the Exile as consequences of Israel's infidelity; and restoration and rebuilding on the land through YHWH's graciousness in the post-exilic period of reform and renewal. So pervasive is the role of land that even the Hebrew laws on economic life and cultic practices on first fruits, gleanings, tithes, and land redemption are ultimately founded on the acknowledgment of God's ownership of the earth (von Rad 1966a, 87; C. Wright 1990, 6).[3]

Land is unquestionably a concrete particularity that emerges out of the historicity of God's in-breaking. Since we are interested in the economic dimension of God's in-breaking, it is necessary to distinguish the symbolic from the functional role of land because it is in the latter that we find matters pertinent to the economics of scarcity.

Symbolic role

Attributing divine ownership to land is not unique to Israel since even the neighboring Near Eastern peoples readily acknowledge that land's fertility is at the pleasure of the gods who rightfully exercise dominion and ownership. This is evident in the prevalent cultic practices in the region. However, land takes on even greater significance for Israel because YHWH is not merely the God of nature responsible for the fecundity of the earth; more important, YHWH is also the God of history who intervenes in human affairs to give the Promised Land to Israel (von Waldow 1974, 496). Consequently, land has a clear theological significance as the tangible expression of God's special solicitude for Israel. The depth of YHWH's care is revealed further with the later understanding that this land is, in fact, Israel's inheritance stemming from her filial relationship to YHWH.

Land serves as the "memory of faith" because of its social and theological meaning. In its social role at the national level, land is a source of identity; at the family level, it is a means of "belonging" within a community.

> To lose their inheritance was tantamount to losing their identity as a member of the people and the privileges that went with that identity. The right and obligation to participate in the legal assemblies, to act in common ventures such as defense, to be present representatively at the festivals, were all grounded in the inheritance. (Mays 1987, 150)

Theologically, land ownership is the sign of their salvation, a reminder of God's saving act in delivering them from Egypt.

Functional role

Of greater interest and relevance for this study is the functional role of land in the life of the nation Israel. Since human beings are material, the natural world is the realm in which this divine-human encounter takes place; it provides the setting in which such a relationship emerges and blossoms. Included in this is economic life since humans as corporeal beings have to be sustained and provisioned in their material needs for survival, growth, and development. Moreover, as social beings in a finite natural world, they need to share resources and collaborate with each other in availing of the fruits of the earth. Such need for intense interpersonal economic cooperation defines sociality as the other distinctive feature of Israel's moral understanding (Ogletree 1983, 79–81). In both of these cases, whether as somatic or as social beings, humans are in one way or another bound to the land.

Creation is a triangular relationship between God, humanity, and the earth. God is the divine owner of the earth which in turn is given as a divine gift to mankind for its sustenance, a "conferred dominion" (C. Wright 1990, 115). This same triangular relationship and its dual dimension of divine ownership and divine gift is paradigmatic for redemption since the creation of the nation Israel is the first movement in God's saving act. This time, however, instead of humanity and the earth, we have a threefold relationship between YHWH, Israel, and the Promised Land (174–75). Again, YHWH, as owner, confers land as a gift to Israel; it serves as the sphere in which YHWH's relationship with Israel is to take shape.[4]

Land occupies such a central place in Hebrew theology because of its functional role in sustaining the family, the basic unit of interaction between YHWH and Israel.[5] It is the family that bears responsibility for discharging the judicial, military, and cultic requirements of the Law, in addition to preserving and transmitting Israel's historical traditions to subsequent generations. Moreover, the family unit serves as the sole medium by which individuals (including slaves, aliens, and strangers who have to attach themselves to a landholding family) are able to fully identify themselves as the people of YHWH and avail of the protection that comes from such a divine relationship.[6] It is the "locus of the individual's experience of the privileges and obligations of [a] national relationship with God" (C. Wright 1990, 97).

Only landholding families can serve as building blocks of the covenant relationship. In the first place, to be landless is to be separated from the natural family community and to be merely guests on someone else's land; it is to be completely at the mercy of the host, that is, the landowner, for security and livelihood. To be landless is to be dependent, vulnerable, and uncertain about the future (von Waldow 1974, 495–96). Land ownership is a necessary condition for personal or collective sovereignty (Lohfink 1982, 44). Second, as observed earlier, landholding is critical because it is only through the ownership and use of land that families are able to discharge their military, juridic, and cultic obligations. Third, land is the family's tangible and direct link to being identified with and made a part of the Chosen People of God. Consequently, there is a critical link between landownership and family in Israel; the two are inseparable (C. Wright 1990). It is landholding that ensures that the family both survives and flourishes since land does not merely furnish sustenance but more importantly provides economic security. In fact, a common feature of the alien, widows, orphans, and slaves is their landlessness and their consequent need to attach themselves as dependents to a landholding household. Therefore, YHWH's gift and guarantee of economic security for Israel is integral to the covenant relationship.

This economic security is affirmed in the forceful and unequivocal claim of divine ownership of land. Far from suffering from the abuses and whims of a capricious landlord, Israel is ensured protection, fair treatment, and justice from the owner of the land on which she now lives—YHWH. Far better to have God as host than to be subject to fellow humans. Thus, Leviticus 25:23 is not a cultic, political, or territorial claim by God but is rather a theological-economic statement (C. Wright 1990, 58–65).[7] Families on YHWH's land will never want or be landless; they will never be deprived of an economic base. In being a people of the land, Israel realizes that her livelihood is completely dependent on the goodwill of YHWH both as provider and as owner of the land. It is an affirmation of a solicitous YHWH as landlord ensuring the economic viability of guests and sojourners on God's domain. The assertion that land is so central and integral to the Covenant should come as no surprise since economic security turns out to be a constitutive element, a divine gift, as part of God's in-breaking in human history.

> [T]he landholding units constituted the basic social fabric through which Israel's relationship with God was "earthed" and experienced. (C. Wright 1990, 71)

In other words, the socioeconomic milieu provides the medium for a divine-human relationship to be initiated and to unfold and deepen.

In summary, Israel's theology of land is key both to discerning the necessary economic dimension of human flourishing and to appreciating God's gifts of economic security and due order in creation and human affairs. Land is a venue for imparting God's providential love to Israel. However, as we see in the rest of the chapter, land also serves as a channel through which the Chosen People requite God's devotion for them by caring for each other in a tangible way, especially for the vulnerable and weak in their midst.

God's concern for the poor

The economic dimension of God's in-breaking is revealed not merely in the gift of land to Israel but also in God's special concern for the poor. Lohfink

(1987, 5–15) captures the economics of this historicity well as he describes the broader backdrop of God's intervention in human history on behalf of the poor. God's championing of the poor is undergirded by the larger "biblical-theological horizon" of God's lively, manifold interests in the here and now, in material things, in society, and in the bountifulness of creation. At the heart of the ensuing drama that God unleashes is a requisite systemic change in political economy.

The divine-human encounter is neither a disembodied affair nor an otherworldly phenomenon. Rather, it takes place in the setting of human life and community. Moreover, it is not reserved for some unknown future eschatology; it takes place within the current human experience of temporality. And as part of a revealed divine interest in the here and now, YHWH actively sustains the Chosen People and rectifies systemic injustices that beget suffering, destitution, and want in the first place. After all, God's vision in creation is one of plenty and harmony for all. These divine concerns converge in the concrete particularity of the Exodus—YHWH's act of liberating the oppressed and the burdened from their slavery and leading them into a land of freedom and abundance (Lohfink 1986, 1987, 1991). God intervenes in human history on behalf of the poor and the defenseless and provides for them. All these reflect an economic dimension to God's in-breaking in human history. Economic life is not merely a side issue in covenant election; it is integral to the moral vision undergirding Israel's existence. The liberation of Israel in Exodus is "concretely a change of economic system effected by God" (Lohfink 1986, 220). Moses's task at Sinai is to fashion a nation that follows the egalitarian character of YHWH's act of delivering the impoverished from enslavement by the privileged and the powerful in Egypt (Brueggemann 1994, 15).[8]

Economic life as terrain of God's in-breaking

YHWH acts in human history to release Israel from oppression, sets them in a land "flowing with milk and honey," and then hands down statutes and ordinances that serve as a "blueprint for God's projected society" (Lohfink 1991, 43). In providing the Law, God spurs Israel to build herself a nation through which divine righteousness will continue to be made manifest in the world. It signals an ongoing care for the poor, but this time through YHWH's empowering righteousness in human instrumentality. There is an envisioned due order in the economic affairs of humans as an indispensable part of God's in-breaking.

> [T]he true God becomes manifest at the moment society assumes human features; society transforms itself and becomes humane in the measure that the true God becomes visible. . . . The economic transformation is an essential element of the total process. The lordship of the new God enacts itself not exclusively but still decisively in a new form for the human management of economic affairs. (Lohfink 1986, 222)

In summary, God's self-insertion in human history can be viewed in terms of land as a divine gift (von Waldow 1974; C. Wright 1990) and of divine intervention on behalf of the poor (Lohfink 1987). Common to their discernment of the concrete particularities of God's in-breaking is an unavoidable economic dimension: economic security as an end of landholding (von Waldow and C. Wright) and of systemic socioeconomic reforms (Lohfink). Economics is thus inextricably interwoven within the social, cultural, and theological fabric of the life of the nation. It is not the only or necessarily the most decisive factor, but it is nonetheless powerful in the way it can shape outcomes and processes in human affairs and interpersonal relations. Socioeconomics is not merely an appendage but is, in fact, at the heart of Israel's covenant election. This is highlighted in YHWH as the God of nature who provisions creatures and in YHWH as the God of history who bequeaths Israel a land they are to share and tend together as a people.

ECONOMIC LAWS

Israel's laws, statutes, and ordinances reflect the economic dimension of God's in-breaking.[9] They govern economic life on the Promised Land and ensure the continuance of the special care extended by God toward the poor. Besides providing material security, land gives rise to another facet of the necessary economic dimension—the mutual obligations that come with living on God's domain. In receiving this unmerited grant of land, Israel is charged with doing "everything necessary to keep and maintain this gift and not lose it" (von Waldow 1974, 503). In particular, she is to live a morally upright life in sharp contrast to the nations she had displaced from the land (Lv 18:24–30, 20:22). Only in being a contrast-society can Israel maintain her residency on God's land, and it is YHWH's statutes and ordinances that show the way to being a nation different from all the other nations (von Waldow 1974, 505–6). Far from being intrusive and confining, the Law guarantees the continued enjoyment of the land (Dt 28, 4:1, 5:31, 6:1–3, 11:8, 11:31, 12:1).

The Covenant Code (Ex 20:22–23:33), the Deuteronomic Law (Dt 12–26), and the Code of Holiness (Lv 17–26) provide an extended list of statutes governing economic life. Among these laws are mandatory lending (Dt 15:7–10; Lv 25:35–37), interest-free loans (Ex 22:25; Dt 23:19–20; Lv 25:36–37), sabbatical rest and festivals (Ex 23:10–12; Lv 25:1–7, 25:18–24), jubilee releases and land tenure (Lv 25), gleaning restrictions (Dt 24:19–21; Lv 19:9–10, 23:22; Ru 2), tithing (Dt 14:22–29), debt remission (Dt 15:1–3), slave manumission (Ex 21:2–6; Dt 15:12–18), and the preferential treatment of widows, orphans, and strangers. In fact, if there is a single overarching theme flowing through these three law codes, it is the social responsibility that is owed to the *personae miserabiles* (von Waldow 1970, 182; Pleins 2001, 51) in which the vulnerable are singled out for special assistance (Ogletree 1983, 56).

Debt legislation

There are four components to legislation pertaining to debt. The first is the interest-free nature of credit: no interest may be charged to a fellow Hebrew for money or food loans (Ex 22:25; Dt 23:19–20; Lv 25:36–37). The second is mandatory lending in which one is morally obligated to assist a neighbor in economic straits (Dt 15:7–10; Lv 25:35–37). Third are the restrictions on the pledges that may be exacted from debtors. Personal articles such as cloaks may not be taken as a pledge since they are essential for the borrower's health and survival (Ex 22:26; Dt 24:10–13). Nor may one take as collateral anything that is critical for maintaining a livelihood (Dt 24:6). Fourth is debt remission on the seventh year (Dt 15:1–3)—the *shemittah*.[10] A purpose of suppressing loans every seven years is to break the momentum of unpaid debts that simply take a life of their own and continue to grow, thereby making it more unlikely for the borrower to recover from economic distress. This periodic debt reprieve halts the continued slide of the debtor into deeper arrears (Schenker 1998, 36).[11]

Commentators advance two reasons for this array of loan legislation. Given the agrarian nature of Israel and her level of economic development, most debts at that time were from distress loans rather than commercial credit for trade or production. Peasants do not borrow money for production; rather, they are compelled to incur debt because of some exigency (Lang 1985, 99). Thus, one should not profit from the extreme need or misfortune of a neighbor, and one should not exacerbate the borrower's economic plight by imposing additional obligations (Neufeld 1955, 359–61; Lang 1985, 99).[12] Charging interest for distress loans would have been a real onus for the debtor. In the first place, Israel had a subsistence economy with not much surplus to spare to cover the supplementary cost of borrowing money or grain.[13] After all, that people have to resort to hardship loans is in itself already an indication that they are unable to meet their basic needs, and this even before imposing the additional burden of paying interest. Hence, it is not surprising that many end up in debt-slavery or simply choose to remain in voluntary bondage once they find a good household (Ex 21:5–6; Dt 15:16–17). Secondly, as we will see shortly, interest rates on grain loans are much higher compared to money loans.[14] This is the antithesis of the preferential option for the poor because grain loans are most likely indicative of even greater urgency or deeper distress on the part of the borrower.

Given the deteriorating economic conditions of eighth-century Israel, there may be a second reason prompting these statutes concerning debt. In compelling creditors to give up interest, forgive debts, and freely provide loans to the needy, these lenders are in effect also giving up their "stranglehold" on rural peasants (Lang 1985). Moreover, it prevents creditors from using moneylending as a means of enriching themselves and making the poor subservient.[15]

Slave release

Debt-slaves are released after six years of service (Ex 21:2–6; Dt 15:12–18) or during the Jubilee year or upon redemption by a kin (Lv 25:39–42, 25:47–55). The manumission of slaves is not unique to Israel as it was already practiced and codified in Near Eastern legislation (Chirichigno 1993).

Sabbatical year

Besides the weekly Sabbath, Israel is to let the land lie fallow every seven years (Ex 23:10–12; Lv 25:1–7, 25:18–24). These practices are said to be unique to Israel compared to other nations in the Near East (Lowery 2000, 24, 51).

The Sabbath-fallow provides a vision of due order in human community, a blueprint for the ideal social order in three ways. First, it is a foretaste of the eschatological banquet and rest. The rationale for the year of fallow echoes that of the requisite weekly Sabbath (Dt 5:12–15). The Sabbath must be viewed in relation to Sabbath-creation and Sabbath-manna in which God provides bountifully to allow for a recreating pause that savors and celebrates the joy of God's blessings; it is an anticipation of the promised eschatological rest in God (Lowery 2000, 101–2; Miller 1990, 81; 1985, 88). Together with the Promised Land, peace in the here and now is a gift from God to the Chosen People as part of their covenant election (von Rad 1966b). Such rest is also an affirmation of divine sovereignty, as it is only God who is able to give and guarantee rest from the pressing threats, concerns, and demands of the world (Lowery 2000, 88–89; Lohfink 1982, 52).

Second, Sabbath-fallow is a lesson on the proper attitude to scarcity and property that Israel ought to have as a community of faith. It is a statement that pecuniary gain, accumulation, and production are not ends in themselves but are merely means to the much larger goal of delighting and resting in the Lord and in each other. It is an attitude of life in which the Sabbath is a paradigm of how people ought to deal with economic scarcity. Rather than allowing property to "possess" them, humans should instead use property as a means of enjoying God and each other's company. This is no ordinary rest—it is a consecrated rest because it is open to God and is a time for thanksgiving: "The sabbath as a rest that is open to God relativizes human work and pulls people away from their own goals and energies and endeavors so they remember the larger work of God" (Miller 1990, 82; see also Miller 1985, 89–90). Moreover, it is also a statement of faith in the generosity of God's providence. Sabbath-fallow, Sabbath-creation, and Sabbath-manna are thematically related to each other (Lowery 2000, 62–63). The promised triple harvest of Sabbath-fallow (Lv 25:18–22), the abundance of the workweek in creation that affords a day of rest (Gn 1:1–2:4), and the double portion of manna collected in preparation for the Sabbath (Ex 16:22–27) point to the same divine characteristic: YHWH provides the necessary means for whatever God may ask of Israel. Thus, inordinate accumulation and excessive consumption are symptomatic of a lack of faith in the trustworthiness of divine word and sovereignty (Lowery 2000, 101).

Third, the Sabbath-fallow is an instrument of social justice. The sabbatical year is more than just letting the land lie fallow. Sabbath-fallow may be viewed as a countercultural statement of justice that stands in sharp contrast to Pharonic production (Brueggemann 1994, 16). It calls for fellowship and the sharing of material resources with those who have little. At a deeper level, it is an affirmation of the equality of status enjoyed by all since there are no social distinctions that divide people in the feasting and celebration that is at the heart of resting in the Lord (Lohfink 1982, 52). It affords recreating pause to the vulnerable and defenseless such as the servants and slaves, the ones who bear the brunt of work. It is an affirmation of mutual concern for each other's well-being. The feasting, contemplation, and sharing that should take place during the sabbatical, including the restoration of slaves, is eschatological in the sense of living the end time in the here and now. To implement such a regimen requires sacrificial changes in economic behavior. Thus, one could even go so far as to claim that "the primary impetus to social justice in Deuteronomic theology is the command to keep the Sabbath" (Miller 1985, 82, 93).

Jubilee Law

The Jubilee is a radical comprehensive socioeconomic reform that pulls together the preceding economic precepts into a single package: debt release, slave release, and land redemption on the seventh of seven consecutive sabbatical years (Lv 25). That land is sold due to insolvency is not unique to Israel, as we find similar practices in Old Babylon (Chirichigno 1993, 350). There are Near Eastern precedents for debt and slave release and the return of family land (Greenberg 1972, 577–78; Fager 1993, 25). The only difference is that whereas these releases are effected by royal decree in the other Near Eastern countries, Israel regularizes these practices and incorporates them into the nation's laws. Common to all these countries is the resistance to alienating ancestral land.

The return of land is at the heart of the Jubilee Law, which can be viewed as a theological statement of Israel's self-understanding of the role of land in her relationship with God. Land is central to Israel's election, from the promise made to Abraham, to its fulfillment in Joshua, and to the laws that govern life on the land. Land is a birthright from YHWH, the tangible touchstone of this special relationship. For a nomadic and agrarian culture, land is the primary dominant good and the key source of value, livelihood, wealth, power, and security.[16] Israel's claim to the Promised Land is based on God: the Lord of history has given land to her (von Waldow 1974, 496). This is the strongest possible claim that can be made; it is a right that trumps all other claims to the land including that of first occupancy, as in the case of the previous in-habitants who are driven off the land by Israel. God, after all, is the final arbiter and rightful owner whose lawful claims supersede all others (Lv 25:23). Israel accepts land as her inheritance from God, the visible sign of her covenant election. Land therefore signifies an even deeper gift of God's love.

This gift of land figures prominently in defining and shaping the content and quality of Israel's relationship to YHWH in two ways: land is inalienable, and its fruits are to be widely shared with the *personae miserabiles*. The in-alienability of land is reflected not only in the Jubilee Law but in other refer-ences to the right and the obligation of land redemption (e.g., Ru 4:6–8). Likewise, the mandate for nonexclusive usufruct is reflected in the numerous precepts and statutes governing economic life such as gleaning, tithing, debt and slave releases, almsgiving, shared feastings, and so on. There are limits to human ownership and use of created goods because God is the genuine owner, and humans are mere stewards. The proper human posture to prop-erty is humble and thankful stewardship rather than proprietorship.

Land inalienability produces practical consequences that are consistent with the ideal egalitarian character of Israel.[17] In the first place, land tenure ensures a family's livelihood, independence, equal status, and participation in the larger community (C. Wright 1990, 63; Eichrodt 1961, 97). Thus, no-tice the care with which the Promised Land is divided to ensure that every family receives a fair and workable share (Jo 18:1–10; Nm 26: 52–56). More-over, land return and redemption avert economic crises and social animosity that an overconcentration of wealth causes (Fager 1993).[18] Since land is the primary source of wealth-creation in an agrarian setting, the return of patri-monial land ensures that relative inequality will be kept within certain bounds.[19] Whether the Jubilee is viewed as restorative or redistributive, or both, in its goals, it is important to highlight that the law is a systemic, insti-tutionalized approach to safeguarding the welfare of all in the community es-pecially those vulnerable to economic privation (C. Wright 1990, 176–80). Even more remarkable, however, is how it does not rely on the state to imple-ment the law. As with the other precepts on economic life, enforcement is left to the conscience and is a matter of moral suasion, honor, pride, reputation within the community, and fidelity to the Covenant. Thus, recall how King Zedekiak (Jer 34:8–12) and the prophet Nehemiah (Neh 5:1–13) have to ca-jole people into observing the Law. This is also consistent with the egalitar-ian and democratic ethos that animates early Israel's formation.

DISTINCTIVE CHARACTERISTICS

Many of Israel's statues are also found in adjoining Near Eastern nations. (Lohfink 1991; Dearman 1984)[20] In fact, it is believed that Israel adopted these laws from her neighbors and from the people she displaced from the Promised Land. There are Near Eastern precedents for debt remission, slave manumission, and return of hereditary land (Greenberg 1972), though these releases were by royal decree and not regularized like they were in Israel. Scholars are in disagreement over the extent to which Hebrew laws on economic life are similar or different from their Near Eastern counterparts.[21]

Despite evidence on the correspondence of Hebrew and Near Eastern economic laws, there are nevertheless essential differences that set apart the nation Israel as distinctive in her understanding and practice of economic life. In particular, see how these laws (1) are embedded within a systematic effort at structural reform, (2) are merely means to the much larger goal of both personal and collective holiness, and (3) are interwoven within a web of cultic-religious-social practices.

Divinely initiated systemic reform

Lohfink argues that the experience of the Exodus is what makes Israel completely unique in her economic life even as she borrows and adopts her humane economic statutes from neighboring countries. He notes numerous, interrelated critical weak points in the Near Eastern nations' appropriation of these laudable ordinances (1987, 29–30). Besides the gap between their statement of the theory and their actual practice, these adjoining empires and states embed these laws within a social apparatus meant to preserve the status quo. They are written from the perspective of the ruling, wealthy, dominant classes for whom these economic rules are simply matters of personal piety or supererogatory works of munificence.[22] Lohfink observes:

> A breath of "charitable" condescension wafts through many ancient Near Eastern texts. The key figure in care for the poor is almost always the king, the key symbol of the existing social order. (1987, 30)

Besides merely addressing the symptoms and not the causes of poverty, these economic ordinances end up strengthening the very social structure and dynamics that give rise to suffering and destitution in the first place. There is no room at all for questioning, rethinking, and reforming the existing social order. The real issues are thus obscured. Moreover, while Near Eastern laws are expansive in their prologues and epilogues on royal justice and the protection of the weak, they have no social legislation in the texts themselves and are silent on poverty (Lohfink 1991, 37).

In contrast, the Exodus not only reveals God's concern for the welfare of the poor but more importantly demonstrates God's call for and active involvement in radically reforming failed social structures. As part of God's *sedeq,* YHWH restores due order in human affairs, especially in the socioeconomic and political spheres. Israel's liberation from oppression and slavery in Egypt and her entry into a "land flowing with milk and honey" are but YHWH's opening acts in a much larger drama of transforming Israel into a contrast-society meant to be uncommon in her character of mutual respect and compassion (Lohfink 1987, 50). Thus, while the other Near Eastern nations codify *what is* ("an expression of regulatory law at work"), the Hebrews state *what ought to be* (a "prophetic reach for a standard of conduct higher than that of the marketplace") (Meislin and Cohen 1964, 258). Moreover, unlike the absence of laws concerning the poor in the Near Eastern collections, Israel's Law has an extensive selection of mandated remedies for the destitute (Lohfink 1991, 39). Thus, poor relief is institutionalized, regularized, and need not be occasioned solely by royal celebrations or be contingent on royal pleasure alone since the entire community is charged with responsibility for the welfare of the disadvantaged.

> And what now bound them together as the new entity called "Israel" was precisely the ideal of a new life together. The rural egalitarian and segmented tribal society "Israel" was in its own self-understanding a contrast to the feudal Canaanite city-states in the vicinity as well as to their colonial overlords from faraway Egypt. They needed no walled cities because their brotherly and sisterly solidarity was a better protection. They have no social classification of poor and rich because they recognized no authority over themselves except that of their God Yahweh; and they had developed social mechanisms to insure that equality of land ownership and in decision making was repeatedly restored. . . . [T]hey were able to discern quite clearly what wonders Yahweh, to their own astonishment, had done with all of them. (Lohfink 1987, 49)

Brueggemann (1994, 13–14) makes a point similar to Lohfink's in arguing that the Exodus is "Israel's identifying narrative" in which YHWH's act
on her behalf becomes Israel's defining moment for her self-understanding.
The Chosen People's moral consciousness is shaped both by YHWH's radical
act of treating them as ends in themselves (rather than as means to be exploited, as was their experience in Egypt) and by YHWH's providing them
with what they need—dignity and compassion—rather than what they de-
serve. These in turn remind Israel of what YHWH expects of them—treating
one another in the same manner in which YHWH attends to their needs and
failures.

Hebrew economic statutes are part of an ongoing project of personal and
collective transformation—one that demands no mere superficial change
but profound conversion, as well as requires a never-ending, sacrificial self-
giving from one's substance rather than merely from one's surplus. The willingness to embrace such self-denial on behalf of the impoverished stems
from Israel's understanding that it is an obligation owed primarily to God to
begin with. A readily observable Hebrew ethical pattern is the "fulfillment of
one's obligation to God by means of the discharge of one's responsibilities for
one's fellows" (C. Wright 1990, 148).

Lohfink's thesis finds validation in the numerous historical-religious
motive clauses. As we find in the next sections, many of these economic ordinances often end with a reminder of what God had done for them in the
Exodus as a way of motivating people to subscribe to these laws. Such motive
clauses prod the Chosen People to extend to others the same favors they had
received from YHWH, particularly the marginalized and those who have
fallen into great distress. More important, such motive clauses reaffirm a key
tenet of the Exodus: YHWH intervenes in human history in order to establish an egalitarian contrast-society that takes care of its poor.

Mixed cultic-civil-moral laws

Hebrew cultic, civil, and moral legislation are mixed together unlike other
Near Eastern laws; the liturgical, ethical, religious, and economic realms and
claims are inextricably tied together.

> [T]his law in its outward form and in its sense of purpose is a unified en-
> tity, . . . its legal content is interpreted throughout with a single mind. . . .

> It is as a result of this unified basic conception that the lawgiver succeeds in establishing *an inner unity between the cultic and the politico-social ordinances.* (Eichrodt 1961, 91; original emphasis)

Unlike Mesopotamian culture that limits religion to cultic practices and sacrifice, Israel undergirds its civil law with its religion. Observance of that religion, therefore, occurs not merely in rites but through social interaction as well (Gnuse 1985, 12).

In seeking to explain the seeming contradictions within the Book of the Covenant, Hanson (1977, 119–21) observes that despite being drawn from a wide variety of sources (such as long-standing tribal practices, Near Eastern legal codes, and local taboos), Hebrew Law is an organic whole that stems from the people's common confession of a covenantal relationship with YHWH. Thus, the constitutive legal, moral, and cultic structures of this nascent nation are drawn together and then transformed by the same sacral vision and goal of being holy before the Lord.

> Israel, like any new people, experienced the need to order life on the basis of social structures appropriate to its experiences and ideals. . . . But the need was not met in the usual, ancient Near Eastern manner of introducing an institution of civil jurisprudence running independently of the cult, that is to say, as a separate secular phenomenon. Instead, the various legal materials were drawn into the cult festivals themselves, thereby obliging those materials to interact with and be transformed by the central confessions of the religious community. The result is the unique amalgamation of civil, moral, and cultic prescriptions which we find in the core of the Book of the Covenant. (Hanson 1977, 120)

Such integration is evident in a number of ways. In the first place, Israel regularizes many of the humane practices of its neighbors. For example, Near Eastern practices concerning the release of those held in bondage, debt write-offs, and land return take place only at the pleasure of the monarch; the ascension of a new king is often the occasion for such royal decrees. In contrast, slave and debt release are regularized in Israel every seven years while land return is set every fifty years. The social well-being of Israel is not going to be dependent on royal or judicial fiat but is to flow as a natural extension and consequence of its worship life (Pleins 2001, 44).[23] In other words, ritual and social legislation go hand in hand. This dovetails the earlier point that while materially similar to its Near Eastern neighbors, Hebrew social legislation is different because it must be viewed within the larger context of the Exodus and YHWH's defining liberation of the poor and oppressed (Lohfink 1987).

Such institutionalization and regularization of humane economic practices is consistent with the view that the nation Israel is founded to be distinctively different from all the other nations because of its triadic covenant model—an economy of equality, a politics of justice, and a religion of God's radical freedom and fidelity (Birch 1991, 172–82). These three realms mutually reinforce each other. Religion shapes and defines economics and politics by providing them with a foundational, ever-present consciousness of YHWH's expectations, even as economics and politics in their own turn serve to extend religion and the genuine worship of God beyond mere cultic practices to include the just treatment of others. Proper economic conduct is a precondition to satisfactory cultic rites, as repeatedly emphasized by the prophets who observe that God is honored not in holocausts and burnt offerings but in the goodness overflowing from the heart that reaches out to others with compassion (Am 5:21–24; Is 1:10–18).

This cultic-economic-theological linkage is clearly embedded in the social vision of the nation Israel.

> By framing the poverty question as both a matter of persons and structures, and by invoking laws to regulate these circumstances, the Covenant Code far surpasses its ancient Near Eastern counterparts. *Justice for the poor became self-consciously both a civil and religious matter in ancient Israel.* As such, the social praxis of justice making comes under scrutiny in the code. (Pleins 2001, 53; emphasis added)

This ready mixing of ritual, theology, and socioeconomics in Hebrew Law distinguishes the nation from its neighbors (Boecker 1980, 137). The Covenant Code is peculiar in that it has a tripartite division of materials—*jus*, ethos, and cultic law—that, in other cultures, would have been treated separately under law, wisdom, and priestly collections.

This close coupling between economics, politics, and cult is well-illustrated in the Jubilee Law both in terms of the language and rituals used (Lowery 2000, 70–72). The Jubilee begins on the Day of Atonement, a day of purification, rest, and self-denial in preparation for encountering YHWH. The celebration is heralded by trumpet blast, just as trumpet blasts are constitutive of numerous rituals in proclaiming and celebrating royal coronations, the beginning or end of battle, and notice of convocations, new moons, burnt offerings, and sacrifices. The trumpet blast that ushers in the Jubilee year ought to be viewed in the context of the trumpet blasts that heralded Israel's earlier encounter with YHWH on Mount Sinai.

> Jubilee observance, announced with trumpet blast on the Day of Atonement, is a Sinai experience for Israel, a direct encounter with the God who redeems and frees them for all human bondage. The social legislation associated with jubilee—abolishing slavery and usury, redistributing land, allowing the land to rest—reveals Yahweh. *When Israel exercises jubilee self-restraint for the sake of the poor and the well-being of the land, they purify and prepare themselves. In these acts of mercy and justice, Israel encounters God.* (Lowery 2000, 72; emphasis added)

Ritual and worship encompass preparation and purification for the express end of encountering the divine. Social action and ritual easily mix with each other, as seen in Lowery's preceding description of the significance of the Jubilee. Israel encounters YHWH both in its cultic and socioeconomic life as these are intertwined. Economics and social worship complement and mutually reinforce each other as part of the tightly knit cultic-economic nature of the Jubilee Law (North 1954, 219–21).

The inseparability of cultic, civil, and moral laws from each other transfers the venue for enforcement from the external and the governmental to the internal and the personal.[24]

> It is no longer a question of simply carrying out certain external regulations, assisted by the power of the state; *the law has been drawn into the sphere of operation of the spiritual and moral life,* where external compulsion must be replaced by personal moral decision. (Eichrodt 1961, 93; emphasis added)

Thus, personal and collective conversion becomes even more important as a necessary condition for the observance of the Law.

Theocentric thrust

In Near Eastern practice, the kings are charged with protecting the defenseless and providing prosperity to the people. In contrast, within Israel, it is not the monarch but YHWH as king who does all these and more. YHWH is the royal protector and the royal provider (Lowery 2000, 7–21; Psalm 72). Thus, central to YHWH's relationship with Israel is the divine gift of land.

Israel is also distinctive from her Near Eastern neighbors because of her appreciation for the provenance of her laws: YHWH is the lawgiver (Dt 4:5–8). This theocentric feature in Israel's legislation should not come as a complete surprise at all since the unity of its tribes stems not from a common ethnicity but from their shared special relationship with YHWH. It is not race but religion and their consciousness of YHWH as a special part of their lives that bind them together as a nation. Israel is different from her neighbors because she struggles to live up to the demands of the Law out of a desire to requite God's devotion and love for her. This "religious temper . . . [leads to] *the total ordering of the people's life as a revelation of the saving will of God*" (Eichrodt 1961, 92; emphasis added). This theocentric character of Israel's legislation leads to even deeper sources of differences between Hebrew and Near Eastern law collections, as we find in the next section.

Motive clauses

Israel's theological self-understanding shapes her socioeconomic life and what she expects of herself. This is evident in the motive clauses—statements that provide the rationale for the regulations propounded—that are said to be unique to Israel. There is a profusion of motive clauses in Hebrew Law and a marked steady growth in their occurrence as the Law develops and evolves from the Covenant Code to the Deuteronomic Law to the Levitical Code of Holiness. Even more significant, however, is the observation that motive clauses are "clearly and definitely a peculiarity of Israel's or Old Testament law" (Gemser 1953, 52). Nowhere else are they found in the law collections of the Ancient Near East.

The forms, functions, and content of these motive clauses are wide and varied. With respect to content, Gemser (1953) suggests four different kinds of motivation: explanatory, ethical, cultic-theological, and religious-historical. Doron (1978) suggests a slightly different division: humanistic, election-related, reward-giving, and didactic. Of relevance to this study are the clauses in Gemser's cultic-theological and religious-historical categories, and those that highlight Israel's election in Doron's typology.

Sacral motive clauses

Within Gemser's (1953) cultic-theological motive clauses, only those that Doron (1978) classifies as a reminder of their election by God and their concomitant call to holiness are relevant for this study. Nowhere else is this more succinctly and definitively captured than in Leviticus 19:2: *"Be holy because I, the LORD your God, am holy."*[25]

Numerous motive clauses remind Israel of her signal election in God, who sets her apart from all the other nations as God's own child (Dt 14:1), as a treasured possession (Ex 19:4–5; Dt 14:2), and as a holy people (Ex 19:6; Dt 14:2, 14:21; Lv 20:24, 20:26). Moreover, these clauses affirm YHWH as the sole source of holiness, who confers such excellence on whomever God chooses (Lv 21:8, 21:15, 21:23, 22:9, 22:16, 22:32).

Such bestowed holiness, however, is contingent on the Chosen People's fidelity to YHWH's ordinances (Lv 20:22; 22:31); Israel's moral conduct ought to set her distinctly separate from all the other nations (Lv 18:1–5). It is a conferred sanctity that blooms to its fullness in the measure the nation lives up to divine statutes since these serve as venues for God to effect holiness in the nation Israel.

> Consecrate yourselves and be holy, because I am the LORD your God. Keep my decrees and follow them. I am the LORD, who makes you holy. (Lv 20:7–8)

This conscious effort to live up to the standards of God's holiness must pervade all facets of her life, even in domestic housekeeping, as in the case of camp cleanliness (Dt 23:14). There is need to embrace God's saving act of making Israel holy; it is a response that finds concrete expression in the observance of YHWH's mandates. This reciprocal dynamic of gift and response in which the reply brings out the fullness of the gift is well-illustrated in the concluding summary of the Deuteronomic Law (Dt 26:16–19). To be holy is to be wholly other. For Israel this includes being "wholly other" from neighboring communities in the way she organizes herself as the Chosen People. This naturally includes being different from surrounding nations in the way she conducts her economic life (Lohfink 1986, 225). "Israel's sacral traditions are manifest in the substantive content of these special obligations" (Ogletree 1983, 56). These economic ordinances and statutes, when observed, reveal YHWH still at work in their midst.

Religious-historical motive clauses

Religious-historical motive clauses describe God's "holy acts in history" on behalf of Israel, such as her deliverance from Egypt and the gift of Canaan as the Promised Land (Gemser 1953, 60–61; Doron 1978, 73). These "holy acts" of God now serve as paradigms for how Hebrews are to treat one another in conferring on each other, including strangers and aliens, the same favors they had received from a gracious and merciful YHWH. These motive clauses give expression to the "organic connection of Israel's history and religion" (Gemser 1953, 63).

YHWH's act of freeing Israel from slavery and oppression in Egypt now serves as the basis for interpersonal relations, particularly with those who are at risk. This is evident from the wide variety of circumstances in which these motive clauses have been employed: affording a Sabbath rest even for servants and slaves (Dt 5:13–15); the liberal provisioning of slaves about to be released at the end of six years of service (Dt 15:12–15); the generous sharing of one's produce in cultic feasts and celebrations, especially with the marginalized and dispossessed (Dt 16:12); the observance of gleaning laws (Dt 24:19–22); the call for restraint in securing pledges and admonitions against being unjust toward the widow, orphan, and aliens (Dt 24:17); dealing honestly with each other in commercial transactions (Lv 19:35–37); the proper treatment of aliens and even loving them (Lv 19:33); provision of interest-free loans (Lv 25:35–38); foregoing the widespread practice of debt-slavery and taking in people who have fallen on hard times as tenants or hired hands (Lv 25:39–43). Note how these clauses have been primarily employed in laws pertaining to the proper treatment of the poor.

These motive clauses have been described as soteriological (Gemser 1953, 60) because God's saving act in the Exodus serves as the motivation for Israel to behave in like manner—to treat others in the same way God had graciously treated her in her own moment of need. Besides urging the proper treatment of the poor, these clauses have also been used to provide Israel with both hope and promise by affirming God's fidelity to the Covenant despite Israel's disobedience (Lv 26:40–45) and by reiterating the peace and prosperity that flow in the wake of compliance with YHWH's laws (Lv 26:1–13).

Gifts of participation and instrumentality

The importance of motive clauses for this study is not merely in highlighting another distinctive difference between the nation Israel and her Near Eastern neighbors. More important, they ground the basis of Hebrew Law in the God of history's in-breaking in human affairs. The strength of the Law's claim to Israel's compliance partly stems from what God had done for her.

The cultic-theological motive clauses of holiness-election and the religious-historical motive clauses of deliverance are inseparable from each other. After all, Israel's election to holiness is effected through God's righteous act in liberating the oppressed and the disenfranchised, and in regenerating them in a "land flowing with milk and honey." This double divine movement, however, is merely a prelude to a third divine movement—enabling Israel to be holy and righteous in her own conduct toward others. Hence, observe how motive clauses are appended to many of the laws governing the proper treatment of the underprivileged in the Covenant Code and in Deuteronomic Law (Gemser 1953, 63), presumably for extra emphasis and for stronger sanction.

For this study, these motive clauses explicitly articulate the warrants for proper economic behavior—reasons that are only implied in Lohfink's (1987) systemic social reform, or merely relegated as an unspoken but understood larger backdrop in the inseparability of cultic-socioeconomic practices. Motive clauses clearly state the basis for the laws and statutes undergirding the vision of Israel as a contrast-society. The mandated social order is founded on the nation's self-understanding of its election to holiness as God's Chosen People, which in turn elicits a necessary response of righteousness in the way they are to treat one another. Holiness and righteousness are conferred by God; the Law is an invitation to accept such unmerited divine benefaction. This entire dynamic is succinctly summarized in Deuteronomy 6:20–25.

Liberation from enslavement and covenant election are two defining moments for Israel. These events point to a special solicitude for Israel evident in YHWH's in-breaking and could therefore be aptly viewed as two signal divine gifts. However, these two pivotal benefactions from Israel's past now serve as the basis for yet another divine gift: Israel herself living up to the heights of holiness and righteousness to which she is now called.

It should not be a surprise that both Israel's exodus-liberation and her election to holiness are used extensively as motivation for the Chosen People to obey God's ordinances. After all, the social morality and its accompanying sacrifices, embedded within YHWH's vision of Israel as a contrast-society, should be even more intelligible to a people that had experienced election and liberation firsthand. Moreover, conformity to divine laws and statutes is not for the sake of YHWH but is for the benefit of Israel herself (Dt 10:12–13, 11:27–28, 28:1–14, 30:15–20).[26] It is through such obedience that YHWH effects and perfects Israel's holiness and righteousness and thus completes what God had begun in exodus-liberation and in Sinai-election. Thus, one could view these ordinances, laws, and statutes as a divine invitation to participate in the holiness and righteousness of God.

Gemser's (1953, 62–63) explanation for the proliferation of motive clauses in Hebrew Law compared to their complete absence in other Near Eastern legislation provides additional support to this view of the Law as "an invitation to participate in God's holiness and righteousness." In contrast to the other Near Eastern collections' targeted audience of jurists, judges, and priests, Israel's laws are intended for a much wider hearing and readership—the larger populace. These statutes have to appeal to people's common sense and be so compelling to their moral and religious sensibilities as to elicit ready compliance. Thus, there is a profusion of motive clauses in an effort to win hearts and minds.[27]

> [A] national law can never attain its goal so long as it remains a system reluctantly endured and effective only by compulsion; *it must be founded on the inward assent of the people.* (Eichrodt 1961, 91; emphasis added)

The consequence of this expanded target audience is to imbue Hebrew Law with a "truly democratic character," in which "motive clauses constitute an instructive compendium of the religion, theology, ethics, and democratic, humanitarian outlook of the people of Israel" (Gemser 1953, 63). This fits in with many of the observations in the preceding sections:

1. This democratic character of Hebrew legislation reinforces the earlier point that unlike other Near Eastern nations, the care of the poor and distressed in Israel is a task not limited to the king or a few, but is a duty incumbent upon everyone since all have been called to election and righteousness.
2. The organic connection of theology, ritual, history, and economics in these motive clauses confirm the inseparability of cult and ritual from socioeconomic conduct.
3. The "institutionalization" of systemic social reform as part of legislation makes the radical saving act of God in Exodus on behalf of the poor an

ongoing undertaking. But this time, it is the people called to holiness and righteousness that carry on God's righteous act. Moreover, this continued concern for the destitute is constitutive of Israel's self-identity given her understanding of what God unambiguously expects of her regarding the treatment of those at risk.

To be upright in moral conduct is to live up to the vision of God's liberating act in the Exodus, to partake of God's justice, and in the process, to be made holy by God's saving act. Thus, one can view both the laws on economic life and the economic dimension of YHWH's in-breaking in human history as God's way of extending human participation in divine righteousness. However, this dynamic does not end merely with Israel successfully being YHWH's envisioned contrast-society or merely in her participating in God's righteousness. For Israel, to be holy is to be a channel through which God also transforms other nations and peoples to be righteous and holy in their own turn. There is a rightful universal claim that can be made on holy people because it is through them that the Kingdom of God draws in the farthest reaches of the world toward the New Jerusalem in the great "pilgrimage of peoples" (Is 2:1–5, 2:60–63; Lohfink 1991, 225–26). It is in the light of such a gift of instrumentality that one gets to appreciate even further how the historicity and particularity of Israel's encounter with YHWH leads to that which is universal:

> [T]he more deeply the prophets reflected upon the import of Israel's particularity, the more that particularity came to be seen not as a denial of universality or even of social and cultural otherness, but as a concretely historical way into universality. *The universal takes on concrete reality,* that is to say, not by abstracting from history, but *by following the promise which is latent in its open horizon.* (Ogletree 1983, 80; emphasis added)

Of course, the most promising possibility afforded to every human life is that of partaking in the holiness and righteousness of God—a participation that in its own turn can be used as a venue for actualizing the possibilities latent in other lives.

In summary, besides the gift of sharing in divine holiness and righteousness is the added gift of instrumentality in which God enlists humans in the service of divine providence. God draws upon such participated holiness and righteousness to water the arid wastelands still to be made fertile and yet to bloom in their unrealized fullness. YHWH invites Israel to live in such a way as to make God's presence manifest to others. God's in-breaking is ongoing and continues to take shape and emerge through human beings themselves as they respond to the unexpected, unmerited cluster of divine gifts proffered.

Filial relationship

Another difference between Israel and her Near Eastern neighbors is her self-understanding of her filial relationship to YHWH. Given such deep bonds, Israel's observance of the Law should be viewed in the more profound context of Israel as a child partaking of, indeed continuing, her Father's work not only in bringing about due order in human affairs but also in making divine in-breaking continually manifest in the world. It is yet another signal gift that provides even greater depth to the earlier benefactions of instrumentality and participation in holiness and righteousness.

Canaanite and Hebrew cultic practices are no different in ascribing the fertility and ownership of land to the Lord of nature. Israel is in Canaan as a guest because of the graciousness of God. Nowhere is this more clearly seen than in the claim made by YHWH in connection with the Jubilee Law: "[T]he land is mine and you are but aliens and my tenants" (Lv 25:23). YHWH as landowner affords sanctuary and provides sustenance to all sojourners who have been welcomed to reside in God's domain. Naturally by extension, guests and tenants who have been received to dwell on the land are expected to mutually respect each other and treat one another justly, if only because they are each equally under the landowner's charge as his guests and tenants. After all, everyone who lives on God's land is "placed under the direct protection of God, and could be attacked only at the risk of incurring God's enmity"; such surety includes even the thief, the alien, and those who have no economic or social status (Mendenhall 1954, 39). To be on God's land is to be under the protection of God's justice; however, it also means that one must discharge the attendant obligations of such protective justice. As guest and tenant, one has to conform to the established rules of the household.

All these take on greater significance for Israel compared to her Near Eastern neighbors because Israel's relationship to YHWH is more than just merely that of a sojourner to its landowner. Israel is more than just a "feudal tenant" holding land as a grant, residing under her master's protection, rendering service, and discharging duties as a feudal peasant would to its lord (C. Wright 1990, 73). Israel is no mere boarder in constant fear of being thrown off the land for infractions and unfulfilled obligations; Israel is God's own child. YHWH is more than just the God of nature; YHWH is also the Lord of history who gave the land to Israel (Dt 6:10–11, 26:5–10; von Waldow 1974, 496–97). And it is no ordinary gift either because it is bequeathed as an inheritance to one's own child.[28]

We find numerous passages in the Hebrew Scripture in which the relationship of Israel to YHWH is cast in terms of a parent-child bond (C. Wright 1990, 15–22). This is true both at the national level in which Israel itself is referred to as YHWH's child (Ex 4:22; Dt 8:5, 32:6, 32:18; Hos 11:1; Jer 31:9; Is 31:9, 31:20, 49:14–16, 63:16, 64:8; Mal 1:6) and at the individual level in which Hebrews are called God's children (Dt 14:1, 32:5, 32:19; Is 1:2, 30:1–9, 43:6; Jer 3:19; Mal 2:10). Ascribing paternity or maternity (Is 49:14–16) to YHWH is fitting since Israel comes into existence only because God calls her forth to receive an election to holiness as a firstborn.

The God of history has effected an unprecedented switch from having Israel merely as a stranger and tenant on the land (Lv 25:23) to being the land's heir. This move from a tenant-landowner to a parent-child relationship deepens the implications of the economic dimension of God's in-breaking in human history in a substantive manner. The religious-historical motive clauses that remind Israel of her liberation in the Exodus take on even greater moment when viewed as a parent giving birth to a child. From a mere stranger-sojourner with no claim at all on the land, Israel suddenly comes to possess the land as an inheritance. From being an alien away from her own natural setting, Israel now finds herself constituted as a community with a home she can now call her own. From being completely dependent on the graciousness of a landlord-master with whom no ties are shared, Israel still finds herself completely dependent, but this time, dependent on her own parent. Coming from the fringes of society, Israel now finds herself at the center, and in a position to bestow benefactions to the marginalized in her own turn and on her own land.

Land and the economic life it embodies are no longer merely viewed from the standpoint of stewardship as a tenant or guest would; rather, they take on new meaning as an inheritance, which heralds a qualitatively different kind of care for the land—one that is proprietal and paternal in its devotion. In other words, we are no longer speaking of land—and economic life by extension—in terms of ordinary stewardship but of a family trust and legacy to be carefully preserved, nurtured, and then lovingly handed down to the next generations.

The sacral motive clauses that invite and cajole Israel to holiness take on greater depth when seen as the heir coming to be like the parent. The child is invited to be and to do what the parent is and does; it is an invitation to partake of the parent's work. As we have already seen in the preceding sections, the economic dimension of God's in-breaking gives rise to an extensive web of obligations in economic life: the never-ending need for systemic reform that favors the poor, moral economic conduct as a precondition for cultic worship, and conformity to the Law as a venue for participation in God's holiness and righteousness. These demands take on an even more profound significance when cast within the context of family ties because Israel now has the added obligation of a child doing, indeed continuing, the work of the Father. It is no longer merely the case of a tenant or sojourner observing the household rules of the landlord, but that of a firstborn standing in place of the Father-landowner to dispense protection, justice, and sustenance to all who have been welcomed by the Father to dwell on the land. The privileges of "belonging" and being an "heir-owner" bring with them attendant responsibilities of caring for the impoverished and the suffering on one's domain.

The *indicative* of the filial relationship gives rise to the *imperative* of obligations that flow from such bonds (C. Wright 1990, 18). Israel observes the laws and statutes of the Promised Land not merely as one of many other tenants. As a child, she owes the Father even much more extensive duties, which carry even stronger claims for compliance compared to a mere sojourner on the land. Moreover, as an heir, Israel now shares in the divine task of providing shelter and sustenance to all who have been welcomed on the land. This is a particularly weighty task since YHWH as landowner has shown an active solicitude and partiality toward the widow, orphan, and strangers—those who are at greatest risk and therefore deserving of even more protection. It is the appointed task of the heir to help the Father govern the domain. What is more, it is the gift of the Father relying on his child to continue his work in providing for the dispossessed, and in the process, it is the Father letting the child experience for herself the unbounded joy and the depths of holiness and righteousness in self-giving. Thus, the obligation to care for *personae miserabiles* should not be viewed as an onerous imposition but rather as a privilege. After all, the weight of the duties would not have been as grave had the Chosen People not been heirs but merely sojourners on the land. Since a preferential option for the poor is integral to the Father's work as evident in the wake of God's in-breaking (Lohfink 1987), such a marked devotion to the afflicted has similarly become integral to the work of the heir by extension.

Of course, the downside to all this is that infractions likewise carry greater moment as seen, for example, in Hosea 11. Such disobedience hurts all the more and produces much graver consequences because Israel as YHWH's own child and firstborn ought to live up to these laws not out of a mere desire to conform to rules but out of parental respect and, more significantly, out of filial love (McCarthy 1965).

ECONOMIC LIFE AS PARTICIPATION IN GOD'S RIGHTEOUSNESS

Far from desacralizing the divine and being mundane, economic life provides an occasion for humans to live out the promise and the possibilities of their unique historical particularities through which the universal is revealed.[29] Hebrew laws and statutes governing economic life are similar in content compared to their Near Eastern counterparts. Nevertheless, Israel's Law is substantively different because it is theocentric; it calls for systemic social reform; it melds together cultic, civil, and moral laws; it extensively appends motive clauses; and it is ultimately founded on a filial-divine relationship. These differences underscore how the economic dimension of God's in-breaking has been used to elicit human participation in God's righteousness and holiness. Despite material similarities in Hebrew and Near Eastern laws, Israel is different because she observes the Law in order to requite God's devotion for her. Motive clauses spur the Chosen People to live up to their covenant election despite the exacting demands of the Law. In the process, motive clauses hone the nation's moral consciousness and self-identity to a heightened sense of responsibility. Israel is different from her neighbors because her conformity to the Law stems from a keen appreciation of her role in God's continuing work of transforming societies that will someday culminate in the New Jerusalem.

The economic dimension of God's intervention in human history serves as a means for YHWH to confer additional, manifold gifts on Israel. The Covenant, Deuteronomic, and Holiness Codes are viewed by the prophets as the "rules of righteousness" (Mays 1987, 151–53). Thus, to live up to these three law codes is to partake in nothing less than the righteousness of God.

In inviting Israel to attentive and systemic solicitude for the poor and in inducing her to upright living through observance of divine ordinances, YHWH is in effect offering Israel a share in God's *sedeq*. The sequential nature of Psalms 111 and 112 reflects the correspondence of human justice to God's own justice (Brueggemann 1994, 24). This linkage is made even more explicit in juxtaposing Israel's revolutionary political economy with God's characteristic concern for the poor:

> Israel undertakes social practices . . . that are radical in character, embracing an economics of sharing and a politics of equity. That . . . is matched by the revolutionary character of Israel's God who . . . begins with a "preferential option" for those who are to become Yahweh's special people in the world. (Brueggemann 1994, 13)

One can make an even stronger claim than this by tracing the causation itself: the Chosen People's living experience of a God who takes up the cause of the poor shapes Israel's own moral vision and infuses her with high standards of equity and sharing. Israel's unique pro-poor political economy manifests a deeper dynamic that has tapped into the divine righteousness that invariably champions the vulnerable. One could even go so far as to argue that in Hebrew Law, "God's royal honor is at stake in Israel's treatment of the 'widow, orphan, and resident alien'" (Lowery 2000, 7). After all, YHWH as both the Lord of nature and the Lord of history has responsibility for the welfare and safety of all who dwell in God's domain. YHWH puts divine honor at risk in providing for the helpless through human instruments that can, and often do, fail. But it is only through such risk that humans get to share in God's own holiness and righteousness.

Moreover, through such participated holiness and righteousness, Israel also receives the additional gift of serving as the venue and instrument by which others are drawn to partake of God's holiness and righteousness in their own turn. And topping all these is the gift that Israel need not do all these as a hired hand, but as God's own child. Law is an invitation to act in the way God has acted in history. And in this, economic life serves as a terrain for Israel's relationship with YHWH to evolve, grow, and deepen. Lohfink goes so far as to conclude that: "Again and again the decisive question was one of economic relations" (1986, 222). That there is an economic dimension to divine-human encounter is not surprising. What is stunning and of interest to this study is how God employs such an economic realm to provide for a whole array of divine benefactions in a multidimensional participation in divine work now open to humans.

These signal characteristics of Hebrew law codes account for why Israel reaffirms and even tightens these economic ordinances further despite her firsthand experience of the difficulties and sacrificial demands of living up to them. The next chapter examines the impact of scarcity on Law and on Israel's striving.

CHAPTER 5

LAW, SCARCITY, AND STRIVING

The preceding chapter evaluated the economic dimension of God's in-breaking in human history and argued that economic laws and statutes provide an occasion for YHWH to elicit human participation in God's holiness, righteousness, and providence. This chapter examines how scarcity imbues greater depth to such manifold participation as it makes the observance of the Law that much more sacrificial. Scarcity precipitates a more intense striving to live up to YHWH's expectations as evident in Israel's reaffirmation and further development of her economic ordinances that were already exacting to begin with.[1]

CONDITIONAL MATERIAL ABUNDANCE

As the Lord of nature, God could have easily provided a world of superfluity and material abundance and thereby ensure that humans enjoyed "sustenance without care."[2] That such a condition is well within the power of YHWH is clear in Sacred Scripture.[3] After all, it is God who brings forth order out of chaos, light out of darkness, and existence out of nonexistence (Gn 1). Moreover, Adam and Eve are provisioned well in the Garden of Eden and do not want for anything. The Lord's celebrated response to Job's complaints is also quite revealing of the overwhelming power and scope of YHWH's providence. Job 38:25–26 provides an effective image of how the omnipotent divine Creator has much to spare to the point of even bountifully watering deserts and lands where no one lives. What may seem to be wasteful to humans is not at all profligate for a God with an inexhaustible capacity to bestow gifts. This is a God capable of easily satisfying "the desires of every living thing" (Psalm 145:16).

As the Lord of history, YHWH also reveals this overwhelming and limitless sovereign power to provide. God supplies people to the point of satiation in which no one is left in want, as when YHWH provisions the nation Israel wandering through the desert with manna and quail (Ex 16) up to the time when they finally take hold of the Promised Land and reap their first harvest (Jo 5:10–12). Moreover, this unbounded divine capacity to provide to whomever God, as the Lord of history, chooses is clearly manifested when YHWH gives the Chosen People cities and houses they did not build, wells they did not dig, and vineyards and olive groves they did not plant (Dt 6:10–11). Israel's "essential gifts of nature, water, wine, and oil are related to YHWH as the Lord of history" (von Waldow 1974, 496). The Promised Land is repeatedly described as a "land flowing with milk and honey" (Ex 3:8, 3:17, 13:5; Lv 20:24; Nm 14:8; Dt 6:3, 11:9, 26:9, 26:15, 27:3, 31:20; Jo 5:6; Jer 11:5, 32:22; Ez 20:6, 20:15).[4] Since ancient societies refer to the food of the gods as "milk and honey" (Lohfink 1987, 43–44), one can infer from the use of such language that Israel's land is one of plenty where nothing is wanting; indeed, it is a land where they partake from the table of God itself. It is an affirmation that material abundance is intrinsic to YHWH's manifold gifts to them.[5] Thus, whether as the Lord of nature or as the Lord of history, God can provide humans with great material superfluity. After all, God is the "giver of abundant life" (Lowery 2000, 19–21) in all its dimensions, spiritual and material.

God could have easily created a world with unconditional material abundance, thereby granting humans "sustenance without care." Unfortunately, human experience belies such material sufficiency; human life has been characterized by so much want and destitution. This being the case, did the Lord of nature intentionally create a world of material want? Far from it. Sacred Scripture shows that YHWH, as the Lord of both nature and history, envisions and intends the created world to be one of material sufficiency, if not abundance, *although one that is merely conditional*—contingent on human need and human response.

Sabbath prosperity, the "fat" blessing of a benevolent world, is abundant, but not unlimited. Life's goods exist in finite, limited quantity. Not scarce, but limited. God blesses generously, lavishly providing life abundant for each person under God's care, regardless of ability. *But the surplus is limited by actual human need.* (Lowery 2000, 100; emphasis added)

God did not create a world of privation. God is interested in plenitude and riches for a world filled with good things (Lohfink 1987, 10–12). God satisfies the hungry and the thirsty without cost (Is 55:1). There will be an eschatological abundance in the New Jerusalem in which unafraid, every "man will sit under his own vine and under his own fig tree" (Mi 4:4). But such plenteous provisioning and unbounded prosperity come about only if Israel conforms to God's laws and statutes; this is a clear and unequivocal condition that is repeatedly found in the Pentateuch[6] and in prophetic literature.[7] YHWH guarantees boundless prosperity, but only if Israel remains faithful to the covenant (Wheeler 1995, 125–27), only if humans do not impede the unfolding promised bounty of God's providence.[8] Deuteronomy 15: 4–8, 15:11 describes this phenomenon well. Note the jarring incongruity between verse 4 (with its claim that there will be no poor in the nation Israel because of God's generosity) and verse 11 (with its admission that despite God's care, some people will still end up impoverished). The only explanation for this, of course, is the intervening passages that speak of *a requisite cooperation from Israel in letting God provide for them, especially the poor, through each other.*[9] It is through this conditionality to material abundance that God elicits human participation in divine providence and righteousness as described in the preceding chapter. The severity of the material scarcity experienced shapes the manner by which the preconditions to provisional material abundance can be met. In other words, as a central feature of the economic life that occasions human emulation of divine righteousness, scarcity shapes the ease or difficulty with which such participation takes place. It is through the careful observance of the Law that people are able to deal with the problem of scarcity (B. Gordon 1989, 11–20; Ohrenstein and Gordon 1992, 47). Even in the Garden of Eden, God's gift is that of material abundance, albeit one that is conditioned on adherence to the due order of God's creation.

YHWH, as householder and royal benefactor of Israel, provides for all and protects the weak. God creates a world of sufficient material provisioning with much to spare, as can be inferred from the statutes that call for Sabbath-fallow, Sabbath-rest, shared feasts and festivals, tithing, and the cultic destruction of first fruits and burnt offerings. God provides enough to enable such communal feasting and rest. J. R. Porter even goes so far as to claim that the "Exodus itself is not God's supreme achievement for Israel, but rather . . . [it is] his settling of them in the abundance of Canaan" (1990, 112).

Prosperity is the intent of God as part of the established divine order, but it is provisional on the quality of human instrumentality. As already mentioned in the preceding chapter, this in itself is another unmerited gift— participation in divine providence. Key to this human cooperation is the Chosen People's fidelity to the Law. In other words, the statutes and ordinances on economic life not only function as the blueprint for the ideal community that is being built at God's own initiative, but they also serve as a venue for the self-revelation of YHWH as householder, royal protector, and provider of the *personae miserabiles* and of Israel.

ECONOMIC LAWS AND THE IMPACT OF SCARCITY

The following sections examine the impact of scarcity in making the observance of the Law much more sacrificial. The persistence and severity of scarcity can be inferred from the difficulties surrounding the observance of Hebrew precepts on economic affairs.

Debt legislation

The impact of material scarcity in the ancient economy and the exacting nature of loan legislation can be inferred from the *prosbul*, the rampant violation of these statutes described in prophetic and extra-biblical materials, and the high interest rates prevalent in the Near East.

Prosbul

The *prosbul* is a legal device in which borrowers formally declare and promise that their loans will be paid regardless of the seventh-year remission of debts called for under Deuteronomy 15:1–2. Since the latter is interpreted to be binding only on individuals and not on courts, debt is turned over to the courts before the *shemittah* to ensure its payment. In effect, the court serves as a third party that collects the loan on behalf of the creditor (Lowery 2000, 41).

We can infer from this legal mechanism that Israel's debt statutes are taken seriously and are a real encumbrance on creditors. Otherwise, there would have been no reason to go through such legal contortions. In fact, the *prosbul* may perhaps be the strongest argument that can be made that the economic laws of the Pentateuch are enforceable and actually administered given that loopholes are sought to forestall their full operation (North 1954, 90–91). The legal fiction adopted in the post-Talmudic literature with the goal of circumventing legislation should be read as evidence that these laws are observed and fully implemented, and therefore subject to adjustments that accommodate actual economic conditions (Neufeld 1955, 410). Most commentators see the *prosbul* as an artifice to get around the *shemittah*. In response, Hillel, the *prosbul*'s architect, contends that he came up with this legal invention to address the impracticality of Deuteronomy 15:1–2 given that credit dries up as the year of debt release approached (Lowery 2000, 41; North 1954, 90–91).

Whether the *prosbul* is a legal stratagem to nullify the *shemittah* or not, what is important for this study's thesis is its confirmation of the exacting demands made of creditors. Moreover, it also attests to the persistence of economic shortages, which drives people to incur debt in the first place and which in turn requires that credit sources be protected even to the point of having to bend the laws. It is obvious that the *shemittah* has the unintended consequence of hurting the very people it is designed to help; the economically distressed could not get any credit at all since loanable funds disappear right before the seventh-year debt reprieve (North 1954, 185–86). Thus, the Deuteronomist is compelled to explicitly state in Deuteronomy 15:7–10 that it is a moral obligation to continue providing assistance to the needy via loans even with the approach of the *shemittah* and the consequent nonpayment of such debt. Despite this clear and forceful reiteration of the moral obligation to lend, creditors remain unmoved, thus leading to the subsequent need for a legal device such as Hillel's *prosbul* to provide a second-best solution that ensures that lending does not completely stop every seven years to the detriment of the needy. In other words, that the *prosbul* is needed to overcome lenders' indifference even to the strong moral appeal of Deuteronomy 15:7–10 can only mean that the Hebrew loan statutes have a troublesome bite to them that hurts.

Pervasive infraction

Despite clear and repeated statements on debt legislation, there is evidence of widespread violations of these statutes within Israel. Indictments of usury, of the unconscionable appropriation of unlawful pledges, and of profiteering from the extreme needs of others abound in prophetic literature (Neh 5:1–13; Ez 18:5–8, 18:10–13, 18:17, 22:12; Hb 2:6) and suggest pervasive abusive loan transactions (Stein 1953, 168; Neufeld 1953–54, 196; 1955, 410; B. Gordon 1982, 407–12). Many are driven to the brink of debt-slavery (2 Kgs 4:1–2; Neh 5:1–13) or to flight (1 Sm 22:2). Reacting to the deteriorating economic conditions of the eighth century B.C., Amos 2:6–8 harshly condemns those who have capitalized on the needy by selling them into slavery; Micah 2:8–10 severely censures the seizure of unlawful pledges for loans. The large number of biblical references to loans at interest most likely reflects their widespread practice in Israel, and some scholars believe that most of these are commercial loans related to agriculture (Neufeld 1955, 382).

Admonitions against abusive moneylending can also be found beyond the prophetic literature, suggesting both the prevalence of such one-sided exchanges and the nation's deep disapproval of them. Proverbs 28:8 warns usurers of the folly of their greed as their wealth will ultimately end up in the hands of those who will give them back to the poor. Sirach 21:8 and Proverbs 22:7, 22:26–27 consider the wisdom of completely avoiding taking any credit at all because of its often dire consequences.[10] Psalm 15:5 lauds those who subscribe to the Law and lend freely without cost as being worthy to dwell in the sanctuary of the Lord.

Breaches of Hebrew loan legislation can be found in extra-biblical materials. Papyri records describe interest-bearing loan transactions between Jews living beyond the borders of Israel (Neufeld 1953–54, 196; Stein 1953, 169; Gamoran 1971, 133–34).[11]

Opportunity cost

Israel's loan legislation carries a significant opportunity cost considering the high rates of interest that are prevalent in the Near East and in cultures at a comparable stage of growth. For a similar level of development, Ifugaos[12] charge 100 percent interest for loans that are due anywhere from a few weeks to a year and 200–300 percent for each additional year that the debt is overdue. On the other hand, Babylonians and Assyrians charge 20–25 percent for money loans and 33 1/3 percent for grain loans. Interest for unpaid debts is 100 percent for Neo-Babylon and 141 percent for Assyria (Neufeld 1953–54, 194–95). Lenders throughout the ancient Near East charge as high as 100 percent for high-risk credit or during periods of scarce capital (Kahan 1972, 1269).

Neufeld (1953–54, 197) uses Nehemiah 5:11 to calculate interest in Israel at 12 percent per annum for money loans and 18 percent per annum for grain loans, although he finds evidence that these rates may have even been as high as 50 percent for money (silver) loans and 100 percent for grain loans. He finds a 12 percent interest rate as "much too moderate" although consistent with prevailing rates during the Ptolemaic period, which are generally capped at 24 percent.

The widespread abuse of creditors may have prompted Hammurabi[13] to fix a maximum interest rate and to punish violators by making them forfeit their loans (Neufeld 1953–54, 195). The Laws of Hammurabi and Eshnunna cap interest at 20 percent for money loans and 33 percent for grain loans; in Assyria it is 25 percent for money and 50 percent for grain loans (Gnuse 1985, 19). In numerous law codes in the Near East, one finds the following prevailing maximum rates of interest: Old-Babylonian period, 20 percent for money and 33 1/3 percent for grain; Assyria, 25 percent for money and 50 percent for grain; Neo-Babylonian and later Persian empires, 20 percent for silver and grain loans; under the Ptolemies in Egypt, 24 percent is the legal maximum (Maloney 1974).

The well-established legislation on debt in the Near East and rampant usury during that period suggest the widespread practice of borrowing and lending, which in its own turn reflects the severity and persistence of material exiguity. The charging of interest seems to be a common behavior across cultures and reveals how people treat each other in the face of scarcity. In contrast to all these, the Chosen People are not to charge each other any interest at all. The censure against levying interest is a strong and consistent pattern in Hebrew Law and the Talmud (Neufeld 1955, 358).

That the Chosen People choose to forego interest (0 percent interest) in contrast to surrounding nations that institute limits, ranging from 20–25 percent for money and 33–50 percent for grain loans, illustrates the demanding nature of Israel's loan legislation. This disparity in interest-rate caps may be due to the other Near Eastern nations being more developed societies in which the borrowers are mostly merchants, and loans are predominantly for commercial use (Gnuse 1985, 19). In contrast, not only do the Chosen People operate on the basis of kinship and extended families, but Israel is also a pastoral society; the vast majority of loans must have been distress loans. However, this argument is problematic because it only accounts for the early days of Israel. Even as laws are subsequently refined and rewritten in Deuteronomy and Leviticus, legislation on interest-free loans remains unchanged. And this is the case even in a period when Israel is already a settled economy with an expanding and vibrant commercial trading sector. Thus, the disparity between Israel and her Near Eastern neighbors on interest-free loans cannot be attributed merely to differences in their economic development. Israel has ample opportunities to rewrite her laws but nevertheless still chooses to reaffirm the ban on charging interest. If anything, such restrictions become even stricter and more explicit, as we find later in this chapter.

Scholars are in disagreement over the extent to which loan legislation is similar or different between Israel and the other Near Eastern nations. Neufeld (1955, 359) and Gamoran (1971) argue that the provision of interest-free loans is unique to Israel. However, Stein (1953, 165) disagrees and observes that there are interest-free loans in other Near Eastern countries during this period although these are rarely mentioned in documents because they are likely to be noncommercial loans and therefore of "little legal significance." He also concludes that loans without interest are common in Ptolemaic and Roman Egypt (169). Meislin and Cohen (1964, 255–56, 263) find records of interest-free loans, including agricultural debts, in tablets from 2000 B.C. in Assyria. Moreover, they also find evidence of mandatory lending in which tenants and farmers have a right to borrow from their landlords.

Mesopotamian rulers decree debt remission when a large part of the population is so saddled with excessive indebtedness to the point where the economy grinds to a halt (Lohfink 1986, 224). However, one difference in the practice of Israel is the regularization and institutionalization of debt release; the practice is not left to the discretion of the king (Patrick 1985, 112).[14]

Determining whether Israel is unique in the Near East for its loan legislation or not is beyond the object of this research. Three points are important to accentuate for this study. First, taking the four different components of Israel's loan legislation piecemeal and then comparing them with their Near Eastern neighbors' practices is not sufficient. What is even more telling is the packaging of these components into a single comprehensive practice in Israel: the provision of interest-free loans that are automatically written off in seven years, severe restrictions on the kinds of pledges that may be taken, and, to top it all, the moral duty to provide such loans to the distressed. None of the scholars mentioned previously suggest that the other nations combine their own debt legislation in a similar fashion. Such consolidation is enough to make Israel unique and unequivocally spells out the object of loan legislation—a love and genuine concern for the welfare of the impoverished.

A second major inference is the hefty claims that result from combining these four separate components. Taken individually, these four elements are in and of themselves already demanding in what they require. Combined together, they mutually reinforce each others' requirements to the point of making them burdensome for creditors who are morally obligated to extend distress loans, provide these at no interest, refuse to take certain kinds of pledges, and then write off the debt whether it has been paid in full or not after a seven-year period. Deuteronomy 15:7–9 and Hillel's *prosbul* show that these laws are a real hardship for lenders (North 1954, 186). These statutes in effect ask creditors to put themselves at risk of financial loss due to debt remission or slave release (or both) that leads to an incomplete recovery of the principal. At the very least, they are asked to forego alternative uses for their funds, such as extending interest-bearing loans to foreign commercial users (Lohfink 1991, 46). After all, most of the merchants in Israel are believed to be Phoenicians and Canaanites (Kahan 1972, 1269) and according to Deuteronomy 23:20, foreigners may be charged interest for their loans.

Indeed, the moral obligation to provide interest-free loans that are to be automatically written off after seven years carries a heavy opportunity cost when compared to the prevailing practice in surrounding neighbors, and all for the cause of caring for the distressed. This high opportunity cost is by no means unintended since Israel is meant to be a contrast-society. The people are called to share in the plight and need of others with alacrity—empathetic solidarity in its genuine and best sense. Observe an assessment made of the ban on interest:

> Eliminate interest, and borrowers are more likely to be placed in a situation of being deprived of that very real capital which offers hope of their redeeming their debts. An alternative is to outlaw borrowing and lending entirely, but that would be a condemnation of many to absolute starvation in the absence of a comprehensive welfare-state apparatus. *Another*

way around the impasse is to apply moral suasion to have loans given with-
out any hope of return on the part of the lender, but it is impossible to make
such suasion definitive through any legal code which allows the individual
some measure of protection against parting with his property against his will.
(B. Gordon 1982, 415; emphasis added)

In other words, it is ultimately only the conscience that will be able to effectively enforce these precepts on loans; it is difficult for the community to
publicly administer these laws because of the demanding nature of these
debt statutes. Only moral suasion works because of the personal sacrifice required. Thus, even as one can prescribe economic behavior, actual success
can be effected only through an appeal to a change of attitudes (Gnuse
1985, 21).

Third, the size of the opportunity cost may be used as a measure of the
severity and persistence of the scarcity experienced. The more persistent and
severe the scarcity, the higher the expected rate of interest. However, the opposite is true for moral behavior and normative thought: the more severe the
scarcity, the more pressing the need and, therefore, the more important it is
to provide effective assistance freely and readily and at even more conces-
sionary terms. Hence, there is a widening gap regarding interest rates between what is (interest rates as reflecting scarcity and as an instrument of
economic triage in allocating limited resources) and what ought to be (allocation according to need and the preferential option for the poor). The wider
the gap, the more severe the scarcity. The larger the opportunity cost borne
by Israel, the deeper the prevailing scarcity.

Slave release

The chronic nature of scarcity is also reflected (1) in the discrepancy between
the practice of debt-slavery and the egalitarian ethos of Israel, (2) in the large
number of debt-slaves, and (3) in the difficulty of ensuring compliance with
the slave-release laws.

Disparity with Israel's egalitarianism

Personal slavery as surety for debt is standard practice in the Near East, and
it should not be surprising that slavery is a way of life in the region since

these are status-distributive societies in which the elite live off the produce of the lower classes. The practice is adopted by Israel from her neighbors. One becomes a slave when sold as a minor (Ex 21:7–11), seized for unpaid loans (2 Kgs 4:1; Neh 5:5), held in bondage for liabilities incurred involuntarily (Am 2:6), enslaved voluntarily (Ex 21:5–6; Dt 15:16–17), or sold for unpaid debts (Lv 25:47–55; Gnuse 1985, 22). Moreover, there is a distinction between debt-slaves and those who are captured in war (Jackson 1988). Debt, not war or conquest, is the major cause for enslavement in Israel (de Vaux 1965, 83, 172).

That debt-slavery is practiced at all in Israel is an enigma. After all, early Israel is much vaunted for its familial-clannish-tribal unity and mutual self-help. Regardless of which thesis one accepts regarding the formation of the Chosen People—as a nation of liberated slaves from Egypt (Albright 1948), as a confederation of nomadic tribes (von Waldow 1970), or as refugees from abusive Canaanite city-states (Gottwald 1979)—the Hebrews subscribe to an egalitarian ethos and resolve to be a contrast-society because of their shared experience of vulnerability and bitter mistreatment. Enslaving each other is completely out of character with the nation Israel's democratic provenance. Thus, it is not surprising that in the development of slave laws, the Chosen People ultimately do away with debt-slavery (Lv 25:39–43) with a pointed acknowledgment of their own genesis as slaves who had been mercifully freed by God.[15] The priestly redactor strongly and explicitly instructs, in no uncertain terms, that the economically distressed ought to be treated as a hired hand rather than as a slave because no Hebrew may be enslaved as each of them belongs to God, their liberator. That Israel even practices debt-slavery at all is baffling indeed.

A second puzzle has to do with the conditions of slave emancipation. The length of maximum service is fixed at six years after which the debt-slave is to be released (Ex 21:2–6; Dt 15:12–18). This is twice the length specified in the laws of Hammurabi (#117),[16] which set the release of slaves after three years of service. This is an odd disparity considering that Israel is supposed to be more humane than her neighbors.

A third mystery is the gap in the value accorded to slave and free labor. Deuteronomy 15:18 preempts slave owners' recriminations in having to release their slaves by observing that the slaves' six years of service were worth twice that of free labor. Put in another way, the rate for free labor is twice that imputed to slave labor.[17]

It is unclear what the imputed wage rate for slave labor is in the laws of Hammurabi. If Hebrew debt-slaves have the same wage rates as those of free labor, their six-year service could be reduced to three years, which is exactly the maximum number of years specified in Hammurabi #117. If these last two baffling issues are related, then the question is why Israel reduces the imputed wage rate of debt-slaves to half of that of free workers.[18]

Regardless of whether these two issues are related or not, what is important for this study is how they are so uncharacteristic of the Law's merciful care in dealing with the poor as seen, for example, in the protective restrictions imposed on the manner and the kinds of pledges that may be secured from the destitute (Ex 22:26; Dt 24:6, 24:10–13). Moreover, the Deuteronomist is supposed to make the Covenant Code more benevolent in response to the socioeconomic decline in Hebrew society that has become more urban and subjected to monarchial excesses.[19] Yet, the Deuteronomic Code does not change the length of service, it does not impute a higher wage to the debt-slave, and it does not do away with debt-slavery itself. Israel has to wait for Leviticus 25 to finally take the initiative of definitively abolishing the practice (Lowery 2000, 45).[20]

Why then would an egalitarian community tolerate, indeed, accept and institutionalize the practice of enslaving each other for debt default despite its obvious inconsistency with its foundational ethos? Why does it take centuries for Israel to finally assert her self-identity and do away with debt-slavery? Why would a contrast-society that is supposed to be more compassionate than its neighbors double the length of maximum service for slaves before their mandatory release? Why should Israel be lenient and bend over backwards with respect to providing and forgiving loans but not when it comes to debt default and debt-slavery? One can only surmise that a possible response to all of these questions lies in a pragmatism that is compelled to keep the "credit market" working. If this hypothesis is true, the desire not to "rock the boat" and to preserve social institutions that furnish liquidity to the populace only goes to accentuate the material shortages that shadow the period. The practice of debt-slavery as a venue for loan recovery is a jarring dissonance to the munificence of debt reprieve, interest-free lending, mandatory lending, and restrictions on the taking of pledges. This contradiction, especially in the context of a community that is supposed to be egalitarian, can only suggest that scarcity must have been chronic and even severe as to drive people to such harsh practices just like the neighboring Near Eastern states.

Widespread debt-slavery

Phillips (1984, 61–62) argues that the intent of Exodus 21:2–6 is to restore the status of the male Hebrew slave as a free and full participant in the affairs of the community. However, given the difficulty of maintaining such free standing in a harsh and deteriorating economy, Phillips hypothesizes that redactors of the Deuteronomic (Dt 12–26) and Holiness Codes (Lv 17–26) are merely keeping the ideal alive regarding the restoration of people to their equal status. If Phillips is correct, this would be indicative of the impact of scarcity on this contrast-society in making it difficult to achieve the goal of having a community of equals as many are falling into slavery.

Without giving or examining any statistics on the number of slaves, Kahan (1972, 1269–70, 1275) and Feldman (1972, 39–41) infer that slavery could not have been widespread in Palestine because it is more expensive to purchase and maintain a slave than it is to simply hire a free laborer as needed. Feldman calculates that the interest alone (six to eight shekels) on the purchase price of a slave (thirty shekels)[21] is already equivalent to the average annual wage of a free worker. To this one must add the cost of feeding and housing a slave, the risk of the slave running away, the restrictive laws governing the treatment of slaves, and the public opinion against it. Thus, Kahan and Feldman conclude that slavery could not have been significant in Israel; there is little incentive to keep slaves. Moreover, they are usually purchased by wealthy families not for productive use but for household work or concubinage.

De Vaux (1965, 83–84) observes that there is little information on the number of domestic slaves in Israel. He notes that about the only evidence available is Ezra 2:64–65 and Nehemiah 7:67, which provide a glimpse into the extent of debt-slavery in the nation. Of the 49,647 men and women who return from exile in Babylon, 7,337 are slaves, or nearly 15 percent of the remnant population. One out of every seven is a slave. These figures dispute Feldman's claim that slavery is insignificant in Israel.[22] Moreover, one must remember that these slaves would most likely have been debt-slaves. Being a captive nation herself, remnant Israel is highly unlikely to have war-captives among the 7,337 recorded slaves returning from exile in Babylon.[23] Thus, one can infer that most of these 15 percent are debt-slaves. Finally, if debt-slavery is not pervasive as Feldman claims, how would he then account for Jeremiah 34:8–22? Why would the release of slaves be such a burning issue? Why does the question of debt-slaves persistently loom in the forefront as law codes are rewritten and edited in different eras? Moreover, why are the poor bitterly complaining about the need to sell their children into slavery (Neh 5:1–13)? One can only infer that there must have been a fair number of debt-slaves in Israel. That many are driven into debt-slavery can only reflect severe and chronic scarcity in the nation.

The practice of releasing debt-slaves after six years of service is a de facto cap on the maximum amount of the debt that may be recovered through the debt-slaves' service (Lowery 2000, 25).[24] We get a quantitative estimate of the amounts involved by using the information that free labor is worth twice as much as slave labor (Dt 15:18). Thus, a six-year limit to debt-slavery would mean that the cap on recoverable debt is approximately twelve-years' worth of wages since imputed slave recompense is only half of free-labor compensation.[25] That there is need to impose such a limit suggests concerns over the sums that need to be repaid or the length of time it would take to fully repay them. That the vast majority of these loans are consumption-distress loans and that they could get to be so sizable both imply that the material exiguity people have to deal with is deep and persistent (e.g., Neh 5:1–5).

Another indication of the severity of the material scarcity experienced by people is the phenomenon of voluntary enslavement. Exodus 21:5–6 and Deuteronomy 15:16–17 outline procedures for Hebrews who choose to forego their freedom and become permanent slaves. Unemployment among free labor at that time is believed to be high so often that it is not unreasonable to believe that some slaves voluntarily embrace their indentured state at the end of their six-year service instead of having to fend for themselves (Kahan 1972, 1270). That people would make such a choice is surprising considering that a slave receives no wages, is part of the master's household, and is subject to the master's complete authority, which includes proprietary rights over the slave, including decisions on the choice of his wife (e.g., Ex 21:4; Cohn 1972, col. 1655). Economic life must indeed have been harsh and uncertain to make slavery a more palatable choice; it is essentially trading one's freedom in exchange for economic security. Life is hard in Israel because it is engaged in subsistence agriculture that does not produce much surplus to provide a cushion for misfortunes, contingencies, and harsh fiscal exactions (Oakman 1986). Furthermore, as an agrarian economy, the region is subjected to the vagaries of the weather.

It is a life of precarious survival characterized by recurrent material short-ages. Consumption loans are believed to have been common in early Israel (de Vaux 1965, 170–73).

Noncompliance

In reconciling the disparity in the release period between the seven years of Exodus 21:2–6 and Deuteronomy 15:12–18 and the fifty years of Leviticus 25, de Vaux (1965, 83) suggests that the Jubilee Law is a compromise in reac-tion to the widespread noncompliance with slave emancipation. The period of slavery is extended to fifty years in exchange for better treatment of slaves by masters who will receive them not as slaves but as guests or as hired hands. Ginzberg (1932) also views the Jubilee as designed to protect the in-terests of wealthy creditors in view of the length of time involved before the manumission of slaves.

Just as in the case of loan legislation, prophetic indictments provide in-direct evidence that slave-release laws are not being observed. For example, in Jeremiah 34:8–22, King Zedekiak has to strike a covenant with the people to get them to free their slaves in accordance with Deuteronomy 15:12. They release their slaves only to change their minds and take back the freed slaves. What is noteworthy here is how the king has to intervene and cajole people to comply with slave-release laws that they should have been observing in the first place. Moreover, observe how the people, despite the king's interven-tion and Jeremiah's warnings, still choose to disobey the law and keep their slaves. A similar problem can be inferred from Nehemiah 5:1–13. Recall too the cruelty and harshness with which the widow's children are nearly seized as pledges for an unpaid debt in 2 Kings 4:1–7. The breach of both the spirit and the letter of these laws seems to be pervasive.

Deuteronomy 15:18 anticipates the misgivings of slave owners in releas-ing their slaves by reminding them that they got twice the value of work from their slaves in their six years of service compared to free labor. That the Deu-teronomist takes pains to preempt and dispel complaints or excuses from slave owners indicates the demanding nature of this statute. Pleins (2001, 369–70) examines scholars' differing interpretations of Amos 2:6, 2:8, and 8:6; the precise nature of the economic injustice indicted is not clear. What is evident, however, is that Amos condemns creditors not merely for failing to extend assistance freely and readily, but for burdening the impoverished even further by buying or selling them as if they were mere commodities to be traded so whimsically. Gnuse (1985, 23) finds no evidence that slave release was observed at all.

Sabbatical year

For obvious reasons, the practicability of the Sabbath-fallow year is directly related to the issue of scarcity. First, observance of this law depends on the availability of surplus that relieves people of the need to work for a whole year. Second, the Sabbath-fallow is directly related to scarcity because it involves the cessation of production and the need to share one's produce with others. The greater the degree of scarcity, the greater the sacrificial element of such observance and its requisite sharing.

That the law has a direct material impact on scarcity is well-illustrated in the account of the Maccabees' insufficient war provisioning due to the Sabbath-fallow year (1 Mc 6:48–54). Numerous proposals have been advanced to account for how the law is practiced even while having to feed an entire nation. Perhaps the law was a rotating land fallow, not a universal fallow, that simply involved "putting away" part of the land. Otherwise, the poor will have nothing for six years until the next fallow year; moreover, people will starve if the Sabbath-fallow were observed by everybody at the same time (Lowery 2000, 54–55). Alternatively, the sabbatical and Jubilee laws might be early legislation when Israel was still heavily pastoral. Otherwise, there would be no other sources of food (Stein 1953, 164). Others simply claim that there is no evidence that the Sabbath-fallow was ever implemented (C. Wright 1990, 148). Nehemiah 10:31 explicitly states the people's promise to observe the Sabbath-fallow and release of slaves every seven years. That reformers are compelled to reiterate this particular provision of the Law suggests that there may have been widespread infractions of the sabbatical ordinances.

The pragmatic concerns over the sufficiency of food stocks are not lost on the redactors who directly address this particular fear in the legislation itself.

> Follow my decrees and be careful to obey my laws, and you will live safely in the land. Then the land will yield its fruit, and you will eat your fill and live there in safety. *You may ask, "What will we eat in the seventh year if we do not plant or harvest our crops?" I will send you such a blessing in*

the sixth year that the land will yield enough for three years. While you plant during the eighth year, you will eat from the old crop and will continue to eat from it until the harvest of the ninth year comes in. (Lv 25:18–22; emphasis added)

Thus, to observe the Sabbath-fallow year is, in effect, to make a statement of faith in God as provider. However, as we saw in this chapter's earlier discussion of God's vision of plenitude, this promise of material sufficiency is merely provisional. In particular, it is contingent on humans not impeding the unfolding generosity of God's providence through their moral failures. Thus, the issue of whether economic conditions permit the observance of the Sabbath-fallow is dependent not on God's liberality but on the uprightness of human conduct.

The nonobservance of the requisite Sabbath rest is sinful and is often deemed to be the root cause of many other offenses against the Lord. I propose that the causation also moves in the opposite direction. Sin causes the nonobservance of Sabbath rest, especially of the Sabbath-fallow, because moral failure erodes the economic foundation crucial to producing the necessary surplus, without which no Sabbath-fallow can be observed without risk of famine. In other words, only an economy that reflects due order in human affairs can ever hope to fully observe the Sabbath-fallow in practice. After all, producing the necessary surplus that permits the observance of periodic Sabbath-fallow years requires profound mutual cooperation, hard work, and rectitude in moral behavior. This fits within the larger theological framework of the Law. Due order is always a necessary condition for Sabbath rest. Thus, in the paradigmatic Sabbath, God rests on the seventh day, having accomplished the order of divine creative activity. Part of this due order is the material sufficiency, if not abundance, envisioned by God. Thus, one could aptly remark that "the goods of the earth are the sign of the right relationship with YHWH as well as the means to create harmony within the community" (Donahue 1977, 70).

Since Sabbath rest presupposes an underlying due order that sets the stage for the fulfillment of God's promise of sufficiency (Lv 25:18–22), the ease or difficulty with which the law can be observed is a litmus test of the presence or absence of right order in human affairs, particularly in economic life. The inability to observe Sabbath-fallow because of material shortages serves as an early warning signal that people have strayed from the order of sufficiency for all envisioned by God. Consequently, it is not surprising that the Sabbath has been viewed as a distinguishing hallmark that sets Israel apart from all the other nations (Miller 1985, 82; 1990, 83).

To observe the Sabbath-fallow is to avail of God's gift of rest in the here and now (von Rad 1966b). We can experience eschatological rest in the present precisely through our cooperation in letting God's in-breaking establish harmony and justice in human affairs. In celebrating Sabbath-fallow, even at great sacrifice—especially within the larger backdrop of scarcity—we are, in effect, participating in God's righteousness in our proleptic emulation of conditions in the eschaton; that is, by treating one another in the way God intends, we enjoy God's envisioned peace in the here and now rather than having to wait for the end of time. This represents a dual gift from God: a correction of our behavior and the peace this brings about.

In summary, Sabbath-fallow is a goal, a theological self-understanding of what ought to be in human affairs. It is a foretaste of eschatological rest, sharing, and feasting in the abundance provided by God. It is also a litmus test: the degree to which we are able to celebrate it is a measure of the rectitude attained in human affairs that allows us to celebrate it in the first place since there is need to have a surplus to make this law practicable. Sabbath-fallow is a statement of faith in God as provider: God provisions us with material sufficiency so as to be able to accomplish what God expects of us. Persistent and profound destitution comes from moral failure and not from the niggardliness of God's providence. Unconditional material abundance would have removed the requisite human effort that must go into the preparation of the Sabbath, which in turn diminishes the delight that comes with resting in God and in each other.

Jubilee Law

It has been suggested that the Jubilee Law[26] is more an expression of a vision rather than a real attempt at social reform because the statute is simply unworkable (Lowery 2000, 58–59). It would have caused mass starvation to have a whole nation observe a universal fallow at the same time (North 1954, 116). Others simply argue that the Jubilee is observed only for 49 days rather than for an entire year (Hoenig 1969). Most scholars do not believe that the Jubilee Law was ever practiced at all (Fager 1993, 34–36; North 1954; Lowery 2000).[27] This is indirectly corroborated by the land monopolies that are so harshly indicted by the prophets (Is 5:8–10; Mi 2:1–2).

The Jubilee may be more symbolic than a genuine social reform for another reason. Note that the average life expectancy for that period is forty years for males and thirty years for females; the infant mortality rate is 50 percent (Lowery 2000, 8). The Jubilee occurs every forty-nine or fifty years, which is well beyond the life span of the average person. If the Jubilee is redistributive or restorative, or both, in its goals, it would be of little benefit to most people who will not live long enough until the next Jubilee. In this case, one has to give credence to North's (1954) point that the Jubilee does not supersede the Sabbath-fallow years but runs concurrent with them. This way, it would still be possible for people to avail of the seven-year releases (debts and slavery). Nevertheless, despite these releases, land return (the key component of the Jubilee as a redistributive or restorative measure) would be well beyond the lifetime of most people. If this is a serious social reform, one would have expected land return to have been scheduled once every generation (twenty to twenty-five years) at the very least.

How is the issue of material scarcity related to the Jubilee Law? First, the Jubilee Law should be viewed as an ameliorative response to the ravages wrought by material scarcity on families. This vision (or practice of a radical social reform) would not have been necessary in the first place had it not been for recurring material shortages that drive families to destitution and the loss of their livelihoods and ancestral heritage. Scarcity is related to the Jubilee in a second way: by making the observance of the law difficult if not impossible. Land buyers would most likely not be willing to return purchased land, especially not under the hard conditions of subsistence agriculture that produces little surplus, as is most likely the case in that era (Oakman 1986).

Summary

We can infer from the pervasive breach of economic statutes that scarcity is deep and persistent in Israel. Economic historians of the period believe that agriculture provides just enough for farmers in which yields generally produce a fivefold return, fifteenfold at most. The difficulty stems from the excessive fiscal exactions of the ruling classes who treat farmers as their principal source of revenue (Kahan 1972, 1273–74).[28] Life is hard; scarcity is chronic and often severe.

Interest rates for money and grain loans—an indirect, albeit reliable, gauge of want—are high for that period and for similar agrarian or nomadic societies in comparable stages of development. That Near Eastern law codes impose a maximum ceiling on such rates can only mean the prevalence of usurious charges that people are compelled to bear given their desperation. Neighboring kings declare periodic debt remission whenever economies grind to a halt from excessive indebtedness. Temples provide loans at more favorable terms than private creditors (Maloney 1974, 15), thus highlighting loans as a regular part of common life. Moreover, that temples are compelled to provide alternative sources of credit for people is suggestive either of abusive lenders or of unavailable private loans, or both. People still borrow despite high interest rates and the risk of slavery for themselves and their families in the event of default.[29] Many end up in recurring debt-slavery. Slaves eligible for release choose to become permanent slaves, suggestive of the difficulty of eking out a livelihood on their own. This fits in with the economic history of that time, in which unemployment rates are high among free but landless peasants, which in turn leads to lower wages (Kahan 1972, 1269–70, 1275). It is a self-reinforcing cycle of low productivity, little surplus, deeper destitution, and even greater dependence on others in subsequent rounds of economic activity.

The debt amounts involved are sizable. A six-year maximum for debt-slave bondage at half the regular wage rate of a free laborer means a total debt of at least twelve years' worth of wages.[30] Moreover, that families can even lose the total value of their ancestral land demonstrates the size of the loans involved. This suggests the chronic nature of material scarcity in which people accumulate large sums of debt over time as they are compelled to keep on borrowing; it is a continued, unstoppable slide into indigence. The different provisions of Leviticus 25 are even believed to be descriptive of the different stages of ever deepening impoverishment for the family (Chirichigno 1993).

That material scarcity is a perennial feature of Israel's socioeconomic life should not be surprising at all because it is only in the aftermath of the modern Industrial Revolution that surplus becomes a regular and expected part of economic activity. While the conspicuous consumption of the elite in distributive-status societies may suggest some surplus, this inordinate excess by a few is siphoned off the produce of the masses who, for the most part, are in tenuous subsistence living to begin with.

What is the impact of scarcity on the formulation, observance, and development of the statutes, laws, and ordinances on economic life? One can infer the following from the preceding discussion. First, the widespread violations of these ordinances on economic life reflect the severity and persistence of the scarcity experienced. Second, given this chronic condition of material need, observing these laws entails much sacrifice. Third, seeming inconsistencies and contradictions within the same corpus of laws may ultimately be traced in part to the conflicts and difficulties induced by scarcity. These contradictions may be a reflection of the tensions between vested interests within Israel itself (Brueggemann 1994, 17). At the root of such friction between the peasants and the wealthy are the competing claims to the finite economic and social goods of the community.

DEVELOPMENT OF LAW

Despite the scarcity-induced burdens of observing ordinances related to economic life, Israel reaffirms and even further develops and tightens these laws in response to their widespread violation and the deteriorating socioeconomic conditions of the monarchial period.[31] We examine variations in the economic statutes of these three law codes in the following sections.

Exodus to Deuteronomy

Most scholars date the Deuteronomic Code (Dt 12–26) much later than the Covenant Code (Ex 20:22–23:33). The Covenant Code is believed to have been part of a "single widespread customary law" (de Vaux 1965). Stein (1953, 164) argues that it is an early composition when Israel is more pastoral than agricultural. Neufeld (1955, 367–72) also holds to an early composition of the Covenant Code but takes the opposite view that the Code reflects a society that is advanced, settled, predominantly agricultural, and familiar with complicated commercial transactions. Despite their differences, however, both Stein and Neufeld agree on the centrality of kinship as the basis for mutual protection. There are no organized classes, neither kings nor the priesthood; people are homogeneous in their socioeconomic standing.[32] Exodus 20:22–23:33 is a codification of "Israelite common law" targeted to a rural audience (Lohfink 1991, 40). It is a carryover of a tribal setting that reflects familiarity with each other in which reciprocal assistance is expected as a regular part of common life.[33] Assistance to the poor, such as interest-free loans, is deeply embedded as a custom within the ambit of an extended family. Thus, there is little concern in the Code about relative inequality, only about mutual help.

Others argue that the Covenant Code is an ameliorative response to the social dislocations that follow in the wake of rapid socioeconomic changes.

> The Covenant Code might more plausibly be read . . . as a *social charter* designed to regulate a state of affairs in which the members of the small farming communities of the tribal federation had begun to suffer severe dislocation and sought in law a framework for exacting justice for their constituency. The Covenant Code would represent a negotiated settlement between the village elders and the royal house, regardless of which group actually promulgated the Code. (Pleins 2001, 53; emphasis original)

As tribal clans give way to large impersonal cities, nomadic customs are codified in an effort to institutionalize the traditional care of the vulnerable (von Waldow 1970; Mays 1987, 154–55).

The Deuteronomic Code is believed to date from either Hezekiah's reign

Regardless of which theory one accepts regarding the formation of early Israel (conquest, gradual infiltration-immigration settlement, or social revolution),[34] one thing is clear: early Israel is characterized by an egalitarian, compassionate, and democratic ethos in contrast to surrounding Canaanite practices and in reaction to her own bitter experience of adversity and oppression (Lohfink 1987, 48–52; C. Wright 1990, 46). Israel sees herself as a nation different from all the other nations in the way her people care for each other. More important, Israel is animated by her conviction that this is what God expects of her in the unmerited election she has received. The provisions of the Covenant Code, including those on economic life, reflect this unique self-understanding and the Chosen People's struggles to be the contrast-society that YHWH has called them to be.

The Deuteronomic Code is believed to date from either Hezekiah's reign (715–687 B.C.) or the time of Josiah (640–609 B.C.).[35] It seeks to make the Law even more benevolent (Boecker 1980, 83). Weinfeld (1961) hypothesizes that the wisdom literature is responsible for this humanism in Deuteronomy.[36] Others, however, believe that it is the prophetic tradition that brings about the relatively gentler and more compassionate provisions of the Deuteronomic Code (Doron 1978, 74).[37]

The monarchial era is characterized by overall economic growth and the expansion of Israel's commercial activities (de Vaux 1965, 76–79).[38] It is paradoxical, however, that more people are impoverished during these prosperous times. Heavy royal impositions of taxes and forced labor[39] drive people to debt, the loss of their land, and ultimately to servitude. The well-off, however, amass even greater wealth, land, and power, both economic and political. As Israel moves from decentralized clans to a heavily centralized monarchy, social stratification and relative inequality worsen as seen from the increase in debt-slavery, the alienation of land, and the emergence of large estates.[40] There is a general deterioration in social conditions with an increased incidence of marginalization and disenfranchisement. Enormous social cost and suffering are inflicted on the people as a royal-urban society replaces the traditional rural community in ancient Israel (Neufeld 1960). The development of law emerges partly from an increasing concern over the social dislocation of many. Appalled at the greater incidence of landlessness and the demise of landholding families, prophets preach against the erosion of the socioeconomic foundations of Israel as YHWH's contrast-society (C. Wright 1990, 65, 105–9). While it is difficult to be precise about the date of Deuteronomy, its legislation is believed to be a response to the suffering of many during the monarchial era (Lowery 2000, 30–31). However, one must qualify this observation with the caution that parts of the Deuteronomic Code are believed to be ancient legislation dating back as early as the Covenant Code.

On the whole, the Covenant Code retrieves or at least institutionalizes the egalitarianism and the ethos of compassion and mutual assistance of early Israel, while Deuteronomy reacts to social fragmentation and reaffirms and further develops the Covenant Code. The following sections examine differences in the economic ordinances of Exodus and Deuteronomy.[41] In particular, observe how many of these changes are concerned with addressing worsening relative inequality. Early Israel is relatively more equal and therefore not as concerned as the Deuteronomist regarding income or wealth disparities, as evidenced in the latter's changes in the law (de Vaux 1965, 73).[42]

An examination of debt practices is the appropriate starting point in studying scarcity as a phenomenon and its impact on human societies. After all, borrowing resources from others is the most immediate and readily available recourse for people in coping with material exiguities. The stringency or liberality in the terms and conditions of such loans provides a glimpse into the nature and quality of interpersonal ties and relations; they are also suggestive of the severity with which scarcity is experienced. Taken as an articulation of the ideal, these laws are a statement of how people ought to deal with each other even in the face of material shortfalls. Israel's moral development is reflected in her loan legislation: in her more humane provisions on pledges, in the clarifications and more precise language of Deuteronomy, in the mandate to provide loans, and in the nature of interest-free loans.

Pledges

Statutes governing pledges for loans illustrate the increasingly higher moral standards of Israel. In the first place, the Hebrew laws restrict the kinds of pledges that may be held by the creditor and the manner by which they may be taken. In contrast, other Near Eastern laws do not impose limits on either of these. In fact, the laws of Hammurabi even permit seizing people as a pledge (Gnuse 1985, 20–21).

Second, note the disparities in the economic provisions of Exodus and Deuteronomy. Exodus 22:26–27 forbids the taking of a cloak as a pledge, as it is essential for the basic health of the person. Deuteronomy 24:6, 24:10–13 echoes the same prohibition on the use of the cloak as a pledge but expands the restrictions much further. Taking millstones as pledges is banned because these are vital tools for people's livelihood. Moreover, the Deuteronomist severely restricts the manner by which pledges may be taken. In particular, creditors may not enter debtors' houses but must wait outside for the borrowers themselves to bring out the pledge they are giving to secure the loan. Lenders are further admonished not to take pledges from the poor but to return them promptly. Deuteronomy's treatment of pledges is far more developed and detailed than Exodus and may largely be an effort to curb rampant abuses by creditors. Moreover, its restrictions signify essential values, such as a preferential option for the poor and respect for the dignity and the privacy of the impoverished.

Greater precision in Deuteronomy

Exodus has many ambiguous points regarding loans that Deuteronomy clears up. For example, in Exodus it is uncertain if the prohibition on the charging of interest applies only to consumption loans and not to commercial loans (Rasor 1993–94, 168–69). Some suggest that interest on commercial debts are permissible (Neufeld 1955, 398–99; Patrick 1985, 86–87; Meislin and Cohen 1964, 264–65), while others disagree and claim that it is an outright prohibition on all kinds of loans (Gamoran 1971, 131).[43] Deuteronomy 23:19 dispels the ambiguity with a clear statement it appends to the original prohibition; it adds to the ban any and all transactions for which interest is usually demanded. Thus, loans even of a commercial nature are now unequivocally covered by the law.

Some interpret Exodus 22:25 as applicable only if the borrower is poor. The rich may be levied an interest payment because only the poor are mentioned as being exempt from such a charge (Neufeld 1955, 398–99). Again, Deuteronomy 23:19–20 explicitly states that the ban applies to all Hebrews regardless of economic status but not to foreigners.[44] Exodus is vague on either point.

Deuteronomy 15:1–3 regularizes debt remission. In other Near Eastern countries, such mandated debt write-offs are effected via royal edict and are therefore irregular and unpredictable. As a consequence, they avoid the problem whereby loans are intentionally incurred in anticipation of debt forgiveness. In regularizing *shemittah,* the seventh-year debt-release, Israel opens itself to such abuses, which in effect impose additional burdens on creditors. Thus, it is not surprising that the Deuteronomist anticipates lenders' objections by adding a proviso for mandatory lending (Dt 15:7–11). Hillel's *prosbul* is indicative of the severity of such intransigence and the ultimate failure of Deuteronomy 15:7–11. Despite the clear and foreseen moral hazard problem, the Deuteronomist nonetheless still insists on regularizing debt reprieve and continues to ask Israel to accomplish that which is arduous despite the anticipated costs and difficulties.

Mandatory lending

It is believed that Leviticus 25:35–38 should be read as an obligatory provision of credit because Exodus 22:25 and Deuteronomy 23:19–20 only refer to cases in which the loan had already been provided (Neufeld 1955, 358). Mandatory lending, of course, is also the spirit behind Deuteronomy 15:7–11, which addresses the problem of disappearing sources of credit with the advent of the seventh-year debt-release. However, there are other possible reasons, besides a forthcoming *shemittah,* that lead to a tightening supply of loanable funds for the poor.

This additional explicit moral obligation to lend to the needy may reflect people's increasing hesitation to provide loans. After all, given a choice, it is preferable to lend to a foreigner than to a fellow Hebrew because one can earn interest, need not write off the debt automatically after seven years, and need not release slave-labor after a maximum six years of service in the event of default. In addition, commercial borrowers have a much better chance of repaying compared to consumption-distress users. The poor, especially the landless, run a higher risk of defaulting because they do not have a steady and stable source of livelihood. And yet, they are precisely the very people who would benefit the most from such loans. Thus, it is understandable why there is need for the Deuteronomist to have to remind people of the moral obligation to lend to the poor.[45]

Both the prohibition of interest and mandatory lending are designed to help the needy. In the case of interest-free loans a corollary goal is to prevent profiteering from others' misfortunes or needs. Mandatory lending involves sharing in others' tribulations since lenders run the risk of financial loss themselves in the event of default. In the case of non-wealthy creditors, this is a real sharing of risk since the possible loss will come not from their surplus but from their substance.

Interest-free loans

Interest-free loans date back to the earliest days of Israel in its pastoral period when people rely heavily on each other for assistance given their tenuous existence (von Waldow 1970, 185–86). There is a mutual dependence and need for each other, which in turn give rise to accepted standards of egalitarianism. They are willing to sacrifice and share each other's risks and misfortunes since they expect others to do the same for them. Hence, there is parity and sharing not only in outcomes but even of risks, as is the case whenever they lend freely from their substance to tide others in their need or affliction. Codifying interest-free loans is in effect an effort to retrieve this earlier standard of solidarity and mutual help.

In all this, one must not forget the sacrificial nature of prohibiting interest and requiring the provision of loans to the poor because, as observed earlier, there are significant alternative uses for these loanable surpluses. It would be more lucrative and safer to lend to foreigners, especially those engaged in commercial or trading ventures. The continued development of debt legislation in the three law codes serves to affirm the critical service provided by loans in easing material shortages; such continued changes in debt ordinances reflect the need to work out kinks in their implementation. The improvements and clarifications in law also become the occasion to close loopholes that creditors use to get around these obligations.

In summary, the Deuteronomic economic ordinances convey an additional significance: they reveal the aspirations of a people to remain true to themselves despite disruptive and confusing social changes. Referring to differences in the three law codes, von Waldow observes: "These examples show sufficiently how the reinterpretation of ancient ordinances and regulations tried to meet the needs of a new time. But this was not yet all. At the same time new regulations were introduced" (1970, 199). Birch (1991, 161) takes the same position and views improvements in the Deuteronomic Code relative to ancient legislation (such as better "sensitivity to the value of all") as a reflection of Israel's growing understanding and more profound appropriation of YHWH's vision and plans for the nation.

Exodus-Deuteronomy to Leviticus

Despite their extensive debates, scholars are still divided on the dating of the Holiness Code (Lv 17–26) relative to the Covenant and Deuteronomic Codes.[46] Of relevance to this research is the dating of Leviticus 25. Some view it as post-exilic (e.g., Brown, Fitzmyer, and Murphy 1990, 78; Lowery 2000, 57; Pleins 2001) while others see it as early legislation (C. Wright 1990, 126; Eichrodt 1961, 96). The following sections examine the implications of both where appropriate for this study's thesis.

Debt-slavery

There is a discernible pattern over time, indeed a revolution, of overcoming a master-slave class struggle in the Hebrew Scripture:

> Of basic importance for the real revolution is the insight that each person among the people of God was originally a slave who has been set free. The understanding of what it is to be a slave is the basis for a twofold revolution which comes from God: (1) There is a changed attitude toward the slave's need for humane treatment and (2) there is a change in his external situation. (Wolff 1973, 272)

Moreover, Chirichigno (1993, 185) observes that, compared to the laws of Hammurabi, the Hebrew laws concerning slaves are more humane by extending to chattel-slaves the same rights afforded to members of the community (e.g., Ex 21:20–21, 21:26–27).[47]

There is a progressive improvement in the treatment of slaves over time, as shown by a comparison between the Covenant and Deuteronomic Codes.

For example, Exodus 21:7 does not call for the release of maidservants after six years of service, unlike male servants (21:2–6). This is revised in Deuteronomy 15:12, which explicitly states that both men and women debt-slaves are to be released. Or take the case of the actual manumission itself. In contrast to Exodus, Deuteronomy 15:13–15 takes pains to emphasize the importance of provisioning the freed slave with a strong and pointed reminder to the master that it is God after all who provides such goods in the first place. There are important practical ramifications to this revision because freed slaves would most likely revert back to debt and ultimately slavery if they are not given access to economic resources with which to sustain an independent subsistence. The quantum leap, of course, in enhancing the chances of freed slaves to keep their freedom occurs in the Jubilee Law. By combining release from bondage with a debt write-off in addition to land return, Leviticus 25 ensures that the freed slave possesses a stable economic base (land) from which to derive a livelihood that guarantees such independence and freedom. Thus, the juxtaposition of debt-release, slave manumission, and land return in the Jubilee is most likely not a coincidence or a mere rehearsal of economic statutes but a genuine attempt at a lasting radical socioeconomic reform. This is consistent with the fervent spirit of reform in the immediate postexilic period.[48]

Sabbath

Sabbath legislation (Sabbath day, Sabbath-fallow, and Jubilee) is a statement against the abuses of the monarchy:

> Sabbath anticipates and ritually celebrates an in-breaking world that reverses the severe conditions of peasant and village life under ancient monarchy. It rejects the "natural law" of scarcity, poverty, and excessive toil for the laboring majority alongside luxury, leisure, and excessive consumption for the court-connected few. It assumes instead a divinely sanctioned social and cosmic order characterized by social solidarity, natural abundance, and self-restraint . . . a world of release for those who struggle on the margins of royal economy, a vision of hope for a better life. . . . *Sabbath is both a prophetic critique of the royal status quo and a visionary call to build a better world.* Sabbath is a foretaste of God's perfect rule. (Lowery 2000, 102; emphasis added)

The reiteration and refinement of Sabbath legislation across Exodus, Deuteronomy, and Leviticus could therefore be viewed as a theological restatement and reassertion of their self-understanding of the kind of community God envisions for the nation Israel. The dating of the Holiness Code does not pose a problem for the inferences we draw about this legislation.

In summary, it is important to note two phenomena that together are indicative of a people laboring to be faithful to its election: (1) the impact of scarcity that makes the observance of statutes on economic life burdensome and (2) refinements in the terms and conditions of the law codes' economic ordinances, both of which suggest a nation Israel wrestling to respond morally to changing socioeconomic conditions. There is ample evidence to believe that material scarcity is deep and chronic, making compliance with the laws on economic life truly sacrificial. Despite the exacting and often unmet requirements of the Law, the Chosen People nevertheless reaffirm these statutes and make them not only more humane but even stricter largely in response to the deteriorating socioeconomic conditions during the monarchy.

The strongest, and the most ideal, claim that can be made for my thesis is to say that the development of the Law (in becoming more humane) paralleled the Chosen People's experience of the increasingly adverse effects of scarcity. Notwithstanding their already considerable sacrificial demands, these economic ordinances could be described as being developed further and made even more exacting because of Israel's self-understanding of what God expects of her, as made clearly evident in the motive clauses appended to the reformulated ordinances. Recall the increasing frequency in the use of these clauses in moving from the Covenant Code to Deuteronomy to the Holiness Code (Gemser 1953). Unfortunately, in the absence of a definitive chronology of these three law codes, I cannot make the claim that the development of the Law was in response to Israel's experience of worsening scarcity. The most that I could say is that changes across these economic ordinances reveal the Chosen People's efforts to adjust their laws according to YHWH's expectations in the face of evolving socioeconomic conditions.

Birch argues effectively that the moral authority of the Law stems from Israel's ongoing relationship with YHWH: "[T]he law codes in their narrative setting are themselves witnesses to the journey of the community Israel, constantly discovering God's will for them anew" (1991, 165). Such a dynamic human-divine interaction inevitably and necessarily finds expression in changes that Israel effects in her social structures and common life in the wake of her ever-deepening understanding of her Covenant election.

Inconsistencies within the Law reflect a struggle to respond to the harmful consequences of changed social conditions. Hanson's (1977) explanation for the contradictions found in the Covenant Code applies just as well to accounting for the incongruities in the economic statutes of the three law codes. Hanson asserts that the strange admixture of incompatible provisions within the Law[49] must be viewed in the context of a tradition-in-process as the nation's legal and social structures and processes are slowly transformed by its religious confession. Birch echoes Hanson's position and concludes that disparities within the Covenant Code stem from:

> [An] Israel inevitably affected by the social practices of surrounding culture, but placing those practices in tension with *patterns of societal relationship which grow specifically out of the uniqueness of Israel's God and experience in relation to that God.* (1991, 161; emphasis added)

Contradictions among the law codes' economic statutes suggest a people wrestling to react appropriately to the problems of their times.[50] There is a *dialectic quality* to their nation-building as the Chosen People seek to live up to the ideals of their covenantal relationship in the face of great hurdles. Thus, discrepancies in the Law flow from the striving of a people endeavoring to understand and to make their own the efforts of a loving God at work in human history. As Birch observes, "Development of the implications of Israel's faith for its social structure and practices continues to be reflected throughout the law codes" (1991, 161). Scarcity prompts an even greater, more deliberate, and intensified effort to live up to YHWH's laws. The Chosen People struggle to be righteous; scarcity causes such aspiration to become an even more profound participation in God's holiness and righteousness. Scarcity does not make their task any easier, although it also makes their striving that much more meaningful and heartfelt.

SCARCITY, ECONOMIC AGENCY, AND COVENANT ELECTION

God's in-breaking in human history exhibits a necessary economic dimension that is amply and effectively reflected in the laws and statutes governing economic life in the Promised Land. Such in-breaking is significant for this study because it is through the concrete particularities of this historicity (e.g., land and God's concern for the poor) that we get a glimpse of how socio-economic life serves as a terrain for the evolution and deepening of this divine-human relationship. I end these two chapters on the Hebrew Scripture by offering insights and conclusions that can be gleaned from the impact of scarcity on economic agency in covenant election.

God's gift of instrumentality

The Exodus is a self-revelation of God's deep concern for the economically exploited. Lohfink (1987, 5–15) situates such a divine liberating act against the larger backdrop of a God with a lively interest in creatures, in the here and now, in society, and in plenitude—interests that unleash a drama. While already a gift in itself, this drama spawns even more gifts in its wake, such as human instrumentality and participation. In other words, not only are humans the object of the drama unleashed, *they too will be the subjects through which God shapes, unleashes, and continues the drama.* This is particularly true in economic life—a realm that lends itself well as a sphere for participation in God's righteousness, holiness, and providence.

There is a necessary economic dimension to this divine in-breaking because YHWH as the Lord of nature exercises dominion and sustains all who dwell on God's domain. As part of their created nature, human beings are corporeal and need to consume and use material goods for their survival and basic health. Even the neighboring Near Eastern peoples clearly recognize that their continued sustenance is at the pleasure of the gods of the lands, the gods of nature who provide for them. As Creator, God is both protector and provider for the fragile nature of human beings. However, there is another element to this economic dimension in divine-human relationship that is not prescribed by human nature: the divine gift of human instrumentality.[51] God chooses to provide for and sustain human beings through each other. God brings forth and maintains due order in the natural world and human affairs through human beings themselves, as is readily evident in the laws and statutes on economic life. A distinctive feature of Israel's experience is our unmerited role in God's governance.

YHWH has used the economic dimension of the divine in-breaking in human history as an occasion to let humans partake of God's holiness and righteousness. Such invitation can be established by considering both (1) what God could have done but did not (furnishing the world with unconditional material abundance) and (2) what God did do instead (providing only for conditional material abundance, contingent on human response and instrumentality). Paradoxically, God provides this gift of instrumentality through scarcity.

Law as a venue for unfolding instrumentality

Land has twin roles that mutually reinforce each other: as a tangible evidence of Israel's special relationship to YHWH (symbolic role) and as a venue and means for sustaining that relationship (functional role). Land not only serves as the terrain for Israel's encounter with YHWH, but it also provides the setting in which content is provided to that relationship. This is particularly evident in the people's mighty struggle to conform to the statutes on economic life and to tailor and develop these further in ways that better reflect life on a land that is both under divine ownership and a divine gift.

It does not matter whether the Hebrew laws on economic life are materially similar to their Near Eastern counterparts or not. What is important is the basis for these laws—the *indicative* of what YHWH did for Israel in the Exodus and the *imperative* of what YHWH now expects of her in her life on the land entrusted to her care. What makes the economic ordinances of Israel different from all the other nations is their underlying rationale and dynamic: in faithfully observing these laws, Hebrews are in effect accepting the invitation to emulate God's *sedeq* and are allowing YHWH to make them holy just as YHWH is holy (Lv 19:2). The Chosen People are able to requite YHWH's devotion and love for them through their love for and devotion to each other, and in so doing, the people themselves serve as a channel through which God continues to sustain Israel with divine providence.

Scarcity and the Law

God does not provide humans "sustenance without care"[52] but sustenance with active interpersonal engagement. It is a sustenance with struggle, a heroic one, as seen in the exacting demands of living up to the Law and in the statutes' further development.

God's vision is material abundance, but that abundance is conditional on human response. God could have mitigated the sacrificial demands of the economic ordinances by attenuating the degree of scarcity in creation. The less severe the material shortages, the less care that is needed for sustenance and the less interpersonal friction in the economic realm. By requiring much deliberate and sustained effort, scarcity deepens Israel's partaking of God's righteousness. The self-donative nature of these laws in the face of scarcity, the reaffirmation and subsequent strengthening of these statutes despite such burdens, the motive clauses that account for the Chosen People's openness to such self-denial, and the sincere desire to address the deteriorating social conditions of their time all point to a human instrumentality straining and striving to live out God's holiness and righteousness.

Distinctive features of such instrumentality

An important word of caution: in highlighting the importance of human response and moral conduct, we run the risk of turning material prosperity into a reward for human effort. We must not do so. It is important to remember that this conditionality pertains to human beings not impeding an unfolding world of plenty as originally envisioned and created by God. After all, the land is an unmerited divine gift to Israel to begin with; the "land of milk and honey" is not given to the Chosen People as a recompense for some accomplishment (von Waldow 1974, 505; C. Wright 1990). The Deuteronomist (Dt 9:4–6) emphasizes the utter gratuity of land as a divine gift. Lowery argues that "universal prosperity is simply the way of the world as God called it into being and intends it to be" (Lowery 2000, 86).[53] Thus, it is not a question of humans bringing about material abundance through their own efforts and through their faithful observance of the Law. It is rather humans "bringing about" such material sufficiency simply by not hampering or spoiling the unfurling abundance of God's providence through their sinfulness.[54]

God could have easily willed a world of "sustenance without care" but did not. Rather, God created an order of sustenance that requires much effort, sacrifice, and collaboration, albeit with a concomitant growth in grace, holiness, righteousness, and mutual care.

CHAPTER 6

PARTICIPATED RIGHTEOUSNESS: INCARNATIONAL AND INSTRUMENTAL

We now turn our attention to what can be inferred from the New Testament regarding the warrants, nature, and manner by which economic life is a venue for participation in God's righteousness. Since economic ethics is merely part of a much broader moral life, this chapter situates upright economic conduct within God's righteousness using Pauline theology.

NEW TESTAMENT ETHICS: DIVINE INITIATIVES AND HUMAN RESPONSE

The first task in theological economic ethics is to examine the larger moral life in which economic agency is embedded and unfolds. Moral conduct is essentially about letting the Holy Spirit actualize in us what Christ has already won (Bottorff 1973, 426). Hence, it is important to have an overview of the specific nature and dynamics of what has now been made possible by Christ.

However, New Testament ethics is so broad and diverse that some scholars doubt whether it could be synthesized and presented as a homogeneous whole. The texts should instead be allowed to speak for themselves (Matera 1996). On the other hand, some believe that such an integration could (and should) be done and have presented their own constructive proposals accordingly (Hays 1996; Lohse 1991; Schrage 1988; Verhey 1984; Schnackenburg 1965). Despite the multiplicity of emphases and perspectives among New Testament authors, a common feature stands out in particular: the texts form a narrative of divine initiatives desirous of and eliciting a human response—one that struggles and fails but is nonetheless always welcomed and aided by grace.

New Testament ethics could be said to have three different dimensions that correspond to the manifold ways by which divine initiatives are manifested: Christological, eschatological, and pneumatological. It is Christological because Jesus Christ is the exemplar of the moral life; the righteousness of God made visible through the Incarnation; the Emmanuel (God in our midst) that heals, reassures, lends courage, feeds, and renews people in their brokenness; the Word of God that teaches and concretely points out the path that leads to enduring treasure. In his own passion, death, and resurrection, Jesus Christ reveals how to embody the most profoundly promising possibility of human life—being fully alive to God. This soteriological dimension highlights the saving act of God through Jesus Christ that breaks the power of sin. It is Jesus Christ who gives human beings a fighting chance of rising above sin. Sin is no longer inevitable, and it could be put behind us as we look forward to a new horizon now open to us. And all this is possible because of Christ's death and resurrection. Thus, moral life is founded on faith in Christ and a baptism that leads us to participate in his dying and rising to new life.

New Testament ethics has an eschatological dimension because the re-created moral life founded on Christ is ever forward-looking. Its hope for the fullness and completion of God's reign necessarily changes and shapes moral conduct. The future is made accessible and can be lived in its first installment in the present. Thus, in writing to the churches he had founded, Paul invariably reminds them of how their expectation of Christ's imminent second coming ought to make a difference in their personal and common lives; they can no longer remain or persist in their former ways. In fact, their faith in Christ finds expression in their changed hearts (1 Thes 4:1–12). The tension between present and future eschatology—the here and the not yet—imbues

New Testament ethics with its dynamism. It cannot stand still or be idle; it is fevered in its desire to participate in the building of the Kingdom of God and will be ever unrested and unsettled until Christ comes again in glory.

Finally, New Testament ethics has a pneumatological[1] dimension because:

> [What] was made possible in Christ is actualised through the Holy Spirit. . . . [I]t is the Holy Spirit which brings the eschatological reality of freedom in the present moment. (Bottorff 1973, 426)

Despite their share in Christ's victory over sin and despite their re-creation in a new age, human beings are nevertheless still embodied and situated in a world where sin lurks. After all, in contrast to the fullness of the *parousia* (the second coming of Jesus Christ), the present eschatology has an incomplete state to it, thereby imbuing the Christian moral life with a distinctive quality of yearning. The Holy Spirit guides, empowers, and directs such striving.

The Christological, eschatological, and pneumatological facets of New Testament ethics accentuate the points of contact between divine initiatives and human response. They situate the grounds of moral life within salvation history. Just like these three dimensions of divine initiatives, human response can also be characterized in terms of its constituent elements.

MORAL LIFE AS PARTICIPATION IN GOD'S RIGHTEOUSNESS

Pauline framework

Pauline writings provide a scriptural basis for the claim that economic life is, in fact, a venue for human participation in God's righteousness. We are able to glean and piece from this single corpus a complete framework that encompasses Christology and eschatology, an examination of their implications for moral life, and an articulation of specific admonitions on economic relations. Paul moves with ease from the most general, abstruse points of theology down to their application in the prosaic affairs of the household in response to churches' manifold questions and problems regarding practical matters of living together as a community.

From a theological standpoint, Paul is also the most ideal New Testament author to use for this study because he himself is steeped in the notion and language of participation. In fact, Sanders (1977) goes so far as to argue that Pauline participationist categories such as being "in Christ" or "in the Spirit"[2] ought to be the central focus of scholars and not "righteousness," as has been the case in Western scholarship. Byrne disagrees with Sanders and notes that participationist categories and righteousness are not mutually exclusive; they reinforce each other and ought to be used together.

> It is not a matter of choosing between righteousness and participationist categories. . . . It is a matter of seeing that *the nub of Paul's distinctiveness lies in the way participationist categories are placed at the service of righteousness, i.e., are presented as the way in which the required righteousness is produced.* (1981, 571; emphasis added)

In his exegesis of Romans 8:1–11, Byrne (1981, 567–70) seeks to illustrate how these participationist categories are, in fact, the "distinctively Pauline mode of conceiving the working-out of the righteousness of God in the Christian" (571). We find the same conclusion in Hays (1987, 272), who also observes that a central theological motif of Pauline ethics is "participation in Christ."

Byrne's point on the need to situate righteousness within participationist categories is precisely the very exercise of this and the next chapter—tracing how economic ethics flows from human participation in God's righteousness. Thus, I use Pauline literature in the following sections as a basis for establishing the nexus between moral life and its partaking of God's righteousness.

Pauline usage of "righteousness"

Before proceeding further, it is important to ascertain what is meant by "God's righteousness." Scholars disagree on whether "righteousness of God" refers to righteousness as God's innate quality (subjective genitive)[3] or whether it refers to the righteousness communicated by God to humans as a gift (objective genitive).[4] On top of this, there is also ambiguity over whether Paul uses "righteousness" in its theological or moral senses (Blackman 1962, 1029). Käsemann (1969, 168–82; 1971, 74–75) shows that it is both, since justification as a *gift* (including consequent ethical behavior) cannot be separated from the *Giver*.

Käsemann (1969, 174) arrives at this conclusion by arguing that righteousness cannot merely refer to a quality of divine nature (subjective genitive) as it is fundamentally a relational term. Thus, he notes that in Hebrew Scripture and in later Judaism, the term refers to "faithfulness in the context of the community." Furthermore, we cannot ignore the numerous Pauline passages on the term "righteousness" that refer to the state of redeemed human beings. Since righteousness is indisputably a quality that is proper to divine nature alone (subjective genitive), it can become a human quality only as it is communicated by God (objective genitive). What is a power in God becomes a gift as soon as it is imparted (from subjective to objective genitive). Such sharing requires a divine act. For Paul, "righteousness of God" is a "phrase expressing divine activity, treating not of the self-subsistent, but of the *self-revealing God*" (Käsemann 1969, 174; emphasis added).

Faith versus good works

Given the critical importance of human response in attaining the ideal economic life, should New Testament teachings on economic ethics be properly described as works-righteousness? This question is, of course, nothing new as it falls within the long-standing Catholic-Protestant dispute on whether faith alone justifies. A thorough assessment of the theological debate on faith versus good works is beyond the scope of this work. Moreover, all that is needed for this study's thesis is to validate the claim that good works are integral to the life of righteousness. This is a conclusion that fits righteousness both as it covers our sinfulness with the merits of Jesus Christ (which is its forensic dimension, and is the Protestant view) and as it transforms people who subsequently lead upright lives (which is its ethical character, and is the Catholic position). Thus, I am able to readily employ literature from both Protestant and Catholic authors for this study.[5] There is abundant scholarship that not only supports the claim that economic life, and for that matter all of moral life, is a venue for partaking of God's righteousness, but also illustrates how such sharing is in fact actualized.

Using Romans 6:1–8:13, Byrne (1981) examines the basis of ethical presuppositions in Paul and concludes that it is pointless to present faith and good works as a dichotomy. After all, moral behavior is, in its essence, Christ living out the righteousness of God in human lives. Furnish (1968) observes that the *imperative* flows and derives its power from the *indicative,*[6] that is, we live up to the demands of morality with alacrity because of our self-understanding of our redeemed and transformed personhood.

Bottorff (1973) contends that *ethics* flows from *justification* through a faith that has to be constantly realized in action in the here and now. In justification, faith procures the power of God's righteousness; in ethical behavior (including economic ethics), faith bears fruit and manifests its authenticity and power in the Holy Spirit. Ziesler (1972) holds similar views but from a different approach: the *ethical* flows from the *incorporative* dynamic in which humanity dies and is born anew as a "Corporate Christ." Moral renewal necessarily rises from the restoration of the relations between God and humanity through Christ—a single encompassing sweep that "includes both the facts of our redemption, and the subsequent life of the redeemed" (1972, 166).

Hays (1987) concludes that the proclamation of the Gospel (*kerygma*) cannot be separated from conduct because faith is not merely an intellectual concurrence, but a lived assent. It is a whole reorientation of life precipitated by a profound conversion (*metanoia*). Good works are the fruits of such repentance and reorientation. Matthew's greater righteousness and Mark's repentance find completion and full expression only in changed lives (Keck 1984; Verhey 1984; Hays 1996; Matera 1996). In his exegesis of Galatians, Hays (1987, 288–89) remarks that its theological and exhortatory (paranetic) sections converge on the person of Jesus Christ; Paul's ethics is founded on his Christology. Galatians 5:6 summarizes the core of Paul's ethics in "faith working through love." For Hays, this is nothing else but the "Law of Christ," which is realized in moral life through mutual "burden-bearing" just as Jesus bore our burdens. Faith in Christ means embracing the Lord as our exemplar. Faith and conduct are inseparable.

Achtemeier (1962a, 99) maintains that righteousness is fundamentally about the restored divine-human covenant relationship in Jesus Christ; it is not primarily about human moral shortcomings or achievements. The latter is merely consequent on the divine act of restoring the relationship. Thus, while it is not the focal point of righteousness, right conduct is nevertheless expected since it is the fruit of justification. Hence, the gift comes with its demands, the indicative with its imperative. This is particularly evident in our relationship with other humans (97–98).

There is much in Pauline writings to affirm James's (2:14–26) characterization of faith without works as being dead. Paul would be the first to acknowledge that conversion and life in Christ do not mean that believers will no longer fall into sin. One only has to look at the numerous moral problems brought to Paul's attention by the churches. Nevertheless, despite these vestiges of sin, Paul expects a sincere effort in changing personal moral behavior as part of the justification received in Christ (Rom 6:1–4, 6:15–19). Believers cannot simply go on with their former way of life as if nothing had fundamentally altered in them. Faith is not faith at all until it is actualized, that is, acted upon, and this is readily observable in the manner by which lives have changed or not. After all, justification is not a mere abstract theological concept meant for speculative thought; it "has very practical consequences, even for conduct in legal and economic matters" (Dahl 1977, 103–4). Put in another way, faith has pragmatic consequences, and it must bear fruit accordingly.

Using Paul's theology and ethics, one can make a case for the inseparability of faith and good works. Nevertheless, humans cannot claim ultimate credit for attaining an exemplary economic life inasmuch as such right order is at its core a manifestation of God at work in their midst. There is a seamless connection between the saving action of God, on the one hand, and ethical behavior from a re-created, transformed humanity, on the other. Hence, observe the ease with which Paul, in his letters, moves back and forth, so readily and so frequently, between Christology and moral theology, that is, between dogma and exhortation (*paranesis*). Ziesler succinctly summarizes this tight and inseparable link when he notes that "'righteousness' is best taken ethically, . . . is God's, and . . . in Christ it becomes ours" (1972, 164). We are now in a position to delve deeper and examine further some properties of the moral life that are essential for this study's thesis.

NATURE OF PARTICIPATED RIGHTEOUSNESS

It is not essential for this study to resolve the "faith versus good works" debate. I am interested only in developing my proposition that economic agency as participation in God's righteousness is both incarnational and instrumental. Since both Catholic and Protestant positions converge on the point that good works are integral to the life of righteousness, I will be using authors and materials from both sides of the debate as I examine the incarnational and instrumental nature of participated righteousness.

Incarnational righteousness

Human participation in God's righteousness can be properly described as an incarnational righteousness because of (1) its provenance—Jesus as the In-

carnate Righteousness of God—and (2) its appropriation by embodied beings. This twofold reason for calling it incarnational is succinctly summarized
by Paul in 2 Corinthians 5:14–21, where he describes the dynamics and elements of human participation in God's righteousness: who makes it possible
and how, who sustains it and to what end, its juridical and incorporative
effects, and its expected impact on ethical behavior.[7] The following sections
examine in greater detail the features of this participated, incarnational righteousness.

Human righteousness comes through Jesus Christ—
the Incarnate Righteousness.

Human righteousness is incarnational because it is founded on a Christological bedrock. And this applies to both the forensic (relational) and ethical
usage of the term "righteousness." Byrne provides an excellent starting point
for discussion in this regard.

> [T]hrough association with Christ by faith and baptism the Christian is
> drawn into the sphere of the righteousness of God; *it is through living out*
> *or rather, allowing Christ to live out this righteousness within oneself that*
> *eternal life is gained.* Such a view does involve . . . a return to an "ethi-
> cal" view of righteousness. But the totally christological base of such
> righteousness—the fact that it remains always the righteousness of God
> communicated in Christ—excludes . . . any sense of a righteousness
> held by human beings over and against the operation of God. (1981, 558;
> emphasis added)

God acquits humans and deems them righteous despite their sins because of their redemption through the Righteous One—Jesus Christ. In
dying and rising with Him through baptism (Rom 6:3–11; Col 2:12–3:5),
humans also share in no less than *Incarnate Righteousness* itself since Jesus
is the righteousness of God made manifest (Haughey 1977). Achtemeier
(1962a, 94–97) describes this phenomenon in the language of participation.
Through his obedience, Christ restores the covenant relationship that had
been sundered. Through faith and baptism in Christ, humans participate
in this restored relationship not merely "as if" they were righteous but as
they are "in fact" righteous. Thus, participation in Christ is the doorway

to justification. This is the forensic or relational use of the term "righteous" whereby deserved punishment is remitted and divine-human relations are once again restored. Note that the Christological foundation of such a juridical dimension of "righteousness" is well-acknowledged in the literature (e.g., Käsemann 1969, 1971; Schrage 1988).

In contrast, the Christological roots of the ethical usage of "righteousness" is not as well-established, and we find evidence for such a lacuna in the long-standing debate on whether justification comes by faith alone or through good works as well. As we can see from the preceding quote, Byrne sees no tension at all between faith and good works because it is still Christ who is responsible for all ethical behavior. He repeats the same point well by emphatically noting that: "Christians do not appropriate to themselves the righteousness of God. Rather, in Christ they are taken up into it" (1981, 574–75). All these echo the crux of Paul's self-understanding: "I no longer live, but Christ lives in me" (Gal 2:20).

Finally, since Christ is the manifestation of God's righteousness (Rom 3:21), a case for the incarnational nature of human righteousness can be made on the basis of Käsemann's (1969) point that the gift is inseparable from the Giver. As noted earlier, scholars are not in agreement on the precise usage of "God's righteousness" in Paul—whether it pertains to the personal attribute or act of God, or whether it refers to the imparted rectitude received by humans. Byrne (1981, 558) adopts Käsemann's position, and we see this reflected in Byrne's thoroughly Christological presentation not only for the forensic but also for the ethical side of human righteousness. In other words, we cannot separate Christ from the righteousness (juridic and moral) that is conferred on humans as a gift. Human righteousness is completely steeped in and inseparable from the ambit of the Incarnate Word.

Participated righteousness is incarnational because it is embodied in human lives.

There is a second reason why human righteousness is incarnational: because of the manner by which it is manifested in the here and now. In the preceding quote, Byrne ascribes a Christological foundation to ethical behavior because Christ's saving act is powerful in its transformative effect. Commenting on 2 Corinthians 5:21, Hays describes the implications and the profundity of this righteousness that is re-creative in its impact:

> [Paul] does not say "that we might *know about* the righteousness of God" nor "that we might *believe in* the righteousness of God" nor even "that we might *receive* the righteousness of God." Instead the church is to *become* the righteousness of God. . . . The church incarnates the righteousness of God. (1996, 24; emphasis original)

Human righteousness is not merely a matter of being covered in the merits of Jesus Christ; it permeates the very being of the new creation in Christ, given the all-embracing, deep, and life-changing manner by which such divine righteousness is given as a gift. The capacity for moral life is strengthened and reconfigured.

> The believer enters not just a private relationship to Jesus, but a new humanity, in which he becomes a new kind of man. Thus there are not only social or corporate implications, but also ethical ones, *for he now shares in the risen life of Christ, which means power including ethical power.* (Ziesler 1972, 168–69; emphasis added)

This is in complete agreement with Byrne's (1981) position, which we have just examined. There is a progression from "the revelation of righteousness through Christ to the manifestation of righteousness" in ethical behavior (Bottorff 1973, 425).

Incarnational righteousness is socially embedded.

There is a discernible pattern in the preceding description of what constitutes human righteousness: it has a communal nature. In stressing the incarnational nature of the righteousness received, Hays (1996, 24) refers to the church and not to the individual alone. Ziesler (1972, 168–69) even goes so far as to explicitly allude to "the social and corporate implications" of righteousness.

There is a necessary social dimension to human participation in God's righteousness because of a shared source, a common righteousness-in-Christ. Romans 5:12–21 succinctly describes the further strengthening of bonds across all men and women, given their common experience of salvation in Christ. A "new unity of mankind in him" emerges, which Ziesler (1972, 164–65) calls the "Corporate Christ."

Dahl examines the doctrine of justification and finds an intrinsic social function to it.

> Justification does not simply involve the individual and his salvation. Paul's perspective includes history and eschatology: Adam, mankind and Christ, the promise to Abraham and the Law given to Moses, the gospel preached to Jews and Gentiles, God's work in the past and in the future, . . . the unity of Jews and Gentiles . . . , and the all-encompassing ultimate goal of God's plan for his creation. Obviously, the doctrine of justification is not primarily social; it is theological and soteriological. *But the framework which Paul uses to locate the doctrine is social and historical rather than psychological and individualistic.* (1977, 110; emphasis added)[8]

This social dimension to Paul's vision of the moral life is undergirded by his ecclesiology, which is as universal in its scope as it is organic. First, Käsemann (1969, 180–81) argues that Paul's vision of a salvation for all humanity fits in within the historicity of his framework. The ever-widening scope of God's activity reveals a worldwide mission as the present eschatology moves into the future eschatology. Beasley-Murray's (1976) exegesis of Romans 9–11 makes a similar observation regarding the gift of God's righteousness being extended to all nations. Käsemann (1971, 76–78) is emphatic that this encompasses even the "ungodly"; Paul's righteousness is, after all, a doctrine of justification of the ungodly.

The theme of universality in the wake of the new dispensation is also evident in changed relationships. "There is neither Jew nor Greek, slave nor free, male nor female, for . . . all [are] one in Christ Jesus" (Gal 3:28). Dahl (1977, 109) observes that Paul intentionally writes this bold claim within the context of his exposition on justification. The believers' social circumstances at the time they receive the gift of faith are inconsequential and irrelevant. Thus, it is meaningless to compare the status of slaves relative to the free because within their shared faith-life, both are free and slaves at the same time—free in Christ and slaves to Christ (1 Cor 7:21–23). The transformative power of Christ is radical not only in the way it re-creates individuals, but also in the manner in which it recasts relationships.

Second, this social dimension to Paul's ethics springs from his ecclesiology, in which all are members of one and the same body in Christ (1 Cor 12). In this organic unity, the ties that bind people to each other are not merely metaphorical but functional. This is immediately apparent in the way Paul puts a premium on mutual love, respect, and assistance (Rom 13:8–10; Gal 5:14–15) in resolving the churches' practical problems that are presented to him. Thus, he is deeply dismayed that members of the same household of faith would take each other to court instead of resolving their differences among themselves (1 Cor 6:1–11). He repeatedly urges the community to bear with one another and with each other's burdens (Gal 6:2) and to generously provide one another with a wide berth of accommodation even to the point of inconvenience to oneself, as in the case of his advice to the strong to forego eating meat for the sake of not scandalizing those who are weak (Rom 14; 1 Cor 8; 1 Cor 10:24–33). And he extends such liberality even to injustices, as in the case of simply quietly bearing unredressed harm to oneself, all for the sake of peace within the community (1 Cor 6:9). And, of course, Paul is untiring and unabashed in soliciting alms for the poor of Jerusalem, constantly reminding the churches of their solidarity with one another and of the need to pass on to others the same unmerited favors they themselves have received from the Lord. Many more examples can be cited to reveal a heavily social nature to Pauline teachings founded on his deep appreciation that personal moral life is set within and inextricably linked to the larger context of the household of faith. As Dahl remarks: "The Pauline formulation of the doctrine of justification has a clear social relevance: it implies an understanding of what Christian community is, and it provides guidelines to show the members of that community how they ought to relate to one another" (1977, 108).

A socially embedded understanding of righteousness is relevant not only for morality but also for systematic theology. One's perception of the link between faith and good works may be affected by whether one acknowledges a social dimension to justification or not. Hays (1987, 269–71) is critical of Betz's (1979) exegesis of Galatians, in which he separates *kerygma* from conduct. Hays ascribes this common flaw among many post-Reformation scholars to their predisposition toward an individualistic view of justification whereby the only relation of consequence is that of the individual and God. Hays asserts that this is not consistent with the intended corporate audience of Galatians.

Participated righteousness has a larger social backdrop to it. After all, as we have seen in Hebrew Scripture, right relations is a constitutive element of righteousness (Achtemeier 1962b). Just as the Kingdom serves as the nurturing womb for the individual in the Gospels, so does the household of faith in

Pauline literature. In both cases, God always works and encounters the individual within a community of faith. Moreover, God commissions the individual, but always for work on behalf of others and not for the self. We observe this throughout salvation history from Adam, Abraham, Moses, the judges, the kings, and the prophets all the way down to the new dispensation—the apostles, the disciples, and even the Messiah himself. Thus, Barth even goes so far as to imbue a thoroughly social character to Pauline righteousness by claiming that the individual can find salvation only through others who have themselves also found grace: "Because God in his judgement and acquittal has caused righteousness to come to fellow-man and has procured for him divine justice, my 'right' before God is as great and as small as my joy and enthusism over that which my neighbor has been granted and which through him is reflected on me" (1968, 267). The added benefit to viewing justification as a social event is that it binds people to each other by virtue of their shared dependence on grace. For this reason, "justification by works" should be viewed with much caution since it segregates people from each other depending on their differences on what constitutes good works (241).

Finally, a substantial social content can be ascribed to justification because of its ramifications for moral conduct. The social character of righteousness derives not merely from the nature of the gift (the indicative), but also from its attendant demands (the imperative). As we have already seen, humans are justified only because of their participation in the covenant relationship that has been made right anew through the obedience of Jesus Christ. Such participation in a restored relationship between the divine and the human necessarily overflows into right relations between humans themselves. Thus, those who have been justified are under obligation to treat others (both the godly and the ungodly) with the same kindness and grace with which they have been accepted by God in the renewed covenant relationship despite their lack of any merit to receive such favor (Achtemeier 1962a, 97–98; Blackman 1962, 1028). In Hays's (1996) typology of "community-cross–new creation,"[9] we become a new creation in the context of the new community in Christ.

Incarnational righteousness situates itself in the midst of the world.

Barth (1968) can arguably be criticized for overstressing the social character of justification at the expense of personal responsibility and the individual's relationship with God. His position can be moderated by noting that justification is not achieved exclusively by associating with the justified. Thus, we leave the doors open to however and whatever means God may choose to impart the gift of faith. Whether one fully accepts Barth's arguments or not, the necessary social context he assigns to justification leads to an important insight for incarnational righteousness: those who have been justified by grace are not called to run away from the world and withdraw in a triumphalistic shell of isolation.

> The social character of justification and of the Gospel calls as little for a glorified worldliness or secularization as its [sic] supports a glorified churchiness and sacralization. What is necessary is a renewal of the church *and* the world. Neither of them is to be triumphant in its own right. The victory and honor belongs to Jesus Christ only who makes all things new. (Barth 1968, 265; emphasis original)

This requisite wholehearted engagement with the world is also affirmed in the clearly historical framework within which Paul develops his doctrine of justification.[10] Justification is set within history whereby God takes the initiative of reaching out to humans right where they are, as we have seen in the Incarnation. To use anthropomorphic imagery, it is akin to God coming on site to where people are in order to save them from their troubles. This, of course, says much about the here and now, even with its disordered human affairs replete with sinfulness, ingratitude, and betrayal. It is the chosen terrain for the divine-human encounter and its resultant re-creative gift.

The ramifications for social ethics of this incarnational dimension to human righteousness should be fairly obvious by now. First, human righteousness, far from fleeing from the world, positions itself in the heart of the world.[11] The justified can do nothing less, given the example of the Incarnate Word itself situating the divine in the midst of the human, embracing it, and enveloping it with divine initiatives. The individual, redeemed in Christ, stands in solidarity not only with the rest of the human community, but with the whole of creation itself. The Kingdom of God is not merely an inner spiritual transformation of the heart. An exclusively spiritualized understanding does not capture the scope and the realism of Christ's sovereignty, which extends to the whole cosmos. As Verhey remarks, "The kingdom is something people enter, not something that enters people. It is a state of affairs, not a state of mind" (1984, 13).

Paul's ethical teachings point to an appreciation that the Gospel of Christ is not an otherworldly *kerygma,* but one that calls for saints to live in the here and now, complete with its failures and victories, its recriminations and joys, and its quarrels and mutual love. For example, take his treatment of slavery. He asks Philemon to accept Onesimus back under the changed interpersonal relationships heralded by the new dispensation as a brother "both in the flesh and in the Lord" (Phlm, v.16). Verhey observes that the juxtaposition of "flesh" with the Lord in this verse is significant: Paul "does not separate the unity, equality, peace 'in the Lord' from the 'real world' [referring to the flesh] of Philemon and Onesimus. *The unity is eschatological, but it is not docetic* [disembodied]; it must have some 'fleshly' expression" (1984, 115; emphasis added).

Paul himself exemplifies the incarnational nature of righteousness. Despite his keen sense of an imminent eschatology and the great urgency of preaching the Gospel, Paul does not simply walk away from the cares of the world to devote himself full time to otherworldly, spiritual matters. In fact, he works as an artisan to support himself and is critical of those who no longer see any need to work in anticipation of the *parousia* (2 Thes 3:6–12). Moreover, Paul's indifference between living in the world or dying to be with Christ (Phil 1:21–24) reflects an acute grasp of the essential nature of his mission in the temporal world. Käsemann describes the worldliness of Paul's justification.[12]

> Paul's doctrine of justification is about God's *basileia* [kingdom]. The apostle generally expresses it in anthropological terms because he is concerned that it should determine our everyday lives. God's *basileia* seizes territory wherever we are and will be entirely human. Otherwise it would be illusion. . . . Justification is the stigmatization of our worldly existence through the crucified Christ. Through us and in us he simultaneously reaches out towards the world to which we belong. (1971, 75)

Note the tension in simultaneously being in the world but not of the world. Observe too the role of human agency as Christ reaches out to the rest of the world through the justified, a reminder of the great moment attached to being ambassadors of Christ (2 Cor 5:20). We examine this phenomenon shortly in the next section, but suffice it to say for now that the instrumental quality to human righteousness flows from its incarnational character in being embedded in the earthly and in the not-so-perfect.

Finally, the best illustration of the worldliness of incarnational righteousness is Jesus Christ himself. The nature of authentic poverty is revealed by Jesus who empties himself for the unworthy and the undeserving despite his own divinity (Phil 2:5–8). Genuine poverty is an attentive, never-ending, decisive, and complete obedience to God's will at every moment and in the very circumstances we find ourselves.

> He . . . emptied himself out of obedience to the Father, minute by minute, in response to the circumstances of his life. When he would preach, he was called to heal (Mark 1:37–45); when he would rest, he was called to teach (Mark 6:31–34); when he was to teach, he was called to feed (Mark 6:35–44); when he would live, he was called to die (Mark 14:33–36).
>
> Since the faith of Jesus consisted in the obedient hearing of his Father's Word, and since that Word came to him, not alone in prayer or in the study of Scriptures, but in his encounters with other men and women, the obedience of his faith was *articulated* by his response to their needs. He placed himself as an attentive servant to others, precisely because this was . . . the only way he could, as a human being, discover what being a servant of God meant in concrete terms. (Johnson 1981, 77–78; emphasis original)

To encounter and to live up to God's will is to situate oneself not in an abstract or in an intellectually disembodied world but in the concrete setting of human affairs, just like Christ in his Incarnation.

Like Jesus, we encounter God's will through manifold venues and agents and in the particular and often untidy circumstances of human affairs. And this includes economic life, just as when Jesus preaches in itinerant poverty with not even a place to call his own (Mt 8:19–21; Lk 9:57–59), when he humbly accepts solicitous material support from others (Mt 27:15; Mk 15:41), when he addresses the physical and economic needs of others (Mt 14:13–21; Mk 6:32–44; Lk 9:10–17; Jn 6:5–13), and when he deals with mundane matters such as taxes (Mt 17:24–27). Jesus's obediential hearing of God's word accentuates for us the material conditions of the Kingdom of God that also serve as the terrain for our response to God's initiatives; it is in such a setting that we discover and live out God's will in our interactions with others. Thus, even as Jesus is not concerned with building an earthly kingdom (Jn 18:35–37), he is nevertheless attentive and sensitive to meeting and alleviating the physical needs and sufferings of people. Jesus exhibits the same interests that Lohfink (1987, 5–15; 1986) ascribes to YHWH: a lively concern for the here and now, and a desire to provide everyone with plenitude. In other words, economic life is an avenue for divine-human interaction. It is not peripheral to discipleship but is, in fact, constitutive of it just as we found in YHWH's in-breaking in Israel's history.

Incarnational righteousness is an ongoing participation.

In reviewing key passages on righteousness in Paul,[13] Byrne characterizes the "righteousness of God revealed in the Christ-event as an on-going righteousness in some sense communicable to human beings" (1981, 574). Temporality is an unavoidable constraint of human nature where neither the past nor the future are accessible. The past cannot be relived, and the future cannot be anticipated in the present. Thus, salvation history itself is subject to the passage and constraint of time. Nevertheless, human participation in God's righteousness through Christ is ongoing because, as we will see shortly, the life of faith has to be sustained for its every moment in the same way that the creative act of God is ongoing since human existence has to be sustained constantly if we are not to revert back to nonexistence. Thus, the present moment is laden with both invitation and possibilities of yet unknown, un-attained heights in human participation in God's righteousness. For this reason, the assent of faith is not a one-time event but continues apace with every single moment. *There is neither pause nor rest away from God.* This makes the gift (the indicative) that much more special, but at the same time, it also makes the accompanying demand (the imperative) that much more daunting.

Righteousness is not a static gift but one that produces abundant fruit. Hence, we come to a second set of characteristics for human righteousness—it is instrumental, indeed a leaven for the world in which it intentionally positions itself.

Instrumental righteousness

Are we led to works-righteousness as we strive to live up to these prescriptions for the ideal economic life? As already mentioned, it is beyond the scope of this study to rehearse the theological debate on faith versus good works. Instead, I take the inseparability of faith and good works as a given and use it as a starting point to examine how ethics flows from justification. This type of ethics can be aptly called instrumental righteousness and has the added benefit of preventing us from falling into either extremes of the debate. On the one hand, it precludes any misconceptions that moral behavior is self-sufficient and completely autonomous from grace. On the other hand, it also acknowledges the distinctive human contribution to attaining the ideal economic life. From chapter 3, we have seen that to be a secondary cause is to contribute something real and distinctive to the final effect produced by both the principal and the secondary causes. This singular human input is faith.

Acceptance of the gift of faith is the particular human contribution to instrumental righteousness. Commentators are in agreement on the inseparability of faith from righteousness; the former is the doorway to the latter. The defining scriptural text to this, of course, is Romans 4:1–14.

Faith is inextricably linked to righteousness and defines the latter's qualities. Thus, in what follows, I examine the nature and dynamics of faith and trace their effects on human participation in God's righteousness. In particular, I argue that faith, and consequently instrumental righteousness, (1) is genuinely free, even as it is enveloped in grace; (2) is empowered and actualized by the Holy Spirit; (3) is necessarily realized in action and ethical behavior; and (4) bears abundant fruit in the here and now. Divine grace vivifies these four qualities, illustrative of the divine-human tandem when speaking of instrumental or secondary causality.

Grace-enveloped freedom

Instrumental righteousness is encompassed by grace, but is nonetheless free. We can glean two insights that play off each other from Bottorff's (1973) examination of Pauline justification and ethics: an all-pervading presence of God and freedom in human action. In the first place, Bottorff suggests a two-tiered foundation to Pauline ethics. The righteousness of God as revealed in Christ and at work through the Holy Spirit is the only, and the proper, starting point. Sin is no longer inevitable for humans; its enslaving grasp has been sundered by Christ. Moreover, the dynamic power of God's righteousness is made manifest in the human heart. The second-level tier is a human faith, which has two sides to it. On the one hand is the human openness and assent to divine initiatives in the here and now; its flip side is God's faithfulness in sustaining human faith. After all, faith is a gift extrinsic to humans; it must be constantly maintained by grace.

It is true that the assent of faith unleashes the power of God's righteousness and its fruitfulness in ethical behavior. Nevertheless, it is grace, not the human assent, that brings forth fruit; human assent merely provides the occasion for such a flowering. It is grace that gives rise to faith and sustains it. Thus, humans cannot claim credit for the fruits of their openness to divine initiatives because God's grace is all-encompassing, not only as it provides the possibility for such human faith to begin with, but also as it preserves it in its operations.

Despite the ubiquity of grace in human faith, one must still acknowledge the reality of human freedom to avoid determinism. Humans are not merely marionettes in the face of the all-pervasive and decisive nature of grace because they have a genuine role to play (Bottorff 1973, 426). Thus, people fall into sin even after baptism; likewise, they can choose to repent for such sinfulness and thereafter lead exemplary lives. Moral conduct does not earn justification but is rather the evidence of justification by faith. There is an authentic human input to rectitude in moral conduct even as we acknowledge that its animating source comes from grace. The authenticity and the place of human freedom is better described when cast in the language of a divine invitation waiting for a human response: "[M]an must do what God makes possible. . . . Christ's obedience figures prominently into this scheme [referring to justification], but *man may never rely entirely on Christ's obedience because man is called to obedience, too*" (Bottorff 1973, 422; emphasis added).

Christ won justification for humans through his obediential hearing of God's word and his unswerving fidelity to discharging the will of God. If Jesus, the Incarnate Righteousness, is expected to exercise a genuine act of the will to be obedient, how much more for participated righteousness? Authentic human freedom is a precondition to a live, active, and responsive faith. And there is great moment and instrumentality in rendering such an obedience, for in so doing, humans participate in no less than God's saving and providential activity.

> God's power reaches out for the world, and the world's salvation lies in its being recaptured for the sovereignty of God. For this very reason it is the gift of God and also the salvation of the individual human being when we become obedient to the divine righteousness. (Käsemann 1969, 182)

Spirit-empowered freedom

The potency of instrumental righteousness comes from Christ as mediated through the Holy Spirit. The self-diffusive nature of goodness that we encountered earlier in Aquinas's metaphysics (part I) can likewise be found in Pauline theology.

> Unactualised power is no power at all. Thus righteousness as the power of God is made possible for us through Christ . . . and becomes operative in us through the action of the Holy Spirit. (Bottorff 1973, 426)

It is not sufficient for Christ to have won over death and liberated us from the inevitability of sin; the very power itself that secures such victory is being proffered so that, now that the hold of sin has been broken, humans may indeed walk away from sin. The freedom that is offered humans is not merely a *freedom from* bondage; this is only the prelude to even greater gifts that follow. Of even greater moment is the new horizon it opens, for freedom is first and foremost a *freedom for* something.[14] And thus, we have Christ's gift of the Holy Spirit that comes with human participation in God's righteousness.

The dynamism of God's righteousness is such that even its vitality is imparted; its power cannot be contained as it seeks to give of itself. More than just liberating humans from the clutches of sin, the righteousness of God made manifest in Christ confers its puissance to produce abundant harvest. Such power is realized in the here and now in human lives through the action of the Holy Spirit. It is the Holy Sprit that empowers humans to actualize what Christ has made possible.

It is the Holy Spirit that brings to the human person the potent nature of God's righteousness. And it is this dynamic that in turn gives rise to ethical behavior. Righteousness in Christ is action-bound and inevitably fruit-bearing because of the self-diffusive nature of God's love. Human freedom means that assent to the aforesaid self-diffusive divine initiatives is a genuine decision. However, there is an essential time dimension to such faith. Unless it is in act, it is merely potential. Faith is actualized *only as it is realized in action at the present moment* (Bottorff 1973, 426–27). Note the two constitutive elements: (1) a realization in action (2) in the here and now. We discuss these necessary features in the next two sections.

Instrumentality as ambassadors of Christ

The striving implanted

The tension between the "here and the not yet" is a perennial feature of Christian life. This incompleteness within the trajectory of salvation history parallels and produces a corresponding gap in human participation in God's righteousness. Even as we have become the righteousness of God through Christ (2 Cor 5:21), the fullness of salvation and all its attendant gifts are yet to come in the eschaton. Thus, human participation in God's righteousness in the present eschatology is characterized by a striving—constant, profound, and deep—that cannot but leave one unrested and unsettled. This is the animating dynamic that pushes moral life to reach for ever greater heights. Paul (Phil 3:12–14, 3:20) is an excellent illustration of such a restless hunger ever yearning for completion and perfection (Käsemann 1969, 170), as is Augustine.[15]

The means provided

Such striving does not exist in a vacuum. Far from it. This yearning is precipitated, indeed implanted, by the gift of God's righteousness to begin with. And the wondrous thing about it is that the gift also brings with it the means, the enlivening spirit, and the enduring vigor to keep up the pursuit. Righteousness is an attribute—a power—that is proper to God alone. It has been communicated to human beings through Christ, a power turned into a gift that brings with it the Giver itself. Righteousness as an innate divine attribute has the character of a power. Power is dynamic by nature and is unrelenting in actualizing itself. In so doing, the Giver lends its power and dynamism to the gift's recipient: "God's power becomes God's gift when it takes possession of us and, so to speak, enters into us, so that it can be said in Gal. 2.20, 'It is no longer I who live, but Christ who lives in me'" (Käsemann 1969, 173; see also 174–75). Thus, even in striving, it is grace that takes the initiative, provides the sustained impetus, and brings human participation in the divine to its fullness.

The manner of pursuit

It turns out that the gift itself also points out the way toward filling such hunger. It is service to others, one's self-donation, that holds the key to satisfying such striving in the period before we reach the haven of the future eschatology. This requisite service dovetails the social character of human righteousness—we receive it as a gift as a community, we strive together as a community, and we reach for fullness together as a community. This service for others is not for our own account, or for others'. It is rather a service pursued on behalf of the Giver of the gift: "[T]he total realization of a lordship over us occurs when such lordship acquires power over our hearts and enlists us in its service" (Käsemann 1969, 175).

Note how we have reached a full circle: The Giver gives the gift that provides us a foretaste of what is yet to come in its fullness. Suspended between the present and the future eschatology, such incompleteness implants an unsettled and unrested striving within us. Yet, it is the gift and the Giver too that not only points to us the way to assuage that hunger (through service), but also provides the power to sustain us in the pursuit of such completion. Grace truly envelops human participation in God's righteousness.

One implication must be highlighted: having been enlisted in the service of the Giver to minister to others, we have truly become not only an incarnational righteousness of God but also an instrumental righteousness of God. In serving others, we become channels through which the Giver grants the gift to others who have yet to receive it. Thus, Paul speaks aptly when he concludes that we who have been justified are "ambassadors for Christ, as though God were making an appeal through us" (2 Cor 5:20) to those who have yet to accept God's gift of righteousness.

To be enlisted in the service of communicating divine righteousness to others, prompted no less at God's behest, is itself another gift added to the earlier benefaction. Incarnational and instrumental righteousness turn out to be a series of gifts building on each other. Human participation in God's righteousness is not merely superficial but has a real function, and that in itself is also a gift.

Finally, if faith and good works are inseparably bound, then justification's transformation of the human person must necessarily lead to moral conduct. And this is not simply the case of an imputed righteousness; it is an effected righteousness in which people are not merely *declared* righteous but are actually *made* righteous. The righteousness received from God requires a lived response. And as we move toward the fullness of the future eschaton in the course of our response, it is appropriate to remember that righteousness is not an object that is kept and "possessed"; rather, it is a state of life that one grows into and then shares with others.

[R]ighteousness . . . [is] both demand and gift. . . . Talk of "imparted righteousness" is therefore imprecise. *Nothing is imparted, but something is lived in.* (Ziesler 1972, 170–71; emphasis added)

Righteousness is not righteousness at all unless it produces harvest, abundant harvest, and it produces fruit only as it unleashes the power that it has received as gift.

Since moral conduct is the flip side of justification, it is not surprising that there is a good fit between *kerygma* and *paranesis* in Pauline literature. Note, for example, the juxtaposition of the ethical teachings of Romans 12–15 with the dense theological discourse on the life-changing righteousness of God for the rest of the letter. Culpepper (1976) argues that this is intentional on the part of Paul, who wants to illustrate concretely for his audience the proper response of gratitude and commitment to God's initiatives on their behalf. If Culpepper's thesis is accurate, it would further validate Furnish's (1968) point that the indicative and the imperative are inseparable in Pauline literature. Paul's ethics is an integral part of his theology; his ethics brings completion to his theology.

The present moment and instrumental righteousness

There is a peculiar quality to faith in that it can exist only in the present moment. Faith from the past cannot be stored for use in the present or in the future. It has to be constantly actualized and renewed. Every moment can be said to be compartmentalized from each other since every present moment is unyielding in its demand for nothing less than a faith that is *in act*. To better articulate this particular feature of faith, we again use Aquinas's distinction between necessary and contingent existence as an analog. God provides creatures with existence and has to sustain them in such continued actuality for every moment of time lest they revert back into nonexistence. After all, only God has necessary existence and all others merely participate in it. The requirements of faith can be described in similar fashion: faith reverts back to nothingness unless it is sustained and renewed for every moment of its existence. Hence, it has to be constantly *in act*.

Another way of making the same point is to differentiate faith as an action from faith as an object and to note that they are mutually exclusive. Bottorff observes that unless faith is in action, it becomes a mere object, a past "event that may be scrutinised, investigated, and in a certain sense possessed" (1973, 427). And to possess it as an object is to open the doors to turning it into an object of a "boast" or claim against God. But such is not faith at all. Only when faith is *in act* is it properly in the subject rather than a remote object. And it has to stay in the subject and cannot be removed from the person to become a separate object. Since it has to be constantly *in act*, the key consideration is whether faith is alive to God in the here and now, and not whether it was alive to God in the past or will be alive to God in the future. Indeed, there is gravity in the present moment.

We should cross-reference the importance of the present moment with two earlier points. First, that faith must always be *in act*—always in the subject rather than a separate object—fits the eschatological terrain well. God's reign is yet to be revealed in its fullness in the future. Nevertheless, we live in a new dispensation characterized by a nearly realized eschatology in which we are already afforded a foretaste of what is to come—the future reign of God breaking into and at work in the present. Hence, one can view the present moment, indeed every moment, as the setting in which faith and God's immanent reign intersect to produce abundant harvest in the present, including right conduct in economic life. Human response to letting faith bloom dovetails the eschatological feature of God's initiatives: the gift of the future, breaking into the present, is accepted, actualized, and manifested in human action in the here and now.

Second, the need for faith to be constantly alive to God (*in act*) fits the earlier point made on the two inseparable sides of faith: personal assent and God's unfailing fidelity to humans. These are two sides of the same coin because human faith is a gift, and it has to be constantly sustained by God. This is consistent with another earlier observation regarding the ongoing communication of God's righteousness through the Christ-event.

PAULINE ECONOMIC ETHICS

In summary, human participation in God's righteousness is incarnational and instrumental. These dimensions can be differentiated by noting that incarnational righteousness reveals what Christ has won for us, while instrumental righteousness manifests the Holy Spirit, actualizing what Christ has made possible.

Far from being works-righteousness, moral conduct flows as an attendant effect of justification. Moral life (including economic agency) is an avenue for participation in God's righteousness. The warrants for this claim lie in the inseparability of the indicative and the imperative (Furnish 1968), of justification and ethics (Bottorff 1973), of the objective and the subjective (Blackman 1962), of the gift and demand (Ziesler 1972), of the Giver and the gift (Käsemann 1969, 1971), and of the juridic and the moral. Thus, a well-founded understanding of human righteousness must begin with the thoroughly Christological nature of both its juridic and ethical dimensions. It is not a tension of faith *versus* good works, but a seamless dynamic of faith *and* good works, because both have Jesus Christ as their source, impetus, and object.

The value of Paul's letters for this study's thesis does not lie in the content of his teachings on economic life. Rather, the key contribution is the illustration of how his economic ethics is grounded in his theology. As I argued at the start of the chapter, Pauline literature is the ideal material to use for establishing how economic agency, and moral conduct for that matter, is a participation in God's righteousness. This stems from its comprehensive sweep that encompasses both a theological understanding of justification and its concrete application to real-life problems. Thus, it is best to end this chapter on participated righteousness with a thumbnail sketch of how Pauline economic ethics flows from Pauline justification.

We can glean at least three teachings on economic life from Paul's writings: the obligation to work even in the present eschatology, his artisan work-ethic of self-sufficiency, and sharing resources with the marginalized and the community. Paul harshly reproaches those who use the imminent *parousia* as a reason for no longer working. He emphasizes the obligation of honest work so as not to burden others and in order to provide assistance to those who are truly in need. His position clearly stands within the incarnational dimension of participated righteousness. Even as we await an imminent *parousia,* we are nonetheless still embodied beings with temporal needs and duties to fulfill, particularly to our dependents and the poor. These imperatives are in no way nullified by the new age inaugurated by Christ. Note further that despite his theologizing, Paul's admonition for honest work is indicative that this is not an "other-worldly ethics." Paul is keenly aware of the responsibilities of the present moment, pedestrian as they may be, as we can see from his constant reminders in his letters on the mutual duties in the household of faith.

The eschatology is not an excuse for foregoing our temporal liabilities; if anything at all, it gives us cause to be even more assiduous in discharging our obligations. We see this in Paul's life itself. He refuses to claim his rights as an apostle for material support from the churches because he does not want to encumber them or distract them from hearing and receiving the Word of God. This is an example of instrumental righteousness, of being an ambassador for Christ so that others, in seeing the example of our lives, may be attracted to the Gospel of Christ. In fact, in urging the Thessalonians to hard work, Paul proposes that in doing so, they also provide the additional service of edifying people (1 Thes 4:11–12). This concern for others—in not wanting to burden them, in providing them with instructive example, and in paving the way for their reception of the Gospel—reflects yet another dimension of Pauline ethical norms: a keen appreciation for the public ramifications of our conduct. This is consistent with the socially embedded nature of incarnational righteousness.

Finally, his constant counsel to provide for the poor of Jerusalem reflects many of the elements of incarnational and instrumental righteousness: a material expression of the faith that bears fruit in the earthly order, social concern, a worldly-wise engagement rather than withdrawal or isolation from the larger world, an acute appetite for doing good on behalf of God as Christ's ambassadors, and an appreciation for the exigencies of the current order even as we await an imminent *parousia*.

Paul's economic ethics bears the marks of a participated righteousness that is rooted in the temporal order even as it is already looking forward to the transcendent. In being grounded in terrestrial realism, his ethical teachings reflect the need for faith to be always *in act* in an incarnate world. This brief sketch is a quick preview of the next chapter's fuller treatment of how economic agency serves as a venue for participation in God's righteousness in the new dispensation.

CHAPTER 7

ECONOMIC AGENCY IN KINGDOM DISCIPLESHIP

Economic agency is an important and necessary, though by no means exclusive, venue for partaking of God's righteousness. Using Pauline theology, the preceding chapter examined moral life as a conferred righteousness exhibiting incarnational and instrumental qualities. It now remains for us to fit in the nature and dynamics of economic life within the larger terrain of moral conduct as a participated righteousness in the Kingdom of God. Using Hays's (1996) framework of community-cross–new creation, this chapter argues that economic agency as a follower of Christ (kingdom discipleship) is about effecting God's envisioned material sufficiency in human affairs.

MATERIAL SUFFICIENCY

Material sufficiency, if not abundance, is a gift intended by God as part of divine Creation-Providence. Destitution and want are not what God intended in creating us; the gift of God lies in plenitude and fullness, not only in the future eschatology, but also for the present.

A key scriptural text to establishing the claim of material sufficiency as constitutive of God's creative act is the passage from Q[1] that explains the utter futility of anxiety over our material provisioning inasmuch as God unfailingly sustains all creatures. Thus, Matthew 6:25–34 and Luke 12:22–31 observe that the birds of the air, the lilies of the fields, and all of creation are resplendent and supplied well in their needs. In like manner, there is no cause for people to worry over what they are to eat or drink or wear because God loves humans even more and would surely provide just as well for them. Instead, we are invited to occupy ourselves simply with pursuing the Kingdom of God, and everything else will fall into place.

In his examination of biblical and patristic views of economic life, B. Gordon (1989, 43–58) succinctly describes the New Testament solution to the economic problem of scarcity as founded on "seeking the Kingdom." He considers Matthew 6:31–33 to be pivotal[2] and builds his entire exposition around it. Scarcity will be solved as a by-product of the building of the Kingdom, something that is "added incidentally" as we devote ourselves to pursuing God's reign.[3] Want and destitution would not even arise if only people were to trust God's righteousness to the point of living righteous lives themselves (Haughey 1977, 279–80). Severe shortages of material provisions are man-made.

Three points must be observed from this vivid image regarding divine providence. First, material sufficiency, perhaps even abundance, is intrinsic to the gift of creation. Thus, the birds of the air and the lilies of the fields have enough for their needs. It is in the nature of things that the earth has enough for all creatures that it bears. Of course, Genesis 1:26–31 is even more foundational and explicit regarding God's intention of letting the earth fill human needs. Second, the certainty that the earth will provide what people need is founded on God's unfailing providential care. God's concern for the birds and the lilies is evident; how much more for human beings who have been created in the divine image and likeness, the only creatures to have been created for their own sake. Hence, humans could freely throw themselves with abandon to God's providence. Third, sufficiency in human material provisioning is merely conditional. It is provisional on human conduct, particularly on their conformity to the demands of the Kingdom of God. After all, only human beings are imbued with a genuine freedom that can act contrary to nature and to God's plans. Thus, chronic want and poverty are reflective of the misuse of reason and freedom. Far from being the norm in human affairs, these conditions are, in fact, a gross aberration, contrary to Malthus's ([1798] 1960) claims.

Those who respond to God's invitation of kingdom discipleship bring in their wake flowing abundance. They also receive the extra gift of being instruments and participating in divine providence. And even for those who choose not to seek the Kingdom but adopt an economic life of dissolute and wanton waste, greed, and idolatry, God nonetheless still sustains them through the efforts of the faithful disciples. More than that, God corrects the injustices they inflict and the damage they wreak on the community through the plenitude that flows from the efforts of the selfless disciples of the Kingdom. Economic agency, and for that matter moral conduct, furnishes an excellent venue by which God provides for us (including the unworthy and the undeserving) through each other. This is also true in the manner by which God corrects inequities and heals human brokenness through our efforts. Given divine omnipotence, God could have easily worked all these without human mediation and its attendant flaws. Yet God chooses to do otherwise and in the process bestows still another gift—the opportunity to participate genuinely in divine righteousness. Procuring this envisioned material sufficiency in the Kingdom, however, follows a dynamic of community, cross, and new creation to which we now turn our attention.

ECONOMIC AGENCY IN PARTICIPATED RIGHTEOUSNESS

Hays (1996, 193–205) suggests three focal images in studying and synthesizing New Testament ethics: community, cross, and new creation.

> Community—because the "church is the countercultural community of discipleship, and this community is the primary addressee of God's imperatives" (196).
> Cross—because "Jesus' death on a cross is the paradigm for faithfulness to God in this world" (197).
> New creation—because the "church embodies the power of the resurrection in the midst of a not-yet-redeemed world" (198).

I adopt Hays's tripartite model to examine the nature of economic agency as it unfolds in moral life.

Hays's "community-cross–new creation" lends itself well as an overarching framework for theological economic ethics. After all, economic life is intrinsically relational by nature (community), sacrificial in its demands (cross), and potentially life-enhancing in its impact (new creation). Thus, one could arguably claim that of the different spheres of society, economic life is a quintessential realm in which human participation in God's righteousness is most apparent, most tested, and perhaps most effective.

Economic agency is a constitutive dimension of the human response to divine initiatives. After all, there is an attendant tangible particularity to the overarching framework of community-cross–new creation in New Testament ethics. "Community-cross–new creation" is not merely an abstraction to facilitate moral discourse. Just like Hays (1996, 196), I use these terms to refer to "the concrete manifestation of the people of God." "Community" pertains to people struggling to live together and mutually support each other with all the realism of their joys, bonds, tensions, and difficulties; "cross" encompasses the real suffering and burdens that people bear; "new creation" is the liberating state that follows in the wake of their conversion (*metanoia*). "Community-cross–new creation" is a narrative of the here and now.

This dovetails our earlier finding on the worldly-wise engagement of incarnational righteousness. We are called to be righteous not at some future point in time or in the New Jerusalem, where the lamb and the lion will graze together and where there will be no more strife and no more tears (Is 65:17–25; Rv 21:1–4). Incarnational righteousness is for the here and now—complete with the blemishes and failures of our sinfulness; it is not otherworldly. Thus, it is not an ethics that seeks to withdraw or isolate itself from a dualistic world of light and darkness. Rather, it is an "ethics of response and engagement": response to God through a vigorous engagement with the world, not to be of the world but to be its leaven. It is an ethics that situates itself in the heart of a redeemed world, an ethics that does its share in bringing such a world to the fullness of God's reign. This is in sharp contrast with the admonition in the book of Revelation for a complete, decisive break from the larger culture deemed to be evil (Perkins 1994, 58–59).

Economic life is a necessary part of this avowedly worldly-wise ethics. Within the here-and-not-yet terrain, people of the new covenant will have to live their newly found and transformed lives still embodied and subject to its nature. Lofty as the present eschatology is given its end, it nevertheless still has a necessary material dimension. Humans, after all, still have to work and provide for their basic needs of food, clothing, and shelter. They still have to work with each other and share the finite fruits of the earth. People still fall through the cracks, are marginalized, and are unable to provide for themselves; they too still have to be cared for with dignity and respect. Thus,

B. Gordon (1989, 44, 50) points to the practical ramifications of Jesus healing the sick; he not only frees them from their illnesses but also liberates them from economic dependence on others in their helplessness. Jesus is not engaged in an exclusively spiritualized mission of preaching and teaching; he is also active in alleviating the dire temporal suffering of people.

Even as he is so keenly aware of an imminent *parousia*, even as he is so preoccupied with the urgency of preaching the Gospel, and even as he spends himself to bring people to Christ, Paul nevertheless still labors to support himself. Even as he preaches the abstract finer points of a theology of justification in Christ, Paul nonetheless also urges people to live out the implications of such faith in Jesus Christ in the good works of sharing their abundance with those who had fallen on hard times. Paul appreciates the incarnational nature of a believer's life in Christ and how it produces fruit in the present. The inseparability of the indicative and the imperative and of theology and ethics in Paul points to the transcendent intersecting the temporal. Indeed, the ethics of the here and now, the "ethics of response and engagement"[4] unfolds on a temporal moral terrain, a terrestrial plane with a constitutive material, economic dimension. Hence, economic agency is an unavoidable part of the human response.

Since economic life is a venue through which humans partake of God's righteousness, the depth of such participation is partly a function of the moral quality of economic agency in the community. There are material conditions to discipleship not only because people are embodied, but more important, because the Kingdom of God is being built precisely through the worldly-wise ethics of the temporal. Economic agency has its role to play in contributing to people's holiness.

Community

The path to full actualization of what has now been made possible by Christ is through the Holy Spirit and *with each other*. Economic life matters in discipleship because there is a necessary social dimension to the Kingdom of God, and economic agency is a major part of that social nature. Moreover, economic labor is unavoidably joint work with and for others. Relationships and economic interactions mutually shape each other. Since humans are distinctive for their intellectual faculties and since they are social by nature, relationships are key and integral to what makes a person human.

Economic life and righteousness are closely linked to each other because both are about relationships. One dimension of righteousness, in both its juridic and ethical senses, is that of due order in interpersonal affairs (Achtemeier 1962b). On the other hand, economic life is fundamentally relational: wealth can confer autonomy by removing the need to depend on others; a finite earth requires sharing; production processes necessitate collaboration; complex socioeconomic structures reflect a tight network of interdependence; economic processes spawn externalities with wide ripple effects. More than just merely reflecting established practices in market operations, however, such economic exchanges further reinforce and lock in the nature of such relationships. Economic interaction has the power to ennoble or demean, to build up or destroy the common life. In fact, relationships are expressed, encoded, and assigned value by the manner in which we conduct exchange (Perkins 1994, 57).[5] This being the case, economic agency can be wielded as an instrument for promoting and establishing right order in human affairs. Thus, scriptural economic ethics is about correcting debased relationships by articulating the ideal and then tailoring societal structures and practices accordingly. For example, at the root of the Hebrew and New Testament economic norms is the call to treat each other with mutual respect as equals, as brothers and sisters, children of the same God. This invitation finds concrete expression in the summons to unreciprocated giving, almsgiving, land restoration, debt remission, slave release, and in the extensive positive obligations of the Gospels.

As observed earlier, incarnational righteousness is socially embedded. Hays notes that the community is the "primary addressee of God's imperatives" (1996, 196). Barth (1968) even goes so far as to claim that individuals are justified only as they are in community. Moreover, there is a constitutive social dimension to human nature. The human person can survive and thrive only with others. Furthermore, economic life is relational and requires collaborative work within the community. Note how the social dimensions overlap: participated righteousness is social to begin with, as is the participant (the human person), as is the venue for such participation (economic life). Whichever way we turn, interpersonal relations are integral to human flourishing. How people treat each other is an important determinant of moral integrity, both for the individual and the community.

Two implications relevant for our study should be highlighted. First, a social dimension means that people are bound to each other by an intricate web of mutual duties. In contrast to contractual social theory (Barker 1980), these are ties we simply cannot walk away from since they stem from the social character of both nature and grace (salvation). And if we take seriously the social dimension of human nature and accept the obligations that bind us to each other, then economic rights have a legitimate place in community. This means having to relinquish our own claims over the finite goods of the earth for the sake of others. It also involves having to sacrifice our own standard of living and working longer hours to meet the unfilled basic needs of others. To accept the embedded social nature of incarnational righteousness is to acknowledge the extensive claims people have on us and to accept whole-heartedly the broad scope and weight of our charge. These are no trivial matters.[6] Thus, we have a formidable array of positive economic obligations in Sacred Scripture.

A second implication has to do with taking responsibility for our collective morality. There is a joint duty to forge an upright corporate person. After all, if personal faith necessarily leads to personal ethical behavior, the Corporate Christ (of which we become members by virtue of our justification) that Ziesler (1972) speaks of must also necessarily express itself in upright corporate moral conduct. It is not only the individual members of the Body of Christ that must bear witness to the transformative power of Christ; the entire Body itself has to provide such witness. For economic ethics, this brings us into the realm of social justice and its concomitant individual and collective responsibility to correct sinful structures of society. This fits in well with the Synod of Bishops' (1971, #6) claim that work on behalf of justice is constitutive of the preaching of the Gospel. It is beyond the scope of this study to weigh the validity of this claim, as the literature on the ensuing debate it provoked is extensive. Suffice it to say that to accept the social nature of incarnational righteousness is to be actively engaged in shaping the corporate behavior of the community. This too is no trivial matter.

Taking responsibility for others and the community finds concrete expression in living up to the economic standards of the preceding chapters: a sharing that is motivated neither by self-interest, by a desire for domination, nor by self-advancement, but by a genuine love for others, especially those who are unable to fend for themselves. New Testament teachings on economic life that speak persistently of duties and obligations parallel the socially embedded nature of human participation in God's righteousness.

Cross

Upright economic agency supports faith's need to be constantly *in act*. The nature of economic life correlates well with faith's characteristic need to be always *in act*. Incarnational righteousness requires faith to be an ongoing lived assent; instrumental righteousness situates faith neither in the past nor in the future, but in the present. Both features of participated righteousness point to a never-ceasing response to divine initiatives that includes producing abundant harvest along the lines of James's understanding that faith and good works are inseparable. This divine-human engagement occurs across all spheres of life, including the economic realm. After all, as we have already seen, participated righteousness unfolds not in isolation from the world but in and with the world. Economic agency can be of help to a blossoming faith, but it can also be a hindrance.

Economic life presents an extremely difficult, if not hazardous, terrain in which faith is supposed to produce abundant harvest; in fact, it can even ruin the human response in faith. Four points are particularly important for this discussion. In the first place, economic goods can easily be used for inappropriate goals. As consumption goods, they are so satisfying in the pleasure they can provide; as positional (Hirsch 1976) or dominant (Walzer 1983) goods, they are alluring in the honors, prestige, and power they can bestow. Thus, economic life can be used for improper ends, produce idols, and retard the development of faith. To resist all these enticements in order to live up to one's positive economic duties and obligations is to be virtuous indeed.

Second, as already suggested in the preceding section, the demands of community life can be enormous and costly to one's own personal welfare and preferences. The scope and strength of economic claims that others can make on us are as deep as they are extensive. The need to take responsibility for moral corporate conduct is likewise a real challenge because of the phenomenon of atomization in which individuals, on their own, are unable to change market processes and outcomes. Moreover, it is often difficult for the community to arrive at a consensus given legitimate differences in viewpoints arising from their diversity in life experiences. This makes the task of correcting sinful structures and processes of society that much more intractable, complex, and demanding. Friction is unavoidable, and much persistent personal effort and dedication are necessary.

Whether in direct interpersonal relations or in dealing with the structures of the community, the requirements of faith entail more than just living up to the demands of justice. After all, there are many gray areas in economic processes and outcomes in which the stipulations of justice are unclear. In such cases, one has to depend on the goodwill of people who would go beyond measured claims in treating one another. There are also the duties and obligations that come from love in which we voluntarily sacrifice our own comfort or preferences in order to make life a little easier for others. There is often need for selflessness so that others might fare better.

All this is best illustrated in Paul's advice with respect to resolving disagreements pertaining to religious dietary restrictions. He urges the strong to take upon themselves inconvenience and sacrifice so as not to scandalize the weak (1 Cor 8; Rom 15:1–9). Paul himself provides an excellent example of this when he describes the extent to which he goes out of his way to be all things to all men and women in order to accommodate the weaknesses of others—and all with an eye toward removing obstacles and making people more receptive to the Gospel he is preaching (1 Cor 9:19–23). The spirit of giving others a wide berth of forbearance, not out of justice but out of the goodness of one's heart, is the antithesis of the self-interested *homo oeconomicus* of the modern, competitive economy. Attaining proper order in economic life necessarily entails much self-abnegation and effort on the part of the individual eager to live up fully to the demands of faith.

Third, living up to the self-forgetfulness that faith bids in economic life is not something that can be readily fulfilled with merely a one-time act; the self-giving occurs over a prolonged period of time and has to be sustained by the nature of both faith and economic life. Faith, as we have seen, has to be constantly *in act*. There is never a pause or rest away from one's response to God's initiatives. On the other hand, common economic life is a continuous round of transactions, exchanges, and interaction with one another; each of these is fraught with questions of justice, accountability, and trust. Furthermore, given the relational character of production and the need to share the finite fruits of the earth, we can readily appreciate why economic life is fundamentally a moral phenomenon.

The interface of faith and economic agency is neither a one-time nor a sporadic event. There is no end to the self-sacrifice called for in economic life. This parallels faith's own need to be constantly *in act*. Consequently, economic life can be either a particularly effective aid to actualizing faith or a formidable obstacle to its growth. The self-giving required in economic agency is not a one-time act but a recurring sacrifice and matches well the ongoing nature of faith. The burden of such a sustained response (of a faith always *in act*) is mitigated in its demand by the reality that faith is a gift that is constantly sustained by God.

Fourth, not only is the aforementioned burden-bearing constant, but it may also get even heavier over time. There are externalities to economic freedom. We have already seen how participated righteousness is genuinely free despite its instrumental character. Such freedom can add to the burdens of actualizing faith because of the shadow of sin. Sinners may choose to freeride by not putting in their share of burden-bearing, thereby leaving others to compensate for their slack. Moreover, besides the harm wrought on its immediate victims, sin can also wreak extensive and long-lasting damage on social structures and processes. Thus, far from bearing their share of the cost of living together as a community, sinners even add further to the overall hardships that others must bear. Instead of assisting in correcting injustices and flaws within the community, sinners add even more to the ruins that have to be rectified.

The question is not whether there will be a cross to bear or not. The cross is an unavoidable part of economic life in community. Rather, the key questions are whether we are going to bear the cross at all or not, how well we are going to shoulder it, and how the burden-bearing is to be apportioned. The latter question is of primary importance and interest because God's solicitude for the poor invites us in our own turn to be concerned over whether the burden borne by the victims of economic injustices and exigencies (most likely the poor and defenseless) can be lightened, and their sufferings eased by the heroism of the faithful who step up to bear others' share of the cross in order to provide the weak with some relief.

In summary, the image of the cross is properly used for this study's thesis because economic conduct often asks for that which is difficult. The never-ceasing nature of faith and recurring human needs that necessarily make economic life an ongoing activity converge in their requirements and dynamics. Ongoing virtuous economic activity can nurture a faith that needs to be constantly *in act*. But sin can also turn economic life into an encumbrance that imposes heavy burdens on everyone else in the community desirous of living out their faith. However, there is a flip side to the genuine freedom that comes with participated righteousness. Humans can choose to cooperate with grace and use their freedom to ease the load and make life a little easier for others by shouldering more than their own share of the cross.

Freedom can choose to be wholehearted in burden-bearing (Gal 6:2), especially in the face of the zero-sum phenomenon[7] to rival consumption that is characteristic of so much of interpersonal economic interaction.

We have now reached the core claims of this study's thesis. Moral life, including economic agency, is fundamentally a participation (or lack thereof) in God's righteousness. Economic life can either be an avenue for or an obstacle to faith's being *in act*. However, in order to serve a faith that bears abundant harvest in the here and now, economic agency has to be self-sacrificing. At the root of theological economic ethics is an ethos of burden-bearing: foregoing one's own economic claims so that others may satisfy their own, accepting personal inconvenience to accommodate the weak, and sacrificing one's own welfare to improve others'. The finite goods of the earth that have to be shared and the fundamentally communal nature of economic activity invite unending, heroic self-donation. This is among economic agency's most significant contributions to human participation in God's righteousness. The sacrificial demands of economic agency add much to the profundity of such participated righteousness because of their direct association with the sufferings of Christ. Any act of burden-bearing finds its paradigm in Christ taking upon himself the curse of sin so that others, despite their unworthiness, may be liberated from death and live (Hays 1987, 286–88). So it is that our own acts of selflessness find their provenance and strength in Christ on the cross. After all, Jesus, the Righteous One, is also the righteous martyr who gives of himself. There is an intrinsic self-donative nature to God's righteousness in which we participate (Hays 1996, 118–20).

The call for self-sacrifice in economic agency is deep, extensive, and never-ending. This sets the stage for the heroic virtue of the cross and the profound participation in God's righteousness that follows in its wake. Material scarcity makes such effort all the more exacting but all the more meaningful.

New creation

Eschatology and ethics

I submit that there is a sacramental nature to human (free and intelligent) activity. Verhey (1984, 13–14) describes two opposing positions regarding ethics and eschatology. On the one hand, Schweitzer's (1910) "consistent eschatology" situates the Kingdom exclusively at some future point in time, with Jesus's teachings being merely an interim ethics. On the other hand, Dodd's (1936) "realized eschatology" highlights the present reality of the Kingdom to the exclusion of the futurity of God's gifts. Verhey is critical of both and takes the middle ground that there are both future and present dimensions to eschatological ethics.[8]

Of immediate relevance to this study is the consequence for moral conduct of an apocalyptism that sees the present age as evil and hurtling in its predetermined trajectory toward God's Kingdom. Such "determinism and pessimism about this age sometimes render[s] human action and exertion fruitless and inconsequential" (Verhey 1984, 14). Without a first installment of the future eschatology in the here and now, there would be no genuine role at all in the building of the Kingdom of God. This devalues God's gift of human freedom. Thus, true to his position on consistent versus realized eschatology, Verhey argues that while "human action does not establish the kingdom, it is nevertheless called for . . . as the eschatologically urgent response to the action of God which is at hand and already making its power felt" (15). Schrage (1988, 21–22) adopts a similar position and argues for a real human contribution toward the building of the Kingdom in the present. Commenting on the image of the seed growing by itself (Mk 4:26–29), he observes that even as the farmer may not be responsible for the growing and ripening of the seed, the farmer still has to be the one to do the sowing and the harvesting.

Verhey resolves the tension between the present-future eschatology by concluding that God's future act already bears fruit now through Jesus Christ (Verhey 1984, 14). God's future act produces abundant harvest in the present through righteous moral conduct on account of human participation in Christ.

Power, gift, and giver

There are manifold dynamic movements simultaneously at work in the new creation: the self-reinforcing cycle of creation-cross–new creation; the present eschatology advancing through the trajectory of salvation history on its way to the future eschatology; the faith constantly affirmed and lived *in act*; the actualization by the Holy Spirit of what Christ has made available; human instrumentality in an unfolding divine providence. Embedded in all this dynamism is God's threefold causality:[9]

1.   All these movements are possible to begin with as a result of the self-diffusive goodness of God. The wellspring for all these movements is God's righteousness as Formal Cause.
2.   It is God's saving and transformative act that provides all these movements with impetus and force. The dynamic that brings about the end results is God's righteousness as Efficient Cause.
3.   The new creation is, in fact, the restored due order that has been marred by sin. The terminus of all these movements is God's righteousness as Final Cause.

There is a sacramental nature to participated righteousness because of how it manifests and effects (as secondary cause) God's righteousness at work and unfolding in our midst. This is also evident in economic agency. We can find a theological foundation for this claim in Käsemann's (1969, 1971) exposition on the nature and dynamics of God's righteousness in Pauline literature. As we have already seen earlier, "righteousness of God" can refer either to righteousness as an innate quality of God (subjective genitive) or to the righteousness that God communicates and shares with human beings (objective genitive). Käsemann (1969, 174–75) characterizes righteousness (as divine attribute) to be a power not only because of its puissance, but also because of its dynamism. Power is not power unless it actualizes itself; it seeks its full realization.[10]

Käsemann declares that righteousness as a divine attribute is power; it becomes a gift when communicated to humans. However, by Käsemann's own conclusion, gift and Giver are inseparable; the power as a quality that is immanent in the Giver is also communicated with the gift of righteousness when it is bestowed on humans. A transcendent power becomes immanent (in humans) as the Giver's righteousness is imparted and effected through the gift that is communicated. In other words, for humans to participate in God's righteousness is for humans to participate also in the power of God's righteousness (to the extent possible and according to their mode of being and operation). Thus, not only is participated righteousness powerful, it is dynamic in its self-diffusiveness to others. The gift is also empowering.

The whole point of human activity, including moral life, is to bring its possibilities and potential to fruition.[11] It is to be perfect, as the Father is perfect (Mt 5:48), to be holy as the Lord is holy (Lv 19:2). Through their moral conduct, humans actualize the power of the righteousness they have received as gift from the Giver, and to that extent, they manifest and effect God's righteousness in the world as secondary causes. The power of moral excellence, indeed, the power of human freedom is nothing else but God at work in our midst. To repeat, whatever righteousness flows from human rectitude is nothing else but the incarnation of the righteousness of the gift's Giver, God as First Cause.

Social implications

Three implications for socioeconomic ethics come to mind in the face of the sacramental nature of human righteousness in the new creation: a conferred transformative power, an unflagging dynamism, and a real secondary causality.

First, we get to participate in the self-diffusiveness that is innate to the power of God's righteousness. Käsemann associates this self-diffusive quality of God with the dynamism of its power and succinctly describes its activity:

> The key to this whole Pauline viewpoint [referring to God's righteousness] is that power is always seeking to realize itself in action and must indeed do so. *It does this with the greatest effect when it no longer remains external to us but enters into us and . . . makes us its members.* (1969, 175; emphasis added)

Käsemann refers to our membership in the Body of Christ (1 Cor 10:16). What is striking here is the image of divinity seeking not only to give of itself, but to embrace the gift's recipient unto itself. It is a power that is not only self-diffusive but is also unitive.[12]

To participate in God's righteousness is to be just as self-donative and just as inclusive and welcoming.[13] We are restless and unrelenting in *letting the power of God actualize itself in others through us.* Barth's (1968) conclusion that we can find justification only through our association with others who have already been justified is radically communitarian in its understanding of salvation and could be moderated to include other venues of encountering God's gift of justification. What is important for us at this point, however, is his observation that justification can be "communicable" in the sense of letting the power of God in the justified draw those who have yet to accept their justification in Christ. Instrumental righteousness is endowed by Christ with freedom as the power to do good (Sacred Congregation for the Doctrine of the Faith 1986). To be a new creation is to be imbued with liberty as only the children of God can.

Given the radical profundity and omnipotence of its source, participated righteousness can also be consequential in its fecundity. Not only are humans transformed, but they also become transformative themselves. As new creatures, humans can be exceedingly fruitful because their righteousness proceeds from an Incarnate Righteousness (Jesus Christ) that is unremitting and self-giving in its work for the Kingdom of God. Having been changed as a new creation itself, participated righteousness can be transformative of the world around it to the extent that it does not impede the diffusive, dynamic, and self-donative nature of its vibrant Christological fount.

The self-diffusive and inclusive power that is embedded within participated righteousness ties in very well with the social character of human nature and with the heavily communal nature of economic life. Thus, economic life provides an ideal terrain for the consummation of such participated power.

Second, there is a necessary dynamism in the new creation that can turn economic agency into a venue for continued greater depth and growth for humans as new creatures participating in God's righteousness. Verhey (1984, 51) observes that it is the futurity of the *parousia* that prevents the tradition from merely becoming a code of conduct but instead leads to a living tradition of Christ's presence and power in our midst. Thus, the moral community is able to deal with new problems never before encountered, including those of the modern economy. Moreover, with the end as a reference point, incarnational and instrumental righteousness is imbued with an "eschatological wisdom" (Verhey 1984, 42–43) that gives humans a long-term perspective of what truly matters.

Being a new creation is not a static state but a dynamic, continued unfolding of God's righteousness in our lives. Thus, it is a condition in which people can have varying degrees of depth in their participation in God's righteousness. This ties in with faith's requirement that it be constantly *in act*. It has to grow and deepen; to fail to produce fruit is to decline in the vigor of faith and to be at risk of ultimately squandering the gift of participated righteousness.

There are numerous constitutive elements in this dynamism. Hays (1996) notes that his focal images of community-cross–new creation are not compartamentalized from each other but interpenetrate and feed off each other. We could recast his imagery as a self-reinforcing cycle in which living in *community* involves sharing the *cross* of Christ, which, when successfully borne, leads to an even more significant rebirth as a *new creation,* which in turn feeds back to an improved quality in community living to repeat the same cycle again. As the cycle continues to reach ever greater heights as a new creation, so does our participation in God's righteousness take on greater depth. Part of this process of self-actualization as a new creation is working away at our rough edges, and economic life is one avenue for such growth.

A similar cycle is operative when it comes to the New Testament teachings on economic life. As already mentioned, self-donation in economic agency is not a one-time event. It is ongoing. *Metanoia* requires constant renewal to enable people to reject the continued allurements to use wealth as the source of our security and self-respect (a form of idolatry) and as power and control over others. Liberated in our conversion, we can move in freedom to actively live up to our duties and obligations. Since this is not a one-time activity but an ongoing daily commitment, renewal, and sacrifice, we grow ever deeper in our participation in God's providence and governance through our economic activities as a new creation.

A third implication of a participated righteousness for economic ethics is the sacramental role of economic agency as a secondary cause.[14] God provides for us through each other; God redresses the injustices that afflict us through each other. God makes us whole anew through each other. This is a gift within a gift. The righteousness that is communicated by God to humans is the initial gift. Within this is a second gift—the gift of secondary causality, of how God shares with us divine providential work and governance. We see abundant testimony to this phenomenon in the New Testament.

Jesus delegates authority to the disciples to preach, teach, and heal—to do the work that Jesus has been doing. And after the ascension, the apostles continue to perform the works of Jesus, even miraculous healings, including raising the dead (Acts 3:1–10, 9:32–43). And, of course, we have the mandate that Jesus gives to the apostles to preach the Gospel to the ends of the earth (Mt 28:16–20). Jesus as God could have easily done all the work by himself, but chooses instead to share such work with humans.

We have already seen how material sufficiency is contingent on upright moral conduct. Those who let their faith bloom in its fullness produce abundant harvest not only for themselves but for others as well, even for those who are unbelievers and sinners. Thus, we have the image of the seeds that fall on good ground producing a yield that is more than enough to make up for those that had been lost and to leave even a surplus for the next planting season (Mt 13:3–23; Mk 4:2–20; Lk 8:4–15). It also reminds us of the image of the mustard seed—the smallest seed growing into such a size as to shelter many in its shade (Mt 13:31–32; Mk 4:30–32; Lk 13:18–19). These images remind us that moral economic behavior on the part of some will supply for whatever may be flawed or lacking in others, consistent with the Pauline call to make accommodations for the weak out of the goodness of one's heart. Thus, we have people going beyond the demands of justice to give more than is required of them in order to care for those who fall through the cracks of community (state) assistance; love picks up the slack where justice leaves off.

Paul is an excellent illustration of the use of economic life as a venue for human participation in God's righteousness. The lofty and abstract nature of his "indicative" is followed by the down-to-earth precepts of his "imperatives" on economic affairs even in the face of an imminent *parousia:* the affirmation of a work-ethic, the need to share but not to the point of driving oneself to penury, and his complete silence on the need for radical divestment in contrast to the Gospels. In other words, our justification in Christ must necessarily find change and expression even in the most seemingly ordinary facets of our lives.

As we have seen in the earlier discussion of incarnational righteousness, there is a necessary social component to the realism of the Kingdom of God, which, far from being merely a state of mind, is a state of affairs (Verhey 1984, 13). God effects the Kingdom of God through nature itself. However, Verhey (1984, 13) cautions against misinterpreting the Kingdom as a social order whose coming is entirely contingent on human activity because only God's decisive act brings about the Kingdom. Such an erroneous reading leads to works-righteousness and merely serves to highlight the value of using the notion and language of secondary and instrumental causality in which God is acknowledged to be the First Cause even while making room for human participation. Using the language of causality, there is no doubt as to whose decisive action ultimately matters.

Divine providence unfolds through human instrumentality and secondary causality; material sufficiency comes about through mutual burden-bearing and sharing. That God elicits human participation in the establishment of a Kingdom that could have been completely accomplished by divine governance alone is in itself a gift. God provisions us through each other; God restores due order in human affairs through us. And in so doing, God grants us the gift and privilege of participating in divine providence and governance. God effects divine plans through us.

Lohse (1991) sees New Testament ethics not as a list of rules but as a modeling of what it is to follow Christ. Hays (1996) describes the New Testament as metaphor-living. Moral conduct can be viewed as embodying the Gospel in human lives. As a community, we can effect what we signify as a new creation. The New Testament is more than just metaphor-making, it is metaphor-embodiment. As Hays notes, "[T]he community of Jesus' disciples is summoned to the task of showing forth the character of God in the world" (329).

A graced moral life is not merely proleptic in character—anticipating and already living that which is to come. It is also instrumental, indeed sacramental, in inaugurating that which is to come; it manifests and effects God's righteousness in our midst. These are profound, unmerited externalities to individual action: a magnified leverage or a multiplier effect in the ripple effects that individual actions can produce because of grace. There is greater weight and moment to every individual deed, and consequently, even greater responsibility. Hence, this accentuates the importance of how we live up to the imperative of the indicative.

Jesus is deeply immersed and vigorously engaged in providing comfort to people in their temporal needs, a concern that surely extends beyond physical debility to include material deprivation. And because of such a gentle and healing presence, there is hope. Such relief continues to be provided today, including the amelioration of the economic destitution of many. In response to the question of John the Baptist as to whether he is the expected Anointed One, Jesus responds by pointing to his work of preaching the good news to the poor, raising the dead, and healing the blind, the lame, lepers, and the deaf (Mt 11:2–6). Evidence of the in-breaking of the Kingdom in the present is also witnessed in the healings and the healers in our midst. We are healers as part of our discipleship, as a consequence of our transformative participated righteousness that is also empowering.

As a new creation in our participation in God's righteousness, we become "ambassadors for Christ, as though God were making an appeal through us" (2 Cor 5:20). Verhey remarks that a view that holds to an entirely futuristic eschatology necessarily leads to "an ethics of response to the coming act of God" (1984, 16). We can go further than this and provide an even more apt description that it is an "ethics of sacramental instrumentality" in which moral conduct takes on greater moment in the here and now as we become "co-workers" with God in building the Kingdom. The term *sacrament* is used in an analogical sense and in a restricted manner to refer to our actions effecting what they signify: *God's righteousness communicated to us and through us.* Haughey describes this phenomenon well:

> One of the powers the justified "enjoy" is the power to "do" justice in such wise that their actions are intrinsically linked to God's actions in redeeming and reordering the world. . . . That power is nothing less than God's own justice enabling us to perform actions which no human capacities would be competent to perform. Not only are the justified brought into a new order of justice, but they become instrumental in the co-creation of that new order. Those who have received the righteousness of God are capable of reflecting and making tangible the new order which that righteousness generates. . . . [T]he justice of God can be enfleshed in human actions and human structures and human institutions. (1977, 285)

There is a sacramental nature to our response to God's initiatives as we serve as instruments in the unfolding Kingdom. Put in another way, humans are "pressed into God's service" by particularizing and instantiating the Kingdom of God's irruption in the present eschatology. Thus, participated righteousness is also "sacramental" righteousness as a new creation.

In summary, actualizing human participation in God's righteousness takes place in a present eschatology that is unrelenting in its march to the fullness of the future eschatology. The terrain of kingdom discipleship can be described as a self-reinforcing cycle of Hays's (1996) community-cross–new creation animated by divine initiative and occasioned by human cooperation. A deeper examination of the nature of this human response reveals it to be a participation in divine righteousness: the fruit of God's justification and a subjective appropriation of God's completed, objective act of salvation.

In the new creation, a graced human response is an empowered, dynamic secondary cause. Humanity is both the subject and object of Hays's self-reinforcing cycle of community-cross–new creation. As object, human affairs are restored to the due order of divine plans through God's saving and transformative act. As subject, we are enlisted and then empowered by God to effect the cycle of community-cross–new creation as secondary causes according to the proper mode of our being and operation, that is, with the use of our reason and freedom. Moreover, the quality and extent to which we serve as secondary causes of God's providence is a function of the degree to which we allow Christ to unleash through us the power immanent in the new creation.

Economic life as a terrain for all this would not have been possible in a world of unconditional material abundance in which sustenance could be achieved without any care at all. Material superfluity would have vitiated the potent dynamism of community-cross–new creation in socioeconomic life. Paradoxically, the limitations brought on by scarcity become the very stepping-stones themselves to a new horizon of unparalleled transcendence.

PART III

Scarcity and Profundity in Participation

CHAPTER 8

NATURE AND IMPACT OF SCARCITY

This chapter argues that material scarcity occasions a more profound participation in God's goodness, holiness, righteousness, and providence. Johnson's (1981) theological reflection on the relationship between *being* and *having* provides a conceptual framework within which to establish the manifold links between human flourishing and possessions.

NATURE OF SCARCITY

Scarcity as an evil

To establish that scarcity properly falls within the ambit of a theodicy, it is first necessary to examine whether scarcity is an evil, and if so, in what sense it can be considered an evil. Scarcity is an evil to the degree that it deprives humans of necessary subsistence for survival, growth, and development. A dearth in essential provisions is a privation of the goodness that comes from material sustenance.

Is scarcity the result of original sin? It depends on the kind of scarcity in question. As proposed in appendix 1, scarcity can be subdivided into the following typology:

1. Antecedent, formal, or existential scarcity: the need to make allocative choices with their accompanying opportunity costs by virtue of human nature's finitude
2. Consequent scarcity: exiguity that follows in the wake of allocative choices, of which there are two possible outcomes:
   a. frictional scarcity, in which there are unfilled, albeit non-life-threatening, needs or wants[1]
   b. Malthusian scarcity, in which there is severe destitution and unmet essential needs

Existential (formal, antecedent) scarcity is not the outcome of original sin. Even in the Garden of Eden, Adam and Eve are subject to opportunity costs, that is, they have to make allocative choices in how to keep themselves occupied, what to eat, and what life goals to pursue. Moreover, they are expected to work, though without its toilsome features (B. Gordon 1989, 1–3). Unlike God, humans cannot be everything they want to be or be everywhere at the same time. They are limited by their human nature. Thus, even as the Garden of Eden has a superfluity of provisions for their upkeep, Adam and Eve are nevertheless still subject to scarcity in the sense of having to make allocative choices and even compete for social standing, as in the case of deciding whether to obey God or not.[2] Gauthier (1986, 330–37) calls this "scarcity in consumption" over life goals and modes in contrast to "scarcity in production," which pertains to available supplies of material goods. And even after the ill effects of original sin have been finally overcome after the *parousia,* scarcity will still be experienced in the beatific vision because saints will not have the breadth and comprehensive sweep of vision as God does.[3] Thomas suggests a useful and concise distinction:

> [T]he economic condition of man goes back beyond *original sin, which itself is the failure of an "economic" act, a bad piece of calculation for the purposes of obtaining a mistaken advantage.* Original sin is not the origin of economics, but of the difficulties of economics. (1955, 162; emphasis added)

In choosing to disobey God rather than conform to divine plans, Adam and Eve are in effect making an allocative choice. Existential scarcity is necessary if the gift of human freedom is to be meaningful to begin with. Otherwise, without opportunity costs attendant to the exercise of freedom, there is no point to freedom at all. This existential scarcity is not a result of original sin.

Consequent scarcity, however, is a post-Eden phenomenon. Both physical and moral evil contribute toward consequent scarcity—frictional and Malthusian; however, only moral evil bears culpability for such a persistent, unaddressed state of affairs. Definite effects flow from definite causes within the limiting formal perfections[4] of the order of creation, and this includes consequent scarcity. Physical evil precipitates material shortfalls through natural disasters, chance, and contingency in the nature of economic processes or other nonmoral failures of defectible secondary causes. For example, material shortages occur because of intrinsic imperfections in market operations such as business cycles that generate costly and disruptive alternating periods of inflation and unemployment, of booms and busts. Moreover, weather, natural calamities, and disease hamper both the production and distribution of much-needed goods and services. Limitations in human speculative and practical knowledge also affect the availability of provisions, as seen in the economy of tenuous subsistence prior to the Scientific-Industrial Revolution that gave rise to the modern economy of growth. These human causes behind material scarcity are properly attributed to metaphysical evil (Leibniz [1710] 1966), limitations that stem from human nature itself. As a proximate cause of scarcity, metaphysical evil includes the finitude of practical reason and other physical limitations of humans with respect to temporality, skills, talents, and effort. For example, scarcity may arise because humans are unable to work longer hours, or are not smart enough to figure out how to coax more out of the earth, or are so fragile as to need the use of so many more material inputs in order to survive, grow, and develop.

Material scarcity due to nature is antecedent to original sin. Moreover, both Aquinas and Augustine maintain that original sin does not cause ontological changes in creation (Forbes 1960, 196–97; 1961; B. Gordon 1989, 126). That is, whatever impact original sin has on scarcity comes not via nature but through human beings and how they use or misuse such material goods. Original sin does not make nature niggardly in provisioning humans. Rather, original sin leads to a disordered reason and freedom, which cause work to be so toilsome and greed to be so satisfying.

Original sin is responsible for consequent scarcity through sins of omission or commission. The consequent scarcity that stems from physical evil is supposed to be corrected through intelligent secondary causes—human economic agency. As we have seen in part I, it is rational human instrumentality that redresses such natural imperfections; it is human participation in God's governance that actualizes God's envisioned ontological material sufficiency despite the expected material shortages some will face due to a whole array of limiting formal imperfections in economic processes. Rational secondary causes—human beings—are responsible for effecting the divine benefaction of material sufficiency for every person. Such free and intelligent economic activity is an effect proper to their nature and mode of operation; it is these proper final effects that make human beings secondary causes rather than mere instruments.[5] Of course, concomitant to this unique proper effect are responsibilities. Thus, at the very least, chronic Malthusian scarcity ultimately stems from the human sin of omission, that is, from people's failure to discharge their positive obligations such as requisite economic transfers to alleviate the unmet needs of others.

Sins of commission may, however, be an even more direct and predominant cause of consequent scarcity. Avarice, inordinate wealth accumulation, overindulgent consumption, and patron-client relationships (Moxnes 1988) inflict hardship on many. After all, given human interdependence and the limited supplies of the fruits of the earth, private economic behavior can impose wide ripple effects on everybody else in the community for good or for ill.[6] Furthermore, human sinfulness most likely aggravates and magnifies the deleterious effects of the unavoidable material shortages that stem from physical and metaphysical evil. For example, A. K. Sen (1982) argues that famine in the modern economy is primarily a failure in the distribution of entitlements more than it is a breakdown in production.

There is a two-way causation between consequent scarcity and sin (Gustafson 1977, 156–57). Consequent scarcity can push people even further toward self-interested behavior and make patron-client relationships that much more enticing and rewarding, given the increased power or prestige that comes with ownership of scarce goods or social positions. Sin, on the other hand, can aggravate scarcity even further because of the real detrimental material impact of selfish behavior (e.g., diminished supplies due to people's cupidity). There is a self-reinforcing cycle between sin and consequent scarcity that leads to ever deeper destitution. Rabbi Simeon Elezar would even go so far as to claim that because of sin, humans forfeit their "right to sustenance without care" (*Kiddushin* 4:14; Danby 1933, 329).

In summary, existential scarcity stems from both physical and metaphysical evil. There is a need to allocate limited supplies of material provisions because of human finitude. Would that human beings were not corporeal. Or even with their bodily nature, would that people were a little more hardy in their constitution and not require as much food, clothing, and shelter or not be too dependent on material inputs. Existential scarcity arises from human beings' nature and mode of operation. Physical evil, such as natural disasters or climatic disturbances, adversely affects available supplies, thereby requiring even more judicious allocations on the part of humans. Consequent scarcity, that is, scarcity as a condition of unfilled demand or as a state of want and destitution, arises from both physical and moral evil. However, moral evil is ultimately responsible for consequent scarcity because human beings, as free economic agents, are supposed to act as intelligent secondary causes in redressing material shortages that stem from physical evil. Moreover, moral evils, such as war, inordinate accumulation, or immoderate consumption, cause massive destruction or wanton abuse of the finite supplies of created goods, thereby deepening material exiguity.

The metaphysical evil at the root of existential scarcity is not an issue for our theodicy, only the physical and the moral evils that undergird consequent scarcity. The need to allocate (existential scarcity) is not an evil in the proper sense of the word but is part of human nature; it is a metaphysical evil. In contrast to existential scarcity, Malthusian scarcity (as a state of want and destitution) is a privation of the goodness of God's creation that provides for all that is needed for human beings to act and flourish according to their nature and mode of being.

Conditionality and human freedom

The order of creation provides adequate supplies of material provisions based on God's threefold causality (chapter 2 and appendix 3). However, empirical evidence of widespread material want and poverty across human history discounts our world as an order of unconditional material superfluity. Thus, the divinely envisioned metaphysical material sufficiency has to be merely provisional.

All creaturely activities unfold either voluntarily or by necessity, and only rational beings are capable of free created acts. Conditionality pertains only to voluntary action since predetermined activities operate by necessity. Thus, conditional material sufficiency in human provisioning must be contingent on human agency. After all, only human beings are capable of deliberate action in correcting deviations from the initial starting point of an existential material sufficiency. In writing on economic thought and justice, Spengler observes:

> [A] fruitful source of information regarding the development of man's economic thinking at particular times is the set of laws and customs he created in order to cope with what we call economic scarcity. (1980, 117)

The economic order revolves around human beings. In the first place, it is human needs that give rise to such a sphere. More significantly, however, economic life is principally a rational activity. In examining the economic order through the framework of secondary causality, we can see how the economy is largely a human construct. The array of possible permutations in the use of the gifts of the earth is principally and ultimately shaped by human practical knowledge and free will that produce the goods, services, and relations that comprise economic life. Thus, the determinate, specific qualities of the economic order are largely the proper effects of human beings as intelligent secondary causes. The degree to which the actual economic order conforms to divine providence (both as a plan and in its implementation in divine governance) corresponds to the depth to which humans participate in God's governance and providence.

Stringency of conditionality and God's preventive actions

The weight of deliberate, remedial action in effecting or restoring existential material sufficiency falls squarely on human agency. Nevertheless, the stringency of the conditionality behind material sufficiency still lies within the purview of God's action.

We have already established that the existence and continued sustenance of creatures is the sole domain of God as Formal, Efficient, and Final Cause (chapter 2 and appendix 3). Before proceeding further with a theodicy, we must also consider whether ours is the best possible universe that God could have created. If it is, then there is no point in asking the counterfactual question of what if God had provided even more supplies of created goods to preclude material scarcity, since that would have meant a less perfect order of creation to begin with.

Besides the order of parts of the universe to each other and besides the order of all things to God as their ultimate end, Aquinas argues that the universe could still be made better with respect to its other dimensions.[7] Among these are creatures' accidental perfections, including the category of quantity (Aristotle 1941a). Thus, based on the perfection of the whole universe, there are no a priori arguments against possible alterations in God's design of the world, such as a greater supply of created goods.

Since we are concerned not with existential scarcity but with consequent scarcity (aftermath of human choice), can we not then simply base our theodicy of scarcity on God's desire to respect human freedom? We cannot. Economic scarcity is not a necessary condition for the genuine exercise of human freedom. God could have just as easily created a world with no consequent scarcity and still preserve the opportunities for an authentic exercise of the human will. I suggest three such scenarios.

First, it is possible for God to adapt divine activity in such a way as to correct for creaturely limiting formal perfections.

> All that is required of the instrument used by God is that it limit in some way His mode of operation. God adapts His activity to the operation of the created instrument for the production of an effect, *while not being limited,* in attaining that effect, by the particular form of the instrument. (Masterson 1967, 550; emphasis added)

God is not impeded from working directly with creatures without the use of proximate causes (SCG III, 99, #9). Thus, divine governance (God as Efficient Cause) is not necessarily bound to the secondary agents' limiting formal perfections.

Second, God could have simply created a world of unconditional material sufficiency. The unqualified nature of this state would mean that the order of creation is so robust that it is able to more than make up for material shortfalls from physical or moral evil. "Unconditional" means "sustenance without care" (*Kiddushin* 4:14; Danby 1933, 329) for humans; there is no need to allocate because of the superfluity of supplies under such an unqualified sufficiency.

The unconditional provisioning of human material needs is a tantalizing counterfactual alternative because of all the benefits it brings in its wake. An increase in the quantities of available supplies makes the economic task less severe, if not altogether eliminating the need for instrumental economic activity; there is a larger cushion for errors; it compensates for individual and collective finitude and defectibility; and it increases the productivity of personal skills, talents, time, and other gifts, as there are more material goods to work with as complementary inputs. Furthermore, in relieving the human person, indeed the human community, of having to worry about such prosaic matters as human provisioning, attention could be channeled to even more important, more enduring noneconomic activities and goals, such as the cultivation of the human mind and spirit.

A world of unconditional material sufficiency does not eradicate moral evil, but it does limit economic occasions for such evil (e.g., predatory behavior and divisive competition). Observe the difference between the peaceful ease with which the wandering Chosen People are able to satisfy their needs with manna in the desert in contrast to Joseph's Egypt in which Pharaoh eventually ends up possessing everything the people had, including a fifth of all their future harvest (Gn 47:13–26). Moreover, a surfeit in material provisions minimizes the economic consequences of moral evil, as in the case of the zero-sum phenomenon in which excessive consumption or accumulation on the part of some leave many others in destitution; there would have been enough for everyone regardless of the moral failure of some.

The benefits of a less constrained economic life can be extensive given the latter's wide ripple effects. One must remember the pivotal place of economic life in human communities. The economic sphere has the broadest reach of all the multiplicity of particular orders in the twofold order of the universe because it directly touches on all of material creation, both rational and nonrational. It is within economic life that material creation is transformed and then employed for the service of human beings. Moreover, the economic sphere provides and sets the necessary material conditions for the other spheres of human affairs: political, social, and cultural. Indeed, there is much at stake in the question of why God did not create a world of unconditional material sufficiency.

Third, besides endowing the world with a superfluity of goods, God could have also prevented a paucity of material provisions by simply making adjustments in the other sources of scarcity. Thus, God could have dampened the element of chance and contingency[8] in economic processes, or made it less complicated and therefore more comprehensible to practical reason, or made humans smarter, or changed the physical constitution of human beings so as to be less dependent on material goods, or all of the above. In other words, God could have prevented a privation of the goodness of divine providence through many channels without even tampering with human freedom or with the degree to which the human will is defectible. After all, every cause or effect in creation is subject to God as universal cause (ST I, 103, a.7).

God could have calibrated the limiting formal perfections to such a level as to make the natural world rugged enough to withstand physical and moral evil and still be able to provide material sufficiency, indeed, an unconditional material sufficiency that is not contingent on human rectitude. But even if God chooses to provide only conditional material sufficiency and require human cooperation, God could have nonetheless still aligned the limiting formal perfections and the dynamics in the order of creation in such a way as to contain the deleterious consequences of moral failure. Nothing is impossible to God.

There are varying degrees of exiguity in consequent scarcity. On one end of this spectrum is frictional scarcity that merely causes disappointment or inconvenience for unfilled, non-life-threatening needs or wants. On the other end is Malthusian scarcity and its accompanying frank poverty, ill health, and even death. God could have fine-tuned nature to be so robust as to make the material impact of human sin less damaging. What is at stake here is the severity of the injurious consequences of scarcity on human provisioning, rather than whether human freedom is allowed to operate or not.

The subject of our theodicy is why God could not have fashioned an order of creation that would be hardy enough in the face of foreseen human failure. Could God not have made Malthusian scarcity less severe? Could God not have allowed a more generous *room for error* in setting the conditionality of the envisioned material sufficiency? God could have easily made such adjustments in the initial endowments or in the limiting formal perfections of the natural world as to mitigate the severity of consequent scarcity as an evil. Such *room for error,* whether it is expansive or not, shapes the sacrificial effort required of humans and determines the impact of scarcity. After all, the difficulty of the task for human agency is directly proportional to the size of the gap that has to be closed between existential and consequent scarcity. The more severe the divergence, the greater the ingenuity and the more heroic the self-sacrifice and cooperation that will be required of the only type of created activity that is capable of furnishing the necessary remedial action: human agency.

In summary, we can formulate our issue as a question of why God did not create a world of unconditional material sufficiency and thereby protect the goodness of divine providence from material privation. Alternatively, since God could still provide relief to the human condition of chronic consequent scarcity by mitigating the severity of material shortfalls, we ask why God did not make the conditionality of the divine gift of existential sufficiency less stringent. In this way, the original intent of material adequacy could be attained with less human hardship and achieved more often. As it is, the bar for attaining material adequacy seems to be set quite high, judging from the persistent human experience of material poverty and destitution. In other words, God could have controlled the severity of deviations from existential material sufficiency through manifold venues. God could have set the initial endowments of material goods in the order of creation at such a generous level as to already make allowances and provide a cushion in absorbing the foreseen losses from natural and moral evils. Alternatively, God could have simply recalibrated the limiting formal perfections of the natural world that give rise to scarcity. God could have made the world otherwise and provisioned people without undue human hardship, but God did not. Why?

IMPACT OF SCARCITY

Conceptual framework: continuum of *being* and *having*

Johnson (1981) provides an excellent starting point in our examination of the impact of material scarcity on the human response to divine initiatives. His theological understanding of material possessions begins with a reflection on what it is to be corporeal. People are not immaterial minds floating about but are embodied intellect and freedom. This means that *being* and *having,* while distinct from each other, are indivisible; for a human person, the statement "I am" is inseparable from "I have" a body.[9]

In speaking of a corporeal make-up, however, one must carefully distinguish variations in the link between *having* and *being.* Thus, Johnson (39) argues that it is more accurate to say "I am heart and mind" rather than "I have heart and mind." The same cannot be said of the hand: I "have" a hand is more appropriate than I "am" a hand. In other words, parts of the human body have varying degrees of importance and function in identifying who people are as human beings and as unique individuals. For example, the connection between *having* and *being* is tighter in speaking of the mind and the heart compared to other parts of the body. From this, Johnson concludes that there is a continuum of varying degrees of conjuncture between *having* and *being*. It is within this spectrum that material possessions can be located. After all, given people's material nature, *being* requires *having*.

> The body expresses who I am, and the body is who I am. I am a living symbol. I am also, inevitably, a *possessor.* Any thinking about human possessions which does not recognize the irreducible nature of human possessing is fantasy. (Johnson 1981, 39; original emphasis)

Thus, Johnson locates what he calls the "mystery of human possessions" within "the ambiguity of our somatic/spiritual existence as humans" (37).

Functions of material possessions

Symbolic function

There is a symbolic function to human materiality. Who "I am" is partly conditioned, shaped, and affected by what "I have" inasmuch as the body serves both as a venue and the means with which to express the self and to relate to the world beyond oneself.

> The body is a symbol in the way a sacrament is a symbol. It is, to borrow the old scholastic definition, a sign which effects what it signifies. The body not only signals the state of my heart, it makes it real in the world outside my mind. (Johnson 1981, 36)

In other words, the exercise of human intellect and freedom is a function of that which embodies them. That which embodies them can shape, though not determine, the circumstances and the ease with which the intellect and freedom find self-expression.

> [T]he traffic moves both ways. Our bodies speak to our minds as much as our minds to our bodies. When I close myself in a tight knot, my body not only expresses fear and defensiveness but strengthens it. . . .

Because the traffic moves both ways, because my body speaks to my spirit, it is possible for me to place my body in witness to my convictions. It is one thing for me to think or say I believe in the resurrection of the dead; it is another to place my body on the line for this conviction. (Johnson 1981, 36)

We can expand this symbolic function to our material possessions by analogy. Art or, for that matter, the work of our hands, is an expression of ourselves and an outlet for our creativity. Locke ([1690] 1952, #25–51) justifies private property ownership because we imprint our personality on the inert fruits of the earth. The way we dress or furnish our houses, what we accumulate for ourselves, and what we readily give to others reflect our personalities and provide glimpses into our inner selves, into our likes and dislikes, into what we value most in life. Possessions can shape how we are perceived by others. Just as our body language can make a statement of who we are, so can our material possessions. *Having* is constitutive of *being* because the body and material possessions are vehicles for self-expression and contribute toward our self-identity. The body is witness to one's spirit and high purpose (Johnson 1981, 36), or lack thereof; by extension, so are material possessions.

Possessions flow into our self-identity as the tangible affirmation of our efforts, as a source of our security, as a bequest that will outlast us, as a testament to our accomplishments, as a basis for our standing within the community, and, in metaphysical language, as the critical tools and outcomes of our operations as we acquire additional perfections. Scarcity enhances the value of all these and makes sharing or foregoing what we have or rightfully acquire even more sacrificial and self-emptying.

Logistical function

Johnson's model can be further expanded and developed beyond his symbolic meaning of the body (and properties by extension) to include the logistical and relational functions of material possessions, which he does not make explicit in his discussion. As he observes, one has to view the human person not merely as a *being* but also as a *possessor* because of the body. Note, however, that a corporeal nature imposes its own requirements. The body has to be clothed, fed, nurtured, and housed. Moreover, beyond serving as inputs for basic health and survival, material goods are also needed by humans as tools and raw materials for both manual and intellectual work. *Having* is a necessary condition to *doing*. In other words, material possessions are needed for physical, mental, and spiritual survival, growth, and development. Consequently, this logistical function requires the extension of Johnson's model in a second way: the acknowledgment of quantity as an important attribute to consider. Given the functional role of material possessions, it is important not only that one has the possibility and opportunity of possessing, but it is equally essential that one has access to such possessions in sufficient quantities.

Relational function

Possessions shape the possibilities of our interaction with others. They can mediate our relationship to God and with others for good or for ill (Johnson 1981, 40–41). Human beings are not only corporeal, they are also social. Bodies, and by extension material possessions, are instrumental in communicating and interacting with others. Thus, we shake hands, hug, give gifts, and share a meal as we reach out to others. In the case of material possessions, such a relational function takes on even greater importance and becomes even more intense in the context of needing to share a finite earth with others. Competition can make the link between *having* and *relating* adversarial. The more severe the scarcity, the more intense the rivalry, and the greater the chances of engendering animosity as a by-product of *having* and *relating*.

Our bodies' ability to function as a symbol is embedded within a larger social context that shapes, defines, and assigns symbols, roles, and meanings to body language (Johnson 1981, 37). Again, by extension, we can say the same thing of material possessions and personal skills. In a world of scarcity, my possession of something takes on even greater significance and value if others do not similarly possess it, or if others intensely desire to have what I own. Hirsch (1976) describes these as positional or prestige goods such as unique works of art or jewelry. Or take the case of Nozick's (1974) example of people's willingness to pay Chamberlain to watch him play basketball and in the process turn him into a wealthy man. In all these cases, it is the social context that assigns value to these scarce goods or skills. In other words, *relating* shapes the value ascribed to *having*.

As discussed in the preceding chapters, the use or misuse of material possessions can either build up or destroy communities. They can sully or ennoble our relations with others. We can set our source of security on mammon instead of God. Accumulating wealth inordinately can become our overriding end instead of using the goods of the earth to feed the hungry, clothe the naked, or shelter the homeless. We may use such possessions to take advantage of the penury of others by dominating them and making them dependent on us, or we can choose to give without expecting return or gratitude. In fact, most of the scriptural teachings on economic life point to the appropriate manner by which we should use the goods of the earth to fashion communities that are genuinely human and reflective of the presence of God in our midst. Indeed, much good or harm can come from our use of material goods. *Having* and *relating* mutually affect each other.

Scarcity as a venue for freedom

Johnson (1981) does not examine quantity as a critical link between *being* and *having*. This is completely understandable since he is interested primarily in the symbolic function of possessions. However, when we speak of material goods in their role of provisioning human needs or of positioning people within communities, quantity becomes a key element, if not *the* determining factor. The importance of quantity (and therefore of scarcity) is best illustrated by rehearsing the precise links by which *having* promotes or diminishes *being* as noted in the preceding section, namely: (1) material goods as necessary inputs for survival and basic health, (2) material possessions as a venue for self-expression, (3) material goods as necessary inputs for interpersonal relations, (4) the production of requisite goods and services as an occasion for communal collaborative work, and (5) the production of economic commodities as an outlet for personal striving.

Scarcity affects human flourishing through these five channels. Let us examine both the positive and negative consequences of a world of unconditional material superfluity. The most evident gain is the complete elimination of Malthusian scarcity. People would be able to satisfy fully not only their basic needs but also all the material requirements of growth and development. Moreover, given their abundance, material goods can no longer be used to dominate or control others, as has been the case in patron-client relationships (Moxnes 1988). Furthermore, there will no longer be any point to competing over material positional goods (Hirsch 1976). Thus, a world of unconditional material sufficiency eliminates material destitution and want from human experience and also minimizes economic occasions for sin and strife. There are less impediments to people attaining human flourishing.

Unfortunately, there are also losses that come with such plenitude. In particular, there is the forfeiture of instrumental productive activity, a diminished urgency for personal and collective striving, less need for each other, and an attenuated sacrificial dimension in interpersonal economic relationships. Each of these is examined in the following sections.

Scarcity and striving

Gauthier (1986, 330–37) weighs the implications of what human living would be like in a bountiful world in which scarcity in production is completely eliminated. People would have all the material provisions they need. In this utopian existence, instrumental human activity would not be completely eliminated but would nevertheless be severely curtailed. As Gauthier correctly observes in his critique of Suits's (1978) original formulation of this imaginary world of abundance, there is a difference between scarcity in consumption and scarcity in production. Material superfluity removes only the latter but not the former. There will be scarcity in consumption because people are still limited in the kind of life they can choose to live. They cannot be an accomplished concert pianist, a nuclear physicist, a neurosurgeon, a novelist, an engineer, a chemist, and a biologist all rolled into a single life (Gauthier 1986, 334). In other words, people cannot live all possible modes of life; they still have to make choices (with their attendant opportunity costs) on what to expend their effort and time, and how to do so.

Thus, in a world of unconditional material abundance, economic allocation will revolve around consumption alone; there will no longer be a need for any instrumental activity in production. On the surface, this is a tremendous boon, as people can now concentrate solely on the big questions and activities of life without having to bother with the more pedestrian and bothersome task of working and producing to sustain a family. People could simply concentrate on their integral human development and not have to worry about procuring for themselves the necessary material means for such advancement.

Ironically, the loss of all instrumental activity in production can retard human flourishing. From being a most important sphere of human life, economic activity is completely sapped of its bygone contribution of imbuing life with additional meaning and purpose—the seeking, the striving, the sharing, the participation in a collective effort, and the possibilities of relating to others who are also seeking, striving, and struggling. In this regard, Malthus ([1798] 1960) is correct in his theological arguments in the last two chapters of his *Essay*: scarcity and want are necessary for human exertion. Paley ([1802] 1972) and Sumner ([1816] 1850) also argue that scarcity is instrumental for enterprise and creativity. Without these, there would be no impetus for sustained and meaningful effort.[10] Two inimical effects of unconditional material superfluity must be considered: the loss of economic life as a setting for seeking and striving, and the loss of productive secondary causality.

First, as we have seen in Johnson's (1981) formulation of the symbolic function of property and wealth, possessions are a form of self-expression. After all, the process of toiling and sacrificing to acquire such property is in itself an integral part of this self-expression. It is the expenditure of personal effort that imbues the possession with personal meaning and significance. In fact, Locke ([1690] 1952, #25–51) argues that it is the stamp of our personal character in making parts of nature productive that becomes the warrant for private property ownership. The possibility of such personal accomplishment is lost if there were no longer any need to work for one's provisioning.

> If a fulfilling human life must include activities with instrumental value, then paradise can be gained only to be lost. Paradise is gained when all obstacles to fulfillment are overcome, but when all obstacles are overcome, instrumental activities lose their point and cease to afford fulfillment. And with the loss of paradise, we come to a new understanding of the place of scarcity in human affairs. In the broadest sense, it is scarcity that gives rise to activities with instrumental value. If they are necessary to human fulfillment, then scarcity is necessary too. The idea of a human society based not on scarcity but on plenitude is chimerical; *to overcome scarcity would be to overcome the conditions that give human life its point.* (Gauthier 1986, 333; emphasis added)

Superfluity simply removes the role and significance of material possessions as a form of unique self-expression and character formation. Much is lost to the extent that seeking and striving are essential for human growth and development.

Second, there is the loss of real productive secondary causality. Unconditional material abundance minimizes the need for humans to produce. As we have already seen in Aquinas's twofold order of the universe, God uses secondary causes to provide for creatures. People stand out in this regard because productive economic activity requires free and intelligent secondary causality, qualities that properly belong to the nature and mode of operation of human beings alone. Thus, humans are even described as "co-creators" with God because of this unique capacity for creativity. In a world of unqualified material plenitude, most productive activity would cease to be necessary and would simply be inconsequential "games" to preoccupy people with a lot of time on their hands (Gauthier 1986, 330–31). There would be no room for the gift of real productive instrumentality in a world of unconditional material plenitude. Much is lost because *being* is a function not only of *having*, but it is also a function of *doing,* a venue for human participation in God's governance.

Doing is an important function of *being;* unconditional material bounty would take away the need for *doing.* There is less need for striving and seeking.

> [T]he . . . individual is an active being, who finds satisfaction in the seeking and striving that constitute activity as we humans conceive it. . . . [T]he good life must combine attainment with striving. But in so far as the latter is essential, the habitat of the . . . individual must be one of scarcity, whether material, mental or emotional. (Gauthier 1986, 346)

Superfluity eliminates the need for *having* and in the process removes a venue for *being* by *doing.* Scarcity precipitates the need for instrumental activities, building blocks to a more penetrating experience of *being.* Scarcity has a vital functional role to play.

Scarcity and restorative justice

Sharing and *participation*—constituent elements of productive economic activity—are rendered unnecessary by unconditional material bounty. People have less need for each other, and in the process, economic agency no longer serves as a sphere that compels great and deliberate effort from people in according each other the equal status, dignity, and respect they owe each other. A world of "sustenance without care" removes the opportunity for people to make up for what is lacking in others. An essential part of righteousness is due order in interpersonal relationships (Achtemeier 1962b); how we treat one another is in turn a function of what we share with each other. Thus, *being* is a function of *relating*, which in turn is partly a function of *having* and *sharing*.

God created humans for a particular purpose and envisioned possibilities and heights to which they can soar not only in the afterlife but even in their earthly existence. God's interests are not exclusively otherworldly; rather, God is deeply interested and engaged in worldly affairs. Moreover, God is intensely committed to providing humans with all that is necessary for a full life in the here and now (Lohfink 1987). Thus, salvation history is replete with God's track record of repeatedly restoring people after their failures. God makes whole again or provides relief to those who have been hurt across different facets of temporal life, including the economic sphere. For this reason, YHWH intervenes in human history in the Exodus to inaugurate a new economic system to provide aid for an oppressed Israel. And as a continuation of this divine in-breaking characterized by a preferential option for the distressed, Israel is invited to live up to divine statutes and ordinances governing economic life. Indeed, human beings can lend themselves as instruments to God's restorative acts, especially in their economic agency. After all, economic life is an important setting for human participation in divine righteousness.

"The poor you will always have with you."
Is Malthusian scarcity an unavoidable state of affairs in the post-Eden experience? After all, endless toil has become part of the human condition as a consequence of original sin (Gn 3:19). Is unfilled material need the lot of human beings in the order of God's creation?

Even in the aftermath of original sin, God's gift of material sufficiency, together with its conditionality, remains unchanged just as it was in the Garden of Eden. B. Gordon (1989, 2–3) observes that Adam and Eve had to work even in the Garden of Eden prior to the Fall. What original sin imposes, however, are greater burdens and costs that accompany such work. The conditionality appended to material sufficiency becomes more severe given the additional, formidable hurdles of selfishness and sinfulness that exacerbate the toilsome and often ineffectual results of such work. Nevertheless, as part of the Covenant, YHWH intervenes in history and recasts human affairs and social institutions to give impoverished and oppressed Israel a clean slate, a new beginning in a "land flowing with milk and honey" in which each family is given a plot of such patrimony and no one will want for anything

(Dt 8:7–20, 15:4, 26:5–11). Thus, sufficiency, even abundance, is freely given by God as a gift for all, even in the post-Eden era. What is even more remarkable is that this gift of material sufficiency bears within it another gift—the gift of instrumentality. God brings about such plenitude through human beings themselves; it is God, after all, who empowers and makes human effort fruitful (Dt 8:12–14, 8:17–18; Psalm 127). God is not going to do for Israel what she is able to do for herself, even with great effort and risk of failure. Thus, the provision of manna—an instance of "sustenance without care"—stopped immediately after the first harvest in the Promised Land (Jo 5:12). YHWH provisions Israel in her period of landless wandering (Brueggemann 1977), and God will still provide abundance thereafter, but only with and through human effort and cooperation.

Actualizing both of these gifts—material sufficiency and human instrumentality—is conditional on human response. At the center of this conditionality are the economic ordinances and statutes from the three Hebrew law codes that together serve as a blueprint for how to overcome Malthusian scarcity in YHWH's contrast-society. This could be viewed as a second chance, in the wake of Eden, to rectify mistakes and injustices in human economic affairs. It is within this context and the historicity of God's in-breaking to restore due order in creation that one should locate the Old Testament laws on economic life. Far from being bothersome impositions or stifling restraints, such economic statutes and ordinances were meant to be embraced and appreciated as pathways to the possibility of an Eden-like material plenitude in the here and now, but only if human cooperation can be successfully elicited. Laws spelled out what ought to be done to approximate the envisioned due order in God's plan.

Economic transfers

Scarcity heightens even further human interdependence and its attendant obligations that are already intense in economic life to begin with (Gustafson 1977); it accentuates the relational dimension of property seen in the boundaries we set regarding its ownership and use. In fact, market exchange with its implicit cooperation and division of labor may be described as a corrective to material scarcity. Hume would go so far as to claim that justice itself has its provenance in the phenomenon of scarcity.

> Here then is a proposition, which, I think, may be regarded as certain, *that 'tis only from the selfishness and confin'd generosity of men, along with the*

scanty provision nature has made for his wants, that justice derives its origin.
([1739] 1978, 495, vol. 3, II:2; emphasis original)

Whether as part of a theodicy of Malthusian scarcity or of a theology of economic agency, there is a central role for economic transfers. As we have seen in Aquinas's metaphysics, economic transfers are instrumental in reconciling the promise of ontological material sufficiency with the reality of scarcity caused by limiting formal perfections (part I). In the Hebrew Scripture, the theme of *release* undergirds many of the Chosen People's ordinances and statutes: release of debt, release of slaves, release from work (weekly Sabbath), release of land's fertility (Sabbath-fallow), release-return of land (Jubilee), and release of the fruits of the land (gleaning, poverty tithing, shared feasts, and festivals). In the New Testament, economic transfers are also central to the teachings on economic life, as in the numerous admonitions to share, in Paul's collection for the poor of Jerusalem, and in Jesus's invitation for radical voluntary divestment.

Common to all these releases and transfers is a "letting go" of claims people have on highly valued scarce goods, resources, and services. This letting go becomes even more self-donative the more severe the material scarcity. Moreover, this letting go serves the critical function of making up for whatever may be lacking in others, whether as a result of physical evil or of their own or others' moral failures. In fact, in modern economic parlance, these mandated grants in Sacred Scripture are direct and indirect income maintenance mechanisms (Soss 1973). Economic transfers are an essential part of divine providence and God's restorative justice.

The merely conditional, rather than absolute, nature to existential material sufficiency means that some human beings (as parts of the whole) will face material shortages given the variety of circumstances and grades of perfections within the order of creation. This is partly due to natural evil, as in the case of economic chance and contingency. However, such a state becomes a moral evil when these distressed members of the community are compelled to remain in such privation given the failure of other human beings to conform to the order of reason and alleviate such need.

Material sufficiency is embedded within creation, but it can be impeded by moral and natural evils. Such impediments become the occasion for yet another venue for human participation: making up for the economic consequences of others' moral failures or of natural evil. Justice can be retributive or restorative, or both. In the latter, human beings serve as channels through which God restores material provisions to those who have been adversely deprived because of evil. And often, such restorative instrumentality requires great personal expense and self-giving as we have seen in the many scriptural precepts and counsels on economic life. But then, such self-sacrifice occasions an even more profound participation in God's holiness and righteousness and brings out an even greater likeness to God's image.

Thus, the conditionality that comes with the divine gift of material sufficiency can be understood in a dual sense. At first glance, it would seem that such material adequacy is conditioned solely by the fidelity with which people subscribe to divine statutes and ordinances regulating economic life. But there is a second dimension to this conditionality. Material sufficiency is also provisional on the willingness of people to walk the extra mile for each other. It is contingent on the readiness of people to supply and fill, at their own personal expense and with great effort and sacrifice, the unmet needs of others even if such want were due to the latter's own fault or sinfulness. Such envisioned sufficiency is conditional on a willingness to absorb risk and loss for others who are not able to do so themselves, even for the undeserving and the sinners. We see this not only in the economic transfers that can compensate for consequent scarcity due to limiting formal perfections (part I), but we also read about it in the numerous biblical ordinances and statutes on extending assistance to the impoverished (part II).

All this is powerfully and concisely summarized in Deuteronomy 15:1–11. YHWH boldly declares that there will no longer be any poor because of the exceeding fecundity of divine blessings (Dt 15:4). But then God is quick to add that savoring such lavish divine benefactions hinges on the generosity that people themselves are able to bestow on each other (Dt 15:5–10). Such divine munificence can be sustained only in the measure that the Chosen People are willing to share and pass them on to others, especially to those who are impoverished. The Deuteronomist ends the passage with a realistic acknowledgment that despite the overwhelming bounty of God's gifts, there will nevertheless still be poor in their midst, which in turn becomes all the more reason for Israel to redouble her efforts and her own generosity (Dt 15:11). After all, just as the human heart is capable of turning the "land flowing with milk and honey" into a barren scorched desert, the human heart can be just as proficient in cooperating with and letting divine grace restore that which has been lost. God responds to foreseen human failures by drawing in people themselves as transformed and empowered instruments in setting aright the ruins of human affairs. It is yet another example in salvation history of God's characteristic generosity of responding[11] to disobedience with even more gifts, and yet another example of how God rebuilds and re-creates using the very ruins that we have made of our lives. That there will always be poor among us (Dt 15:11) can be viewed both as a reproach and as a promising possibility. It is a reproach because chronic destitution is prima facie evidence that as individuals and as a community we have failed in our responsibilities whether by our sins of omission or commission. Nevertheless, it is also a promising possibility because it provides an occasion for serving as "sacramental" instruments in rectifying or mitigating the consequences of such sinfulness, as is clearly evident in the invitation to take extra care of the impoverished (Dt 15:5–11). In reconciling the seeming contradiction in Deuteronomy 15:1–11, Lohfink asserts:

> In Deut 15:11 we read: "The poor will never cease out of the land." . . . But poverty, which rises again and again, stimulates all brothers and sisters to react against it and eradicate it immediately. Because of this reaction, which always calls forth divine blessing, and because of the functioning system of provisions for the different groups in Israel, what we read in Deut 15:4 also remains true: "There will be no poor among you." (1991, 47)

Integral to divine providence's unfolding abundance is the gift of human instrumentality in which God provides for people through humans themselves (1) as they live up to the laws, (2) as they care for each other, and (3) as they willingly make up for each others' failings even at the expense of their own personal welfare. Just as material scarcity can lead people to prey on each other, scarcity can also turn out to be an opportunity for people to mutually care for each other in heroic and unexpected ways.

Scarcity and sacrificial sharing

Scarcity not only makes economic transfers necessary, but it also opens the possibility of depth, sacrifice, and self-giving in such sharing. The entire spectrum of biblical laws and statutes on economic life is meant to mirror in the here and now the abundance of the eschatological banquet. In the eschaton, no one will be in want, and all will feast and savor each other's company in God's Kingdom. Given the reality of material scarcity, approximating the eschatological banquet in the present is possible only if there is an open and generous apportioning of the finite goods of the earth. Property can serve as a way for people to share meaning and value with each other, especially when such possessions are drawn from their substance and not merely from their surplus, and especially if such properties are precious to those who selflessly dispense them. Letting others partake of our material goods is a mode for meaningfully communicating with and relating to others, especially the destitute. In fact, sharing possessions signifies a giving of ourselves; the more severe the scarcity, the more profound do we pour of ourselves. Unconditional plenitude renders such sharing unnecessary and meaningless.

The use of material goods is either functional (when it fosters human dignity and growth) or dysfunctional (e.g., inordinate consumption or drug abuse). Material possessions can be used for good or for ill. Johnson (1981) already alludes to this when he situates what he calls the "mystery of human possessions" within the "ambiguity of our somatic/spiritual existence as humans" (37).

> Serious thought about possessions must start with the capacity of the human body to express the human spirit, to be the medium of human meaning in the world, to be enfleshed word, and at the same time, *with the possibility for this message to be distorted and misread.* (Johnson 1981, 35; emphasis added)

The message can, of course, be distorted and misread to begin with through our misuse or abuse of what we "have," including our bodies and material possessions.

A common denominator in many of the teachings on economic behavior in both the Hebrew Scripture and the New Testament is the invitation to forego material possessions (either of ownership or of use) in favor of our neighbors. We see this in the Old Testament laws on interest-free loans, debt remission, slave release, land return, almsgiving, poor tithing, and gleaning. In the Gospels, we observe this in the precepts and counsels to share wealth with others and, in some cases, even to radical dispossession in order to follow Christ more fully. In all these cases, we deprive ourselves of the use of such material goods so that others who are more needy than we are may find some relief in their material want and destitution. The more severe the scarcity, the more self-donative is such economic agency. Idolatry becomes an even more enticing option in the face of worsening scarcity because of the higher opportunity cost involved. Perkins describes this phenomenon well, particularly for the modern era:

Since we are constantly encouraged to identify ourselves in terms of material possessions rather than inherited personal or social relationships to others, loss of things may feel equivalent to loss of self-identity. It is this modern privileging of the economic category as a measure of personal independence and self-expression that makes it appear more radical to leave all things to follow Jesus. (1994, 59–60)

Consequently, a progressively self-donative sharing is aptly described as an increasing dependence on grace and as a leap of faith in a God who provides and replenishes those who have poured themselves out selflessly as a libation. It is the same faith that is so evident in the observance of the Sabbath-fallow and the Jubilee—that God will provide a double and triple harvest to enable the Chosen People to accept God's invitation of a consecrated rest.

If God had created a world of unconditional material abundance, if God had removed scarcity as a feature of the created world, there would be no unmet material need at all. There would be no need to differentiate the varied uses of goods and to allocate accordingly. There would be no need and no occasion to share with and to sacrifice for each other.

But God does permit material scarcity to be an attribute of the earth. Material abundance is made conditional on the human response to the divine invitation to let God provide for us through each other. Scarcity presents the occasion for depriving ourselves voluntarily so that others may live; it is scarcity that magnifies the selfless character of any and all economic activities taken in response to divine initiative and invitation. The more severe the scarcity in the way God created the world to begin with, the greater the opportunity cost we incur in responding to God's invitation to reach out to others, even to the point of radical voluntary dispossession. The more sacrificial our act, the more Christ-like we become, and the more profound is our participation in God's holiness and righteousness.

PARADOX REVEALED AND RESOLVED

Economic life is at the heart of the material dimension of our response to God's initiatives. Economic activity is a participation in the building of the Kingdom of God, a partaking that is made much more difficult and challenging in the face of material scarcity.

Why does God not simply create a world of unconditional material superfluity and allow people to focus their seeking and striving on the more substantive and less mundane facets of human life? Why even create conditions of scarcity that occasion conflict and mutual exploitation in human affairs? Why does God not provide initial conditions in material creation that are so robust as to withstand physical and moral evils and still provide everyone with sufficiency?

Whether we use metaphysics or Sacred Scripture, it is clear that God has envisioned a world of material sufficiency, albeit one that is conditional. We find ample testimony for this in Genesis, in the motive clauses of the Law, in the Promised Land "flowing with milk and honey," in the eschatological vision of the New Jerusalem, in the proleptic sabbatical feasting and festivals, and in the Gospel assurance of God's unfailing providence. God could have intervened decisively in human history and permanently locked in the intended plenitude for all, but chose instead to use defectible human instrumentality to effect such divine providence. The gift of material sufficiency will not be unconditional but will be contingent on human effort and cooperation. God is not going to do for us what we are able and supposed to be doing for ourselves together with grace. Depending on how we live up to our obligations, we can bring to fruition God's vision of abundance for all, just as God provides for the birds and the lilies of the fields (Mt 6:28; Lk 12:27). Scarcity magnifies our capacity to make life easier or harder for each other.

Long is critical of the discipline of economics in viewing human action in terms of opportunity costs and, by extension, of scarcity.

> Any action that I take will be inscribed in a world of lack wherein my choice is made possible only by the other options I choose against. Rather than viewing human action as arising out of a plenitude, this metaphysics assumes it is ensconced in scarcity. Death, violence, and antagonism become the source and end of such a metaphysics. (2000, 4)

Unlike Long's pessimistic prognosis, I argue that acknowledging a world of opportunity costs is precisely the stepping-stone toward the metaphysics of plenitude that Long himself speaks of; scarcity has a paradoxical dynamic.

Like many other paradoxes in the Christian faith, material scarcity sets the conditions for an even more consequential plenitude, of divine gift building on divine gift. Scarcity becomes the occasion for a more meaningful economic agency as a perfective secondary cause that participates in God's goodness, righteousness, holiness, providence, and restorative justice.

CHAPTER 9

MALTHUSIAN AND PARTICIPATIVE THEODICIES: A COMPARISON

For felicity in exposition and comparison, I use "Malthusian theodicies" as a shorthand for the formation-of-mind (Malthus) and the state-of-probation (Paley and Sumner) accounts of scarcity. After all, except for Malthus's formulation of original sin and final judgment, they all share similar premises and conclusions regarding anthropology, evil, goodness, and social policy. I refer to this book's constructive proposal that uses Thomistic metaphysics and Sacred Scripture as a "participative theodicy."

SIMILARITIES

There are significant similarities in the cosmology undergirding both theodicies, though each point of intersection also demonstrates differences. In the first place, both employ natural theology to shed light on the conceptual problem brought about by scarcity. In fact, Malthus ([1798] 1960, 126) begins his theodicy with a vigorous justification for why natural theology ought to be the preferred method (over revelation) in making sense of scarcity.[1] He eschews speculative theology in favor of starting with empirical insights afforded by a simple and direct observation of the world around us. Waterman (1983a, 202) suggests that Malthus's theological errors are partly due to his exclusive reliance on natural theology. In particular, his failure to take the Incarnation into account leads to his flawed soteriology.

Just like Malthus, Paley, and Sumner, this study uses natural theology to examine scarcity (part I). Observe that this part of the research completely stands on its own and arrives at a theodicy of scarcity as a participation in God's goodness even before bringing in insights from revelation (part II). Unlike Malthus's formulation, the natural theology of part I does not even have to bring in the Incarnation to be able to account for scarcity in a manner consistent with Christian theology.

Second, just like Aquinas and my participative theodicy, Malthus acknowledges an innate heterogeneity in God's created order (as do Paley and Sumner). Variety is produced not only in the diversity of creatures, but also in their differing grades of perfection. Moreover, they are also similar in their views on how the less perfect contribute to the good of the whole.

> Infinite variety, seems, indeed, eminently her [nature] characteristic feature. The shades that are here and there blended in the picture give spirit, life and prominence to her exuberant beauties, and those roughnesses and inequalities, those inferior parts that support the superior . . . contribute to the symmetry, grace, and fair proportion of the whole. (Malthus [1798] 1960, 137)[2]

Malthus ascribes a different end to this requisite natural variety in creatures: the excitement and formation of the mind.

> The infinite variety of the forms and operations of nature, besides tending immediately to awaken and improve the mind by the variety of impressions that it creates, opens other fertile sources of improvement by offering so wide and extensive a field for research and investigation. . . . Both reason and experience seem to indicate to us that the infinite variety of nature (and variety cannot exist without inferior parts, or apparent blemishes) is admirably adapted to further the high purpose of the creation and to produce the greatest possible quantity of good. (Malthus [1798] 1960, 137)

In the case of Aquinas, the formation of the mind is not the purpose for the variety and grades of perfection found in creatures, even as humans benefit collaterally from such multiplicity. Such diversity in Aquinas is needed to reflect the goodness of God, to the extent possible.

Third, both theodicies encompass dynamic undercurrents. Malthus's formation of the mind and Paley's and Sumner's state of probation imply movement. The same is true for participative theodicy's views on the development of moral excellence that leads to complete goodness.[3] Both approaches highlight the importance of change and self-actualization. A key difference, however, is that in the case of Malthus, movement is accomplished entirely through human effort alone, a Pelagian account of human flourishing. In contrast, participative theodicy begins with God's threefold causality and situates the effects proper to human effort as those of a secondary cause viewed within the larger backdrop of the First Cause.

Fourth, both theodicies perceive a set, predetermined due order in the world. Malthus argues that it is the predictability behind a mechanistic, well-defined order that gives people reason to exert themselves in reaching out for goals. It is this larger ordered setting that assures people of the efficacy of their labor and the means they employ. Had creation been chaotic without any constancy in the laws relating means and goals, people would simply not expend themselves, as everything becomes merely a matter of chance and contingency (Malthus [1798] 1960, 130–31). There is an order to God's creation and it is intelligible.

Finally, the severity of scarcity matters. In referring to the role of scarcity in rousing humans to work, Malthus observes that scarcity, as an evil, "would not act so powerfully as an excitement to exertion if the quantity of it did not diminish or increase with the activity or the indolence of man" ([1798] 1960, 142). In participative theodicy, scarcity also leads to greater and more intense effort, although for human participation in divine perfections rather than the formation of the intellect.

DIFFERENCES

Though meaningful similarities exist between Malthusian and participative theodicies, significant differences lead to marked variances. In the following section, I enumerate twelve such differences that demonstrate the profound conflict between them.

The first difference is specific to Malthus alone and has to do with the need for forgiveness and salvation. Recall that for Malthus original sin is the torpor and inactivity in the human person. There is no prelapsarian phase in Malthus, and since there is no fall, salvation is entirely irrelevant and unnecessary. In contrast, Aquinas's twofold order of the universe is able to account for such exigency through the limiting formal perfections in the order of creation. In particular, human will is defectible and therefore in need of forgiveness and restoration. Even as human beings (as intelligent secondary causes) ameliorate conditions of want and scarcity, participative theodicy is not Pelagian, does not rely solely on human agency, like Malthus's. As mere secondary causes, human beings bring about their proper effects only because of their participation in the First Cause—God. Aquinas's twofold order of the universe is compatible with the biblical notion of original sin as a failed exercise of a defectible human will.

Second, these theodicies have diametrically opposed cosmological starting points: the principle of population for the Malthusian theodicies and existential material sufficiency for participative theodicy. Malthus, Paley, and Sumner incorporate material scarcity and its attendant vice and misery among the necessary "blemishes and imperfections" that constitute the necessary diversity of the world. In Thomistic thought, scarcity too is part of such need for variety and arises from the limiting formal perfections of the secondary causes employed by God as part of the created order. However, there is a fundamental difference in their cosmology when it comes to the envisioned initial starting position of human beings: precarious subsistence living for Malthus, Paley, and Sumner, and conditional material sufficiency for participative theodicy. Both approaches subscribe to a dynamic in which limiting formal perfections give rise to scarcity as an expected, natural phenomenon. However, as shown in part I, such scarcity in Aquinas's twofold order, while inescapable, can be corrected through intelligent and selfless activity. In particular, interpersonal economic transfers are essential for reaching material sufficiency for all despite the chance, contingency, and imperfections in economic processes and despite the defectibility of the human will. In other words, in Malthusian cosmology, subsistence existence and its appurtenant human misery and suffering are set within the order of creation, by God's design. They are natural, universal laws—unavoidable and immutable. In a Thomistic twofold order of the universe, God's providence calls for material sufficiency for all, albeit admittedly a conditional one. God did not envision a world of want and then consign humans to a temporal existence of hard struggle for their upkeep. In other words, Malthusian scarcity is not intrinsic to the natural world in God's plan but is merely accidental, brought about by a lack of moral rectitude.

In affirming the human condition as a state of probation rather than a state of retributive punishment from God, Paley ([1802] 1972, 386) wants to maintain that the human condition is not one of designed misery. However, he goes on to accept the position that the principle of population, with its resultant hardships and subsistence living, is a natural and universal law. This is an inconsistency because such a deterministic human condition is a de facto state of devised affliction. Despite Paley's disavowal, to accept want and destitution as inherent to the natural order of creation is, in effect, to have a world of "misery by divine design."

This difference in the cosmological starting point on human provisioning also reflects deeper and even more significant disparities in views regarding the qualities of generosity and liberality in God as Creator and provider. If God is to have the highest of all perfections, God must also be unsurpassed in generosity. Thus, it is difficult to accept the vision of a God who intentionally creates a world of Malthusian scarcity and misery by design. It is such a pessimistic view of God. And even if we were to grant Malthus's thesis that such destitution is a necessary condition for the mind's formation, could God's omniscience and omnipotence not have found other ways to accomplish the same end?

Third, this difference in initial conditions and endowments has wide ramifications for these theodicies' respective underlying notions of evil. By making the hardship of subsistence living a universal law within the natural order, Malthus has essentially assumed away the "evil" of want and destitution. Hence, Waterman (1983a, 201) aptly describes Malthus's theodicy as a "non-solution of the problem of evil" because "in his system everything that is commonly thought of and experienced as 'evil' has to be regarded as a necessary part of the providence of God, and hence is not really an 'evil' at all, but a 'good.'" The alternative to this, of course, is for Malthus to use a Manichean or Albigensian formulation in which evil is a coprinciple with goodness in God's order of creation. This, however, would have created an even bigger theological problem of dualism. In contrast, participative theodicy views chronic material want and destitution as an evil consequent to moral failure.

Fourth, there are major differences in the notion of evil, and among these is the disparity in the views on the "finality" of evil. For Malthus, evil has to have an instrumental value in all cases.

> [Malthus] never grasped the essence of tragedy since he refused to accept evil as an end in itself, a finality which might crush men without ennobling them. Such tidiness violates modern sensibility, if not our credulity. But it was the cornerstone of a natural religion whose deepest faith lay in God's rationality. (LeMàhieu 1979, 468–69)

Indeed, evil is accepted (perhaps even valued?) for its instrumental role.

> Health and sickness, enjoyment and suffering, riches and poverty, knowledge and ignorance, power and subjection, liberty and bondage, civilization and barbarity, have all their offices and duties, all serve for the *formation* of character; for when we speak of trial, it must be remembered that characters are not only tried, or proved, or detected, but that they are generated also, and *formed,* by circumstances. (Paley [1802] 1972, 388; emphasis original)

The preceding chapters have vigorously argued that there is no *intrinsic* redemptive or *inherent* instrumental value to the evil of hunger, destitution, and other forms of physical destitution. To be sure, such deprivation may lead to some ancillary good. Nevertheless, such Malthusian scarcity is neither necessary in God's order of creation nor envisioned as part of God's providence. It is an evil that cannot be rationalized and should simply be accepted for what it is—an aberration, a deviation from the intended due order of creation. These are evils to be avoided and redressed and not merely accepted for their serviceable utility in human life. At this point it is worth recalling Lohfink's (1987, 5–15) theses in dispelling the mistaken notion associated with the view that ours is a "God of the poor." Lohfink argues emphatically that God did not intend a world of poverty and that God is not merely interested in otherworldly matters. God is keenly concerned with providing creatures with a world of plenitude and riches, and not for some unknown time in the future but immediately in the here and now.

This difference in views on the "finality" of evil is not merely a sterile speculative exercise in philosophical and theological reasoning. It has tremendous practical ramifications because to accept evil on account of its salutary instrumental value is to lay the theoretical foundations for a passive social policy. It is to rationalize and then accept disorders in social life for their beneficial ancillary effects. It is to acquiesce to social conditions that ought to be changed.

Fifth, such an exclusively instrumental view of evil leads to a role reversal between good and evil. Malthusian theodicies not only conclude that such disorders have some value to them, but they even argue that they are necessary and unavoidable if we are to grow in moral goodness. As already observed in chapter 1, the good is desired in the Malthusian theodicies only to the degree that people are repulsed by evil. It is only through its contrast with evil that goodness is able to elicit desire and human action. In effect, evil is a necessary condition for goodness. Malthus is emphatic about this when he claims, "It is highly probable, that moral evil is *absolutely necessary* for moral excellence" ([1798] 1960, 136; emphasis added). This is contrary to the long-standing Christian position that evil is a mere privation of the good (Augustine 1953). Furthermore, such a stance has to presuppose that evil is antecedent to good. This brings us back to Manichean and Albigensian dualism. In contrast, participative theodicy follows the Aristotelean-Thomistic notion of the good as fully independent of evil in being able to elicit human desire and action by force of its own power and perfection. There is no need for evil to "push" people toward the good because goodness is able to attract moral agents by virtue of its own proper excellence. Evil is not a necessary condition for goodness, even if there may be beneficial consequences in its wake. Evil is not intrinsic to the order of God's creation; it is merely accidental (SCG III, 10). Again, understanding this difference in the nature of goodness and evil is not merely a dry academic exercise because it has consequences for social policy. In particular, there is less urgency, if there is even need at all, to ameliorate or eliminate evil in human life if evil is deemed to be a necessary way station to the attainment of the good.

Sixth, the Malthusian theodicies do not examine the sources of material scarcity but simply accept it as a given in God's order of creation working through the principle of population. For example, Paley ([1802] 1972, 387) does not delve into the provenance of scarcity but simply incorporates this phenomenon, together with other disorders, within the requisite chance and diversity in creation. It is not clear to what extent the disorder concomitant to the population dynamics is natural or moral in its origins. We could only infer that Paley, just like Malthus, views such a condition as innate to the natural order. Observe, for example, how Paley sets the phenomenon of scarcity in his theodicy within the context of variety provided by changing seasons and their positive effects on farmers' virtue and character. From the variety that the vagaries of the weather precipitate, Paley slips in the "seasons of scarcity" as analogously beneficial.

> The *seasons* are a mixture of regularity and chance. They are regular enough to authorise expectation, whilst their being . . . irregular, induces, on the part of the cultivators of the soil, a necessity for personal attendance, for activity, vigilance, precaution. It is this necessity which creates farmers. . . . Seasons of scarcity themselves are not without their advantages; the most conducive to health, to virtue, to enjoyment. They call forth new exertions; they set contrivance and ingenuity at work; they give birth to improvements in agriculture and economy; they promote the investigation and management of public resources. (Paley [1802] 1972, 382; emphasis original)

Paley does not delve into scarcity as occasioned by moral failure in the last section of his chapter 26 (378–92), his reworking of Malthus's theodicy. Sumner ([1816] 1850) also ignores it although he does mention in passing that intemperance and extravagance lead to indigence. After all, Malthus, Paley, and Sumner belong to a school of thought that views social evil, including scarcity, as more of a natural rather than a moral evil.[4]

Part I of this book employs a teleological approach to understanding scarcity, but arrives at conclusions very different from a Malthusian theodicy. Even as it acknowledges a Newtonian order undergirding the natural world, participative theodicy nevertheless still concludes that unredressed scarcity stems from human failure. In starting from Aquinas's twofold order of the universe, participative theodicy sees scarcity as the outcome of the limiting formal perfections of secondary and instrumental causes. Given such a distinction, it is then possible to break down scarcity into its origins in natural and moral evil. Furthermore, understanding the dynamics behind scarcity allows one to examine the degree to which such a phenomenon is immutable. In particular, notice that this study's participative theodicy is similar to the Malthusian theodicies in tracing scarcity to physical evil. However, unlike these earlier works, it asserts that unaddressed scarcity is a moral evil in light of human beings' mode of operation as intelligent and free secondary causes (chapter 3). This has ramifications for policy and moral theory.

Seventh, there is divergence regarding accountability for want and destitution. Both theodicies acknowledge the reality and the long-standing experience of material deprivation as a perennial part of human history. For Malthus, the general, dismal human condition of want (in which population growth is always in tension with food supplies) is part of natural law and cannot be changed. Consequently, humans cannot be held accountable for such a collective condition. Malthus observes that human misery comes "from the inevitable laws of nature, and not from any original depravity in man" ([1798] 1960, 75).[5] Not so in the case of participative theodicy. Both material exiguity and sufficiency are conditioned on moral agency. Human beings can be held accountable for unaddressed, chronic material destitution, even those that are caused by physical evil. As seen in part I, human beings, as free secondary causes, need not act by necessity; they can choose to reach out to others and even sacrifice their own well-being in the process. As intelligent secondary causes, humans can discern not only the Creator's vision of material sufficiency for all, but they are also fully capable of acquiring the requisite practical knowledge to remedy the expected material scarcity that emerges from limiting formal perfections. In other words, in Malthusian theodicies, scarcity is inexorably due to nature; in participative theodicy, its interminable state is ultimately traceable to moral failure.

Eighth, Malthus, Paley, and Sumner are quite negative in their anthropology. As seen in the preceding chapter's assessment of the impact of scarcity, participative theodicy also holds the view that scarcity has a role in engendering striving and human effort as part of character formation. However, unlike Malthus, Paley, and Sumner, this study does not locate the need for such exertion in human indolence. The self-respect and pride that flow from personal accomplishments in life are sufficient motivators without need for the threat of pain and hunger to get people moving. Undergirding this latter, unflattering view is an even more fundamental premise—the inability of goodness to attract by virtue of its own power and desirability. Hence, Malthusian theodicies have a "compelled" theory of goodness in contrast to participative theodicy, in which goodness entices people with its own proper excellence. Another implication of Malthusian anthropology is the presumed orientation of people; they are primarily concerned with their personal comfort and welfare. In contrast, the anthropology of this study's theodicy requires that they be outwardly focused on the well-being of others and the whole community.

Ninth, all the preceding differences culminate in the policy implications of these respective theodicies. At first glance, they may seem to be similar given this study's repeated stress on the importance of deliberate economic transfers and the manner by which Malthus ends his *Essay:*

> Evil exists in the world not to create despair but activity. We are not patiently to submit to it, but to exert ourselves to avoid it. It is not only the interest but *the duty of every individual to use his utmost efforts to remove evil from himself and from as large a circle as he can influence,* and the more he exercises himself in this duty, the more wisely he directs his efforts, and the more successful these efforts are, the more he will probably improve and exalt his own mind and the more completely does he appear to fulfil the will of his Creator. (Malthus [1798] 1960, 143; emphasis added)

Malthus stresses the importance of deliberately and assiduously rectifying the evil experienced. This is as far as similarities go, however.

In calling for personal effort in this concluding paragraph from the *Essay,* Malthus refers only to personal advancement—the formation of the mind—and does not say anything at all about the possibility of social change or of the efficacy of personal action on social improvement. In fact, he is against socially mandated poor relief.[6] Participative theodicy takes a different position by asserting that interpersonal economic transfers are not supererogatory but are, in fact, duties that come from both general and distributive justice.

Malthus's position is not surprising given his underlying premises and the larger intellectual milieu of the *Essay* that grounded scientific findings on natural religion and its arguments based on design (LeMahieu 1979, 467–68).

> [B]y stipulating the final cause of his central principle, Malthus was not simply following the "new science" but was also aligning himself with the traditions of the Scottish Enlightenment. With the obvious exception of Hume, Scottish moralists constantly invoked the categories of teleological reasoning in their treatises. Indeed, the Aristotelean distinction between efficient and final cause helped shape *one of the Scots' most characteristic notions: the idea of unintended consequences.* . . . To [Adam] Smith, as to other Scottish theorists, *men's capacity to determine their own destiny was severely circumscribed.* (LeMahieu 1979, 468; emphasis added)

Of course, the most powerful and memorable articulation of such unintended consequences is Adam Smith's ([1776] 1937) invisible hand. Human effort cannot change universal and immutable definite effects from definite causes.

Malthus's principle of population, in which the human community always bumps up against its capacity to feed itself, is part of natural law. In fact, the long-run steady-state equilibrium is that of subsistence living. Consequently, ameliorative social policy is futile as scarcity is embedded within the workings of nature itself. In contrast, participative theodicy views Malthusian subsistence living as neither natural nor universal but the result of human failure and, therefore, subject to remedial action. The fundamental vision of divine providence, seen in its underlying metaphysical starting point, is that of material sufficiency and not a state of tenuous survival with barely sufficient food supplies for a burgeoning population (chapter 2, appendix 3). These are diametrically opposed views on the nature of God's gift in the order of creation: Malthus's precarious subsistence survival versus participative theodicy's conditional material sufficiency.

Such disparity in starting points naturally leads to differences in views regarding accountability for material shortages. For Malthus, the dismal state of a population growth that is inevitably always in tension with food supplies is the outcome of a deterministic process and nothing can be done to eliminate it.

> Malthus always went out of his way to antagonize all those who believed in the amelioration of social conditions. Every effort at the deliberate improvement of conditions was said to come to grief upon the irrepressible tide of human numbers. To relieve poverty directly by state subsidies or private charity, he liked to argue, was to remove the principal check against an increase in population, namely, the necessity for each person to fend for himself and to bear the full burden of his own improvidence. (Blaug 1985, 67)

Moreover, if there is a necessary instrumental value to evil in the overall scheme of God's rationality, then why should social policy alleviate, much less remove, such a constitutive element in the divine order of creation? Subsistence living and its accompanying hardships are intrinsic to the natural order, and no amount of social engineering will be able to change these.[7] In fact, eliminating these would be counterproductive, as people would slump back into torpor, inactivity, and lack of ambition (Malthus [1798] 1960, 129). Such a worldview implies a resigned, passive approach to dealing with poverty.[8] Thus, in the penultimate paragraph of his theodicy, Malthus contends that "it seems highly improbable that evil should ever be removed from the world" ([1798] 1960, 142).

Just like Malthus, Paley calls for a passive social policy. The evils, such as Malthus's principle of population, that excite human labor and exertion are integral to the natural order of creation. These universal laws can neither be removed nor changed. Moreover, to remove them, if at all possible, would be to cause more harm than good in view of their utility.

> [S]o long as bodily labour continues . . . to be necessary for the bulk of mankind, any dependency upon supernatural aid, by unfixing those motives which promote exertion, or by relaxing those habits which engender patient industry, might introduce negligence, inactivity, and disorder, in the most useful occupations of human life; and therefore deteriorate the condition of human life itself. (Paley [1802] 1972, 384)

These views hold equally for his position on wealth inequalities, which he believes are conducive to greater human effort and ambition. Paley's policy posture is most revealing when we examine his views regarding poverty alleviation.

> [E]ven the *acquirability* of civil advantages, ought, perhaps, in a considerable degree, to lie at the mercy of chance. Some would have all the virtuous rich, or, at least, removed from the evils of poverty. . . . And how such a society could be kept in subjection to government has not been shewn, for the poor, that is, they who seek their subsistence by constant manual labour, must still form the mass of the community; otherwise the necessary labour of life could not be carried on; the work would not be done, which the wants of mankind in a state of civilization, and still more in a state of refinement, require to be done. ([1802] 1972, 382–83; emphasis original)

Sumner views poverty similarly although he distinguishes it from its more severe form, which he calls indigence.

Poverty is often both honourable and comfortable; but indigence can only be pitiable, and is usually contemptible. *Poverty is not only the natural lot of many, in a well-constituted society, but is necessary, that a society may be well constituted.* ([1816] 1850, 224; emphasis added)

Both Paley and Sumner see poverty as necessary to a "well-constituted" society. This is entirely consistent with their views of indolence as the human person's natural state. Moreover, it falls within the intellectual climate of the eighteenth century, which sees inequality of wealth as a natural, rather than a moral, evil (Waterman 1991a, 75–76).

In contrast, participative theodicy views chronic material want as a failure of moral agency, whether through sins of omission or commission. It is an anomaly in the order of God's creation, and humans are entirely accountable for them. Poverty is neither natural nor immutable in God's order of creation. It is a disorder that requires an ameliorative response from free and intelligent activity. In the same way that humans often cause such a state of affairs, they are also fully capable, with the help of grace, of restoring or approximating the envisioned material sufficiency of divine providence.[9] Malthusian scarcity is not a necessary evil but is subject to both personal and systemic remedies. In contrast to Malthus's formation-of-mind explanation of scarcity, participative theodicy highlights the freedom of an active participation in God's governance.

Participative theodicy's call for re-centering our understanding of economic activity around universal basic-needs satisfaction complements economic scholarship on merit goods[10] and literature on the philosophy of economics.[11] Certain goods or services, such as education and school lunches, are deemed to be essential for human development and growth. They merit widespread distribution through the extra-market intervention of government or community institutions.[12]

Malthusian and participative theodicies have irreconcilable positions regarding social policy. The former's antipathy toward activist social policies is consistent with, and in fact stems from, its premises: the rejection of the "finality" of evil, the role reversal of good and evil, the inability of goodness to attract by virtue of its own power, a cosmology marred by an insufficient initial endowment, and an anthropology of lassitude and indolence. In contrast, participative theodicy's call for interpersonal transfers of economic resources flows from its belief that human agency is an instrument used by God to provide for our material needs.

Tenth, there is a marked difference in the emphasis of the state-of-probation theodicy compared to participative theodicy. In many ways, the aforesaid divergence on social policy can be traced to even more fundamental
differences with respect to the appropriation of God's gift of happiness.

> [I]f it be true that our ultimate, or our most permanent happiness will
> depend, not upon the temporary condition into which we are cast, but
> upon our behaviour in it; then is it a much more fit subject of *chance* than
> we usually allow or apprehend it to be, in what manner, the variety of
> external circumstances, which subsist in the human world, is distrib-
> uted amongst the individuals of the species. (Paley [1802] 1972, 389;
> emphasis original)

The school-of-probation approach presents attractive features in its arguments: the temporary nature of our current condition and the overriding importance of the manner by which we respond to undesirable states of affairs
(process rather than outcomes). But together with the promise of a higher
and a more permanent condition of happiness in the hereafter, such a down-
playing of outcomes runs the risk of breeding passive acquiescence to social
and personal circumstances that can be and ought to be rectified. Process is
definitely important given the formative nature of human life and experience. However, it cannot be overemphasized to the exclusion or at the expense of outcomes. After all, states of affairs do shape operations in subsequent rounds of activities either in facilitating or impeding the possibility of
succeeding processes. For example, people cannot grow in virtue and character during this period of probation if they die in infancy because of want
and destitution; hard-pressed people, completely preoccupied with earning a
livelihood, do not have the time for the enjoyment of culture and the formation of mind and spirit. Process is certainly important and takes precedence
over states of affairs. However, process in itself requires taking responsibility
for outcomes, if only for the sake of the next rounds of activities and subsequent processes.

Moreover, to view circumstances in human affairs as largely a matter of
chance is to forego personal and collective moral responsibility for social outcomes. Carried to extremes, the school of probation can spawn the very inactivity and torpor it seeks to avoid. After all, what is the point of exertion
and striving if social circumstances are a matter of chance? What value is
there to effort if outcomes are not all that essential? More important, all three

theodicies—Malthus's, Paley's, and Sumner's–suffer from the common flaw that *in correcting personal torpor and inactivity, they inadvertently engender collective torpor and inactivity over their communal good and social outcomes.* This is an unintended consequence of the necessary and instrumental evil they ascribe to the hardships precipitated by Malthus's principle of population.

In this regard, Brueggemann (1985) is correct when he argues that theodicy has usually been a purely speculative exercise in theology. He argues that God can be perceived only in human history, in unfolding social processes and human affairs. Thus, he concludes that evil is neither merely moral, natural, nor religious; it is also social. It is in the context of such a social evil that one could envision a theodicy that involves the need to change social processes. Observe how this social dimension is missing in Malthus, Paley, and Sumner. They view scarcity only as a catalyst to personal striving and effort, and not to collective reflection or joint action.

Part II of this book addresses Brueggemann's concerns as it examines a theodicy of scarcity within the context of human lives and communities. And as we have seen, Sacred Scripture does indeed arrive at a theodicy that is profoundly social. Moreover, both speculative philosophy and theology can be used effectively in discerning and getting to know more about God when dealing with questions of theodicy. Take part I of this book as an example. Despite its ahistorical speculative exercise using natural theology, it nonetheless arrives at a theodicy that is heavily social in its content and prescription. This stems from Aquinas's twofold order of the universe in which the internal order calls for individual parts (of the whole) to be oriented toward each other. Hence, the absence of a social dimension in Malthus, Paley, and Sumner has to do more with the premises they employ rather than the inadequacy of speculative thought itself.

Whether derived from natural theology (part I) or Sacred Scripture (part II), participative theodicy views scarcity as an occasion for both personal sacrifice and collective secondary causality that address the systemic causes of chronic scarcity. That God chooses to relieve scarcity not through a superfluity of goods but through human instrumentality implies the reliance of God on social change and social processes to compensate for nature's limiting formal perfections that engender material exiguity. Rectifying the consequences of limiting formal imperfections is a social process itself. The drama that God's in-breaking unleashes is that of a ceaseless systemic reform for the sake of the impoverished (Lohfink 1987).

This study's participative theodicy strikes a balance between life outcomes and processes. Within the economic sphere, outcomes are important because God's gift of material sufficiency as part of divine providence is not only intelligible and attainable but is, in fact, also the proximate end of human economic striving and effort. Thus, both outcomes and personal or collective behavior (process) converge in their concerns and goals: rectitude in economic conduct that stems from providing for each other's needs as envisioned by God. This point can be made even stronger when we move beyond natural theology and examine Sacred Scripture. Incarnational and instrumental righteousness is social and is not otherworldly in its concerns (chapter 6). It is interested in both outcomes and processes in the here and now. With regard to scarcity, God's gift is plenitude, not want or destitution.[13]

Eleventh, the Malthusian theodicies are Irenaean; participative theodicy is both Irenaean and Augustinian.[14] For Malthus, Paley, and Sumner, scarcity is innate to the natural order of creation as the catalyst that generates human effort; they do not examine scarcity as a consequence of moral failure. In fact, they do not subscribe to the view that the dismal state of humans is a punishment for sin. Paley is emphatic about this:

> Patience and composure under distress, affliction, and pain; a steadfast keeping up of our confidence in God, and of our reliance upon his final goodness, at the time when every thing present is adverse and discouraging; . . . a cordial desire for the happiness of others, even when we are deprived of our own: *these dispositions, which constitute, perhaps, the perfection of our moral nature, would not have found their proper office and object in a state of avowed retribution;* and in which, consequently, *endurance of evil would be only submission to punishment.* ([1802] 1972, 390–91; emphasis added)

Indeed, there would be no merit at all to human effort and exertion if scarcity had been meant to be a punishment for sin. Thus, both formation-of-mind and state-of-probation theodicies are Irenaean in that scarcity and its ensuing hardships serve as channels for personal growth and development.

Participative theodicy is both Augustinian and Irenaean. It is Augustinian because scarcity results from both natural and moral evils. Malthusian scarcity is a punishment that humans bring down upon themselves through their abuse of freedom. After all, definite effects flow from definite causes.

The persistence of unfilled material needs is indicative of personal and collective sinful economic behavior (such as excessive accumulation, inordinate consumption, or sloth) or sinful negligence (such as indifference or inaction on the part of those who are able to help), or both. Sins of commission or omission give rise to Malthusian scarcity. Participative theodicy is Augustinian because *chronic,* unaddressed want and destitution are not part of God's intended order of creation but are, in fact, moral disorders due to rational agents' failure to respond justly and lovingly to material exiguity.

Participative theodicy is also Irenaean because economic activity can occasion a person's growth and development in moral goodness, especially when it is sacrificial given the requisite resource transfers called for in order to effect material sufficiency for all. The economic agent grows in complete goodness given the virtues acquired through rational secondary causality.

Acknowledgment that scarcity also has roots in natural evil allows participative theodicy to be Irenaean just as it is Augustinian. Not all deviations from existential material sufficiency are occasioned by sin; some are due to limiting formal perfections such as chance and contingency in economic processes. Redressing these falls under the aegis of both justice and love. Just and supererogatory acts in response to the scarcity caused by natural evil make participative theodicy Irenaean because of their self-perfective, reflexive impact. Material shortages that arise from physical evil should not lead to chronic or severe want and destitution because humans, as intelligent and free secondary agents, are supposed to remedy such shortfalls, primarily through interpersonal economic transfers and assiduous work. It is through such participation in God's goodness, righteousness, and providence that economic agency is formative and perfective of the person. Such rational response is shaped by the demands of justice or by the utter gratuity of love, or both.

A final difference has to do with the natures of temporal existence and, in particular, of economic life. Given that its object is greater excellence through a more profound participation in divine perfections, participative theodicy can also be viewed as a "state of trial and school of virtue preparatory to a superior state of happiness" (Malthus [1798] 1960, 126). However, participative theodicy is not a state of probation in which conditions are intentionally made intolerable by divine design to prod effort and striving that are critical for character formation. This is a strongly negative view of God as a taskmaster in a divinely created domain of "moral discipline and probation."[15]

Scarcity has instrumental value as a catalyst for people's genuine participation as secondary causes in God's governance and providence. By design, the world already has all the requisite goods necessary for human growth in character. However, it comes with the added gift of conditionality. God effects a world of material sufficiency together with human work. Human failure causes the evil of chronic destitution. For the Malthusian theodicies, life is a proving ground; for participative theodicy, life is not a test, but is rather an invitation to "co-create" with God. The phenomenon of scarcity is not part of the natural order to probe our rectitude but serves as a stepping-stone to a deeper appropriation of God's perfections and activity. Since temporal existence is not a testing phase, the object of life is not to prove ourselves and our worthiness, but to share and communicate God's goodness in the here and now even as we await the even more perfect state of the hereafter. The present is more than just an ethics of response.[16] It is a real chance to leave a lasting mark for all eternity through our contributions to the building of the Kingdom of God. It is at its heart a gift of "sacramentality" in effecting (through a graced free and intelligent secondary causality) and conveying to the larger order of creation that which we signify: *imago dei* (image of God).

In summary, Malthusian and participative theodicies differ widely in their views on the nature of the person, economic agency, goodness, and evil. These disparities are most clearly reflected in their incompatible policy postures on poverty alleviation: passive acquiescence for the Malthusian approaches and active social change for participative theodicy.

CHAPTER 10

TOWARD A THEOLOGY OF ECONOMIC AGENCY

Why would a beneficent Creator permit a world of material want in which sustenance comes only after great effort and often with much attendant strife? This study has argued that the economic agency occasioned by scarcity is a venue for a manifold participation in God's perfections and activity.

Part I uses Aquinas's twofold order of the universe to trace material scarcity to various limiting formal perfections in the order of creation. Given the expected diversity in people's circumstances, the adequacy of human provisioning will vary widely from superfluity for some to frank poverty for others.[1] Only human beings, as free and intelligent secondary causes, are capable of correcting such destitution and effecting the envisioned material sufficiency for all as part of the goodness of God's threefold causality. Such economic agency is a sharing in God's goodness and providence, and it is perfective. It is scarcity that gives rise to economic activity, and it is scarcity that begets greater intensity to such partaking in divine excellence than would have otherwise been the case.

Part II examines insights from Sacred Scripture on this question. In the Old Testament, we find a necessary economic dimension to God's in-breaking in human history manifested concretely in YHWH's gift of the Promised Land to the Chosen People and in God's active solicitude for the poor. The economic statutes and ordinances that flow from such historicity become the means for God to proffer and elicit human participation in divine holiness, righteousness, and providence. Scarcity makes conformity to the Law that much more sacrificial, but that much more consequential as well.

Using Pauline theology, we can view God's imparted righteousness as both incarnational and instrumental in the New Testament. Economic agency in kingdom discipleship effects God's envisioned material sufficiency for all in a vibrant dynamic of community–cross–new creation (Hays 1996). Scarcity provides greater depth to such an unfolding, conferred probity in economic life.

This book offers a fivefold contribution to the scholarship on the intersection of theology, philosophy, and economics. First, it provides an alternative theodicy of scarcity that corrects some of the more problematic anthropology and notions of good and evil in the formulations of Malthus, Paley, and Sumner. Second, it demonstrates the use of metaphysics and Sacred Scripture as analytical tools in assessing the teleology of scarcity. Third, it explores what natural theology has to offer toward building a metaphysics of economics, an emerging area of interest for philosophers and economists alike. Fourth, it lays the groundwork for a theology of economic agency. Fifth, it offers metaphysical and scriptural validation for activist ameliorative social policies.

Reason and faith converge in their assessment of the role of scarcity in God's order of creation. Both Aquinas's metaphysics (part I) and Sacred Scripture (part II) separately arrive at the following five conclusions. First, God's envisioned order is one of sufficiency in human provisioning and not the destitution so commonly observed in history. A world of material exiguity by design simply goes against the goodness that stems from God's threefold causality as Formal, Efficient, and Final Cause (appendix 3). Both the Hebrew Scripture and the New Testament affirm abundant life not merely after the dawning of the New Jerusalem or of the *parousia,* but plenitude in the here and now (part II).

Second, such material sufficiency is merely conditional. It is contingent on human response and cooperation with the varied gifts they have received. In particular, adequate provisioning for all is effected only to the degree that material shortages stemming from the limiting formal perfections of creatures[2] are corrected by free and intelligent activity. Only humans are capable of such rational activity. In fact, within the economic sphere, due order in human provisioning is an effect that is proper to humans alone as self-directing secondary causes (chapter 3). Scripture highlights the centrality of justice and love if want and destitution are to be avoided or alleviated. Covenant election and kingdom discipleship call for personal self-sacrifice in interpersonal economic relations (part II). There would be no poor (Dt 15:4) if only humans take their obligations to each other seriously. Chronic Malthusian scarcity is prima facie evidence of moral failure whether by sins of omission or commission.

Third, God uses such proper economic agency to elicit human participation in divine perfections. Free and intelligent activity is the only venue through which humans attain the accidental perfections necessary for their growth in complete goodness, such as virtues. Such moral development manifests human beings partaking of divine excellence whereby people receive and then communicate God's goodness (part I). Sacred Scripture, on the other hand, establishes a necessary economic dimension to God's inbreaking in human history. Economic life is a sphere through which God bequeaths human beings a share in divine holiness and righteousness. This is evident in the Hebrew and the Christian Scriptures' formidable lists of precepts and counsels pertaining to rectitude in personal and collective economic conduct (part II).

Fourth, economic agency, by which humans grapple with the problem of scarcity, instantiates an array of divine benefactions: (1) a gift of partaking in God's perfections by receiving and then communicating God's goodness; (2) a gift of living in God's holiness and righteousness by treating others with the same measure of justice and love with which they themselves had been treated by God, to the extent possible; and (3) a gift of taking an active part in God's providence and governance whereby God provides for us through each other. This series of gifts is embedded within the conditionality appended to God's creation of a world that, by design, is merely provisional in its material sufficiency.

Fifth, it is scarcity, and not a world of unconditional material superfluity, that provides the venue for a more profound human participation in the aforesaid divine perfections and activity. The severity of scarcity conditions the degree of requisite effort and selflessness demanded of humans in reaching God's envisioned due order in the economic sphere. It is scarcity, not overflowing abundance, that gives us access to the heights of human perfection. Plenitude in virtue, in fellowship, in that which really matters for human flourishing, is occasioned by material scarcity. Ironically, material superfluity would have greatly impoverished us by impeding the signal gift of an even more meaningful appropriation of the excellence of God, especially as we supply for each other's lack at great cost and sacrifice to ourselves. Scarcity serves as a channel for finitude and temporality to blossom into transcendence.

These conclusions reflect both similarities and differences between this study and the theodicies of Malthus, Paley, and Sumner (chapter 9). Participative and Malthusian theodicies begin with an underlying due order that reflects the wisdom of the Creator; both ascribe an instrumental role to scarcity in the perfection of the human person. However, these theodicies differ in the more fundamental premises undergirding their anthropology and in their views on the nature of goodness and evil. Consequently, it is not surprising that participative and Malthusian theodicies hold irreconcilable policy postures.

This study's findings provide the foundational building blocks for a theology of economic agency. Economic activity has a real and consequential impact as a secondary cause in God's order of creation. Economic life is not merely an appendage to God's in-breaking but serves as a terrain for divine intervention in human history. Moreover, not only is economic agency perfective, but it is also a venue by which God provides for us through one another.[3] Indeed, the seemingly prosaic concerns of consumption, production, exchange, and distribution have a place in God's economy of salvation as a fertile channel for sharing in divine perfections and activity. After all, ours is a God with a proven track record of an active and engaged interest in providing plenitude, both spiritual and material, in the here and now.

The contributions of this book are primarily theological rather than economic. Nonetheless, economists have something to take away from the results of this research: a reminder of their provenance as a discipline. Pullen (1981, 52) laments that Malthus's *Essay* is viewed solely as an economic treatise because beneath the principle of population is an even deeper and more significant concern—the question of human perfectibility. Malthus's economic thought is situated within the much wider issue of human progress. Unfortunately, this critical larger backdrop is lost to subsequent commentators.

Scholars have long deplored the direction in which the discipline of economics moved: from a classical political economy with a breadth of analytical vision to a neoclassical economic analysis that is narrowly focused and often engaged in formalistic exercises.[4] Harvey-Phillips believes that the first edition of Malthus's *Essay* with its final two chapters on theodicy marks this turning point:

> The *Essay* of 1798 was very much in the eighteenth-century tradition, in which it was de rigeur to couch a scientific treatise within some sort of philosophic *systeme*. . . . Malthus' system was his theodicy. . . . Its subsequent editions are, however, notably different from the first, if only in the absence of this theodicy. . . . A wedge was thus firmly driven between the eighteenth and nineteenth centuries' approaches to political economy as science. In effect, political economy now became "positive" in the philosophical sense, with any potential metaphysical questions remaining implicit in its axioms. The theological confusion that Malthus seems to have found himself in sometime between 1798 and 1806 would appear to have had, therefore, important ramifications for the subsequent development of the science of economics. (1984, 607–8)

In revisiting Malthus's original question and his theodicy, I maintain that classical political economy and neoclassical economic analysis are not mutually exclusive and can, in fact, richly benefit from each other. The powerful analytical advances achieved in neoclassical economic thought can be wedded to classical political economy's expansive conceptual framework. It is time to situate rigorous economic analysis and policy formulation back within the ambit of a broader interdisciplinary approach. There is much that economics, philosophy, and theology can add to each other.[5] However, great care must be taken in laying the theological and philosophical foundations of economics since underlying premises do have wide and profound ramifications for policy proposals that flow from such economics. Note, for example, how theological and philosophical views shaped the politics and policies of nineteenth-century Christian political economists (Waterman 1983b, 1991a). Or observe the diametrically opposed social implications of the Malthusian theodicies and this book's participative account of scarcity. Getting the economics right is critical, but so is the philosophy and theology undergirding such economics.

A final word for economists. Economics as a task has revolved around Robbins's ([1932] 1952) classic formulation: allocating scarce resources to their best competing uses. Given the findings of this study, I propose an amendment to this long-standing, widely accepted definition: *Economics deals*

with the allocation of scarce resources to their best competing uses with an eye to-
ward effecting sufficiency in material provisioning for all. Mainstream, neoclassical economists are averse to setting goals as part of their profession. They
view their work as a purely "engineering" charge of finding the optimal set of
means to employ for given ends; they absolve themselves of responsibility for
critically evaluating the larger, and often clashing, goals pursued in economic
life. This study suggests a rethinking of such a self-imposed restriction. Economics as a discipline is not merely about allocative efficiency, it is also about
the much larger endeavor of partaking in God's ongoing providential act of
sustaining humans, the only creatures created for their own sake. Whether
they like it or not, economists produce unintended consequences in people's
economic behavior through their analytical discourse. *Homo oeconomicus*, as
a purely calculating economic agent that optimizes a utility set of preferences, detaches economic agency from its much wider context of sharing in
God's perfections and creative act.

Finally, there are profound possibilities embedded within economic life
as a participative phenomenon.

> [T]he consequence of this relation [of participation], which is the fruit
> and culmination of all the prior communications of God, is not merely
> to give the creature a created participation of God, but *to unite him to God*
> *Himself as the internal principle and immediate term of his activity. The crea-*
> *ture here sees and rests in God Himself.* (J. Wright 1957, 71; emphasis
> added)

This entire book has been about the discovery of one proffered gift after another—the gift of partaking in God's goodness (part I), the gift of sharing in
God's holiness and righteousness (part II), and the gift of taking an active
part in God's providence and governance (parts I and II). It turns out that
even this benefaction of a multidimensional participation is itself merely the
prelude to yet an even greater gift: rest in and union with God. Indeed, there
seems to be no end to God's goodness, no limits to God's initiatives on behalf
of human beings.

TYPOLOGY OF SCARCITY

Scarcity pertains to quantity, one of the nine accidents in the ten Aristotelean categories.[1] There are differing views on what constitutes a condition of scarcity. For this study, I make two nested sets of distinctions. In the first set, there is a difference between scarcity as the need to allocate that comes with the corporeal feature of human nature (existential, formal, or antecedent scarcity) and the scarcity that follows in the wake of moral agency (consequent scarcity). Within the latter, I propose a second round of differentiation between scarcity as destitution and great want (Malthusian scarcity) and scarcity as nonessential wants outstripping supply (frictional scarcity).

FORMAL (ANTECEDENT, EXISTENTIAL) SCARCITY

Human beings are corporeal and temporal by nature. As corporeal beings, they require the use and consumption of material inputs that come from the finite fruits of the earth. As temporal beings, they cannot be occupied simultaneously in an unlimited number of activities. Thus, human beings face a constant multifaceted need to allocate—choosing between competing activities they could undertake and between alternative goods or services they could produce, procure, or consume in pursuit of their ends. Put in another way, humans face a surfeit of goals and of alternative means to reach their chosen ends. They simply have to make choices in allocating their time and limited resources.[2] Understood as the need to allocate, scarcity is part of the human condition; it comes with human nature and could thus be appropriately called antecedent or existential scarcity. Meeks (1995, 35) calls this "formal" scarcity.

Robbins defines economics as a "science which studies human behaviour as a relationship between ends and scarce means with alternative uses" ([1932] 1952, 16). Two constitutive elements are implicit in this view: supplies are limited and there are manifold uses for the resource in question. Both conditions must be present. It is commonly believed that material shortfalls are due only to limits in the available stock of a good. While a necessary condition, finitude is not sufficient to constitute scarcity because there also has to be rival uses or users (and therefore competing demand) for the resource. For example, prior to the mid-nineteenth century, crude oil was deemed to be more of a nuisance than an object of value. Even as it was finite in supply, there was not much use for crude oil, and consequently, no significant demand for the resource; it was not subject to competition. Of course, the key change that occurred since then was the discovery of crude oil's myriad uses in industrial society.

Even if there are competing uses, the commodity must come in a quantity so limited as to be less than or just about equal to demand. In a situation in which supply vastly exceeds demand, scarcity does not arise, as there is still no need to allocate. Thus, one could consider sea-water to be a free good; it has alternative uses, but its available supplies far exceed the demand for it. Long before our current sensitivity to the ecological damage wrought by agricultural and industrial production, earlier editions of introductory economics textbooks (e.g., Samuelson 1955, 418, 429) cite air and water as examples of free goods not subject to scarcity. Today, we are only too painfully aware of the need to conserve dwindling supplies of clean air and fresh water.

Given Robbins's definition of economics, one can make the following claims:

1. Scarcity gives rise to economics as an allocative task. Dealing with scarcity is the *raison d'etre* of economics both as an academic discipline and as a human activity.[3]

2. The existence of an opportunity cost is both a necessary and sufficient condition for the phenomenon of scarcity. It is defined as the foregone alternatives to the choice one makes.[4] An opportunity cost arises only if the object of choice has multiple competing, alternative uses that exceed available supplies.

Put in more precise terms, formal (antecedent, existential) scarcity is a state of affairs that describes the unavoidable opportunity costs that humans incur in choosing between competing means to achieve their ends. Such allocative decisions between alternatives have to be made because of the temporal and corporeal constitution of human beings. Formal (antecedent, existential) scarcity follows from human nature itself. The need to allocate per se is a predetermined condition that comes with human nature.[5]

CONSEQUENT SCARCITY

In contrast to existential scarcity, which stems from God's creative act, consequent scarcity pertains to the aftermath of human allocative choices. For heuristic purposes, it would also be useful for us to distinguish two qualitatively distinct conditions of consequent scarcity.

Malthusian scarcity: as deprivation or poverty

Pemberton and Finn (1985, 123–25) point out another, even more popular, usage of the term *scarcity*. Besides economists' definition of having to ration means for competing uses, most people view scarcity as a state of destitution in which essential needs go unfilled and people live in indigence, unable to secure the means for at least a decent, if not a full, human life. Obviously, this latter view is more restrictive. A key difference between the two notions is that most economists do not distinguish pressing needs from superfluous wants.[6] Thus, as Pemberton and Finn observe, many economists see no difference between family A's lack of food and family B's inability to buy a yacht; both are deemed to be similar instances of unfilled demand. Neoclassical economics avoids separating needs from wants since this requires normative judgment and a philosophical commitment to a particular notion of the good, thus violating the discipline's self-professed claim that it is a purely scientific enterprise of positive description. Since human want and poverty are severe conditions of scarcity that signal a major disorder, I refer to this state of affairs as Malthusian scarcity. We could view this as a situation of unfilled needs; human needs exceed available supplies.

Frictional scarcity: as non-life-threatening unfilled demand

Ohrenstein and Gordon (1992, 47–48) distinguish between two kinds of scarcity in Talmudic literature: *Batzoret* and *Kafna*. *Batzoret* is an anticipated shortfall that occurs in the normal course of a market's operations, such as occasional minor interruptions in the distribution system. *Kafna,* on the other hand, is the more serious variant in which there is a severe disruption in aggregate supplies. In both cases, shortfalls occur because of the vagaries of the market.

In the course of human allocative choices, there are expected instances in which not all demand can be satisfied, given the imperfections in the normal workings of the market.[7] Human finitude and defectibility and the vagaries of economic processes often cause disparities between demand and supply even if there are enough resources available. To differentiate these cases from the more exigent variant of Malthusian destitution, I posit a second category of consequent scarcity: as non-life-threatening unfilled demand. This can be properly called frictional scarcity because it emerges from foreseen imperfections or uncertainties in regular market operations. Needless to say, Malthusian scarcity is more severe compared to frictional scarcity. In the latter, demand exceeds available supplies; however, the unfilled demand is for nonessential wants. In the former, demand greatly exceeds supplies; moreover, the unmet needs encompass basic goods that are vital for survival, basic health, and human flourishing.[8] Thus, one can distinguish frictional from Malthusian scarcity by following Pemberton and Finn's earlier distinction between essential human needs versus mere superfluous wants.

These categories are not mutually exclusive. In fact, they are concentric subsets of ever-increasing degrees of exiguity. Existential scarcity is the broadest category. After all, it is the need to allocate by the nature of things that lead to either Malthusian or frictional scarcity. Malthusian scarcity can be viewed as a subset of frictional scarcity in terms of general unmet demand. Consequent scarcity is properly the subject matter of this study's theodicy. Why does a benevolent Creator permit the possibility of material want in human life?

GOODNESS RECEIVED, GOODNESS COMMUNICATED

NATURE OF GOODNESS

Two questions immediately come to mind as we grapple with a theodicy of scarcity. First, why does the paucity of material goods constitute an evil? Second, since Christian thought views evil as a mere absence of the good (Augustine 1953), what is the precise nature of the goodness that is subject to such privation? A theodicy requires that we first establish the goodness that will serve as a datum, the larger backdrop against which evil is to be perceived, appraised, and understood. Thus, it is necessary to examine the nature of creaturely goodness: what it is, how it evolves, and in what manner it is manifest in beings. It is a goodness that flows from the threefold causality of God as Formal, Efficient, and Final Cause.

Uncreated goodness

Aristotle and Aquinas define the *good* as the perfection that all things seek. Simply put, it is the completion creatures desire since it has the "formal character of an end" (SCG III, 20, #1–2). In fact, nothing can be said to resist divine government precisely because all things tend toward that which is good (ST I, 103, a.8, reply).

Goodness has a self-diffusive quality and confers its own goodness where there was none before (ST I, 19, a.2, reply); "it is a creative principle which brings others into being by letting them share in goodness" (te Velde 1995, 21). The unique nature of goodness in God is best appreciated by understanding how goodness comes about in creatures.

Participation is the sole means by which creatures attain goodness. Note, for example, the manner by which they come into being. Existence is the highest perfection of creatures *qua* creatures. To be, to exist, to possess "beingness," is the full actualization of their potency as creatures. To exist, therefore, is to be in act.

There is a stark contrast between the existence of God and of creatures. God has necessary existence by the very nature of God as a self-subsisting being. A contingent existence entails a necessary dependence on something or someone, and such an attribute goes against what we would properly call God. Thus, to be, to exist—*esse*—is the very essence of God. More accurately said, essence and existence are identical in God, *Ipsum Esse Subsistens* (SCG I, 22–23). To be God is to exist necessarily.

Creatures, on the other hand, have contingent existence. To exist is not an indispensable part of their nature; their essence and existence are distinct. Thus, their conditional existence has a provenance external to them, ultimately from a source that is absolute in existence. Since necessary existence can be found only in God, all existent beings must, therefore, derive their existence from God, the one source of *esse*. Creaturely *esse*, therefore, is merely a participation of God's *esse;* it is a derived existence (SCG II, 15; ST I, 3, a.4; I, 44, a.1).

Since existence, the highest perfection of beings *qua* creatures, merely partakes of *Ipsum Esse Subsistens,* all other creaturely perfections must necessarily be derivative themselves, drawn from the perfections of God (ST I, 3–11). Thus, participation is the unavoidable grammar in understanding how goodness comes about in creatures both in the nature of their being and in the mode of their operations.

The goodness given to creation is for the sake of the creatures themselves since divine perfection is already complete by God's nature. Thus, creation and the goodness that is proffered are not necessary by nature but are entirely gratuitous and unmerited on the part of recipients (SCG III, 64, #4 and

#9). Moreover, it is a goodness offered forever as God is immutable; once willed by God, it will continue to be willed in existence (*De potentia* V, 4; J. Wright 1957, 49).

Created goodness

The identity of essence and existence in *Ipsum Esse Subsistens* reflects simplicity as another distinctive quality of God (*De potentia* III, 7). There is no composition in God since God is Pure Act with no tinge of potency. Thus, God's goodness is complete and immutable. In contrast, created beings are composed and are subject to further development (SCG III, 20, #6; ST I-II, 18, a.1). The fullness of their goodness increases or decreases depending on the extent to which they actualize their potency.

Te Velde (1995, 26–30) provides a succinct description of the threefold manner by which goodness is revealed in and by creatures. Created beings' complete goodness has three constitutive elements, each of which is merely participated: (1) *substantial goodness,* by virtue of their being, (2) *transcendent goodness,* by virtue of a relation, and (3) *accidental goodness,* by virtue of added properties. We are primarily interested in accidental goodness for purposes of our study, but first I offer a quick description of substantial and transcendent goodness.

Esse, even if derived, confers goodness to the being (SCG III, 19). As already observed, existence is the highest perfection of creatures *qua* creatures, their most fundamental participation in God's perfection. Thus, there is an intrinsic goodness that comes merely with the act of existence even before any other activity on the part of creatures. This is called substantial or essential goodness because *esse* is inseparable from essence, even as they are necessarily distinct from each other in creatures. In other words, existence is conferred on creatures through their essence; after all, existent beings must simultaneously have an essence through which their existence is actualized. Substantial goodness is intrinsic to the creature's being; it is the goodness conferred by *esse,* even if merely derived. This essential goodness is not subject to further growth or development because a thing either exists or not; it either has essential goodness or not. Thus, it is called ontological (existential, substantial) goodness and is considered to be the primary perfection of creatures.

Substantial goodness, and all other goodness for that matter, is a mere likeness of divine goodness because God does not communicate the very essence of God itself, as in the case of the processions in the Blessed Trinity. Thus, we can speak only of an analogical goodness. Nevertheless, even as it is merely a likeness, it is real and intrinsic because the goodness that comes with existence (God as Exemplary Cause) is effected in creatures by God as Efficient Cause. The immanent form of human beings, even while a mere "likeness of the highest good," is neither a mere logical nor conceptual participation in God but is a real, created participation (te Velde 1995, 26).

Transcendent goodness pertains to the creature's ontological relation to the ultimate end in God. A good that is oriented to the final end takes on the character of an end itself (te Velde 1995, 29). Such participation in the goodness of the end is descriptive of created beings insofar as they are directed to this ultimate end. Since every being seeks and then rests in its own proper good (ST I, 19, a.2, reply), to exist is to be oriented toward God as ultimate end.

> Insofar as the form and perfection of the effect is a likeness of its cause, the effect, in seeking its perfection, turns to its cause and seeks to become as alike to it as possible [ST I, 6, a.1, reply]. In other words, all creatures seek to be united with their origin, since every thing achieves its own perfection in an assimilation with its origin. (te Velde 1995, 33–34)

Thus, creatures' existence (from nothingness) brings with it an orientation to their source as final end; transcendent goodness is implied in substantial goodness. Note, for example, how scholars refer only to ontological (substantial and transcendent) and moral (accidental) goodness when referring to human beings (Stump and Kretzmann 1988; Gallagher 1994; Klubertanz 1967, 465). Ontological goodness[1] is a goodness only in the qualified sense, as it uses an analogy of participation (ST I, 6). In contrast, non-ontological goodness (ST I, 5, a.1, ad.1) pertains to the virtuous, the pleasurable, and the useful (ST I, 5, a.6, ad.3). Put in another way, the first perfection of human beings is in the form they receive, that which makes them what they are. Their ultimate perfection, however, consists of their operation and the term of such activity (SCG III, 64, #11; III, 20); it is the goodness that stems from the actualization of the potency they received in their form.

The complete goodness of created beings is comprised of all three kinds of goodness. For example, human beings are not called "good" on the basis of their existence alone even if the latter is ontological goodness. To be properly good, they must also have the additional perfection of being virtuous. Thus, accidental perfections are central to our study. Before we deal with this third type of goodness, it is necessary to establish first the terrain in which such accidental goodness is sought and attained: the twofold order of the universe.

TWOFOLD ORDER OF THE UNIVERSE

God as Final Cause

All creatures tend to an end and are inclined toward their own proper good as they seek completion and perfection (ST I, 19, a.2, reply). However, creaturely perfections are a mere likeness of those found in God. Since all creatures merely participate in the goodness of God, only God's goodness is perfect and complete. Only the absolute goodness of God provides the finality that brings to an end the search for a good that fills and completes. Only in God do we find Pure Act without any trace of potency left to be actualized, an unparticipated goodness that is self-subsisting. Thus, we are led to two inferences. First, God is the Final Cause, the end of all creation (SCG III, 20, #1; ST I, 6, a.1; I, 44, a.4; I, 65, a.2; J. Wright 1957, 64-65).

> For since every operation is for the sake of some good, real or apparent; and nothing is good either really or apparently, except in as far as it participates in a likeness to the Supreme Good, which is God; it follows that God Himself is the cause of every operation as its end. (ST I, 105, a.5, reply)

Second, by virtue of being merely derivative, every created good has the character of an end only in the measure it is oriented to God as the ultimate end (te Velde 1995, 30). Both claims form the bases for the constitutive characteristics Aquinas ascribes to the order of creation.

J. Wright (1957, 1967) describes a twofold order in Aquinas's view of the universe. First, creation (taken as a single entity) tends toward God for completion and perfection; it attains its ultimate end only as a unity, as a whole. This is properly called the external order of the universe since God as the ultimate end is extrinsic to the universe. Second, creatures constituting the universe are oriented toward each other with the larger goal of bringing the entire unity to its external end in God, their common term. In other words, the internal order of the universe is about parts (of the whole) acting on each other to bring the whole to its ultimate perfection. The universe's external order to God defines the order of parts to each other (*De veritate* q.5, a.1, ad.9; J. Wright 1957, 31). The internal order of the whole (parts to each other) is a function of the whole's orientation to an end external to itself (*De veritate* q.5, a.3). Besides, it is only on account of the external order that the internal order exists in the first place (J. Wright 1957, 5). Observe the dual (internal and external) dynamic movement of this twofold order.[2]

The interdependence of the two orders stems from their inseparability and from their mutual reinforcement. On the one hand, the whole provides the term for the internal order (of parts to each other). On the other hand, the whole's final end is actualized only in the measure that its parts, by being ordered to each other, bring the whole to this external term. Thus, J. Wright describes the universe simply as "the whole ensemble of created beings ordered to one another and to God" (1957, v).

The twofold order embedded in the metaphysical structure of creation bears an intrinsic dynamism. We can infer from such a structure (1) a potency, an incompleteness calling for perfection, (2) a yet–to be–attained end, and (3) a necessary movement from the former to the latter, from potency to act. This corresponds to the operation of God's threefold causality whereby the goodness conferred on created beings via God as Exemplary and Efficient Cause moves forward, grows, develops, and finds completion in God as Final Cause.[3] Thus, we can say that the *telos* (the end) of creaturely existence is activity, and the *telos* of such created action is to move toward God as end; existence is meant for activity, and activity for completion (J. Wright 1957, 189). Such dynamism is true both for the whole and its parts, corresponding to the external and internal halves of this order. Note that the whole and its parts are steeped in the goodness of God's causality through all stages: from the reception of an effected likeness to such similitude's completion in its end. Thus, God's threefold causality is evident in every agent (ST I, 105, a.5, reply).

Role of parts

The whole and its parts replicate the goodness of God. Such similitude includes the self-diffusive character of divine goodness. Of course, the primary example of such diffusiveness is creation itself as an outcome of God's threefold causality.

This self-diffusive quality of goodness is particularly important for the second half of the dual order of the universe. In fact, this diffusiveness is the impetus for the dynamic movement within the internal order. The order of parts to each other is the action of parts on each other to effect (but only as secondary or instrumental causes) and actualize the divine likeness in each other. In other words, parts are said to be ordered toward each other because they are meant to help one another bring about and reveal the fullness of their similitude to God's goodness.[4] It is precisely in such activity of parts within the internal order that the whole is moved toward its external end in God.

That the goodness of many is better than the goodness of one is another rationale given for the self-diffusive character of goodness (J. Wright 1957, 44; ST I-II, 113, a.9, ad.2). The fullness of a creature's goodness requires, as a necessary condition, that it communicate such goodness beyond itself to the fullest extent possible according to its mode of being and operation. Moreover, it is also in such self-diffusiveness that the individual part actualizes its own likeness to God and attains the end proper to itself.

A number of implications must be underscored. First, in actualizing the divine likeness both in itself and in others, the individual part in effect becomes a "principle of goodness" to those around it and within the whole (J. Wright 1957, 44). Second, since all creatures tend toward God (Final End), their individual activities find commonality in the same ultimate end pursued. Individual activity, therefore, is merely part of a much larger common enterprise and contributes to the whole's attainment of its common term.

These two implications provide arguments for why the good of the individual part and of the whole, far from being at odds with each other, are actually necessary conditions to each other; they are distinct, but inseparable.

> It is in this second moment, the moment of created activity, that the universe achieves the unity, intelligibility, and goodness which are proper to it. For when a being by its activity tends toward God as the common good of all, it necessarily shares its own goodness with all others according to its capacity to give and theirs to receive. Hence, *the relations of all parts of the universe to one another, which by reason of individual existence are only dispositions to act and be acted on, are made actual in the common tendency to God in created action*. . . . For by reason of this order, what belongs to anyone belongs to all, and what belongs to all belongs to each according to the capacity of everyone to give and to receive. (J. Wright 1957, 189–90; emphasis added)

The pursuit of their common end provides the occasion for parts to actualize their relations to each other.

Third, the twofold order of the universe cannot be viewed as a mere juxtaposition of the whole interacting in an unmediated fashion with its disparate, constituent parts. For example, individual human beings do not directly interact with an abstract universe. Instead, as individuals, they contribute to and derive benefits from the "whole" (universe, community, humanity) via intermediate human partnerships and associations to which they belong (whether freely or by nature), such as their immediate family, local neighborhood, church, school, professional associations, nation, and so on. At the very least, people are born into a particular household and a specific culture that nurture and provide an environment for their growth and development. By necessity or by choice, people associate with other human beings in their activities. In addition to such cooperative ventures, humans engage each other across manifold spheres of human life: economic, political, religious, and cultural. These, too, illustrate the collaborative nature and setting of most rational activities. All these stem from the multiplicity of particular orders in divine creation.

> From each cause there results a certain order to its effects, since every cause is a principle; and so, according to the multiplicity of orders, subjected one to the other, as cause is subjected to cause. Wherefore a higher cause is not subjected to a cause of a lower order; but conversely. An example of this may be seen in human affairs. On the father of a family depends the order of the household; which order is contained in the order of the city; which order again depends on the ruler of the city; while this last order depends on that of the king, by whom the whole kingdom is ordered. (ST I, 105, a.6, reply)

It is through these *particular orders* that the dual order of the universe unfolds and the accidental goodness of its parts is attained.

ACCIDENTAL GOODNESS

Nature of accidental goodness

Accidental goodness comes from the additional perfections that creatures gain according to their mode of being and operation as they move from potency to act. Human beings, for example, grow more virtuous or vicious depending on their use or abuse of their rational faculties.[5] This category of goodness is called secondary perfection, in contrast to the primary perfection of substantial goodness. Note, however, that the use of "accidental" or "secondary" to describe this category does not mean an inferior or an expendable kind of goodness. On the contrary, these are indispensable and are in fact *the* determining kind of perfection when referring to the fullness of creaturely goodness.

An accident is a form that is external to the essence of the subject. It is a universal that is participated in by the subject in a particular way. For example, redness is a universal, accidental form. This particular red apple (a particular subject) participates in "redness" as a universal. Thus, the redness of this particular apple is an accidental perfection. It is merely accidental because it is not in the essence of apples to be red. Hence, in speaking of "accidental" or "secondary" goodness, we are referring to extra-essential perfections (te Velde 1995, 37). Substantial goodness is called the first perfection because it is the first good that can be said of creatures. Other perfections are called secondary not because they are of lesser quality but because they are posterior to existence. The critical feature we have to highlight for our study is the dynamics inherent to accidental goodness. Again, this property is best understood by contrasting divine and human attributes.

As we have already seen, the very essence of God is sheer perfection, a complete goodness. Because of such intrinsic fullness and perfection, God is immutable and has no need for other creatures or for additional, perfective properties. The very essence of God is absolute, complete goodness—Pure Act without any potency. In contrast, human beings do not enjoy the simplicity of God but are beings composed of matter and form needing to be actualized. Their complete goodness entails a movement from potency to act. This requisite growth and development call for change, and more important, activity. The manner of such further growth lies in the supervenient qualities that build on the perfection that comes with existence. Thus, we gain "additional perfection[s] grounded in accidental principles," a participated goodness via the "accidental sphere of perfections that are added to the essence" (te Velde 1995, 28). Again, it must be emphasized that these requisite changes in the subject (human beings) are called "accidental" not because they are dispensable but because they are changes in the degree of, or variations in, qualities without changing the substance or essence of the subject itself. Accidental goodness is about taking on added properties, and taking on such added properties implies activity. Accidental goodness reflects in a determinate way some particular aspect of perfection in the First Cause as Exemplar.

Accidental forms admit differences in degrees of perfection,[6] and it is this variation in additional perfections that make human beings unique relative to each other. We know from the phenomenon of the *One and the Many* that besides having a variety of creatures, there are also varying grades of perfection in order to better reflect the goodness of God (ST I, 47, a.1, reply). Since they belong to the same species, human beings share the same ontological goodness. Hence, variations in individual perfection can come about only from differences in accidental perfections, especially moral goodness.[7]

Accidental goodness highlights the developmental character of human beings. Over and above their participation in the perfection that comes with existence, there is a need to grow and develop further according to their nature and mode of operation. Of course, since the most distinctive qualities that human beings enjoy relative to other creatures are their intelligence and free will, we expect rational activity to be the key venue by which humans gain their requisite additional perfections.

Central importance of activity

Any being's act is by its nature perfective because of the ontological ordination of all beings to God as Final Cause. Creaturely existence (*esse*) is for the sake of being in act. Thus, there is an inherent dynamism to the order of creation.

> When the creature acts, since through action under the movement of God it deepens its relation to the end, it participates more fully in divine goodness and is thereby perfected. (J. Wright 1957, 66)

Besides serving as the venue by which complete goodness and fullness of being are attained, activity is important for its other properties. In particular, activity communicates (to others) God's goodness in the external effects of such operation; moreover, humans also receive the goodness of God through the reflexive nature of such acts. This is the interior, perfective impact of activity on its agent in addition to its external effects.[8] Activity is constitutive, indeed determinative, of the agent's accidental perfections.

Activity as communicating God's goodness

Unlike some creatures that imitate God's goodness only by similitude, human beings do so through their activity. In fact, human beings receive and communicate God's goodness through their intelligent activity. Parallel to the earlier description of the three components of complete creaturely goodness, the fullness of beings is comprised of (1) their act of existence and (2) their operations.[9] The act of existence, considered as a perfection, is complete in itself because a thing either exists or not. In contrast, the need for activity signifies incompletion, and the object of such operations points to additional perfections desired or required.[10] Put in another way, the human's complete goodness is comprised of its goodness from existing (ontological goodness) and its goodness drawn from accidental perfections from its mode of being and operations, especially moral goodness (SCG III, 20). Thus, the degree of goodness achieved by human beings is a function of how well they actualize the potency of their human nature (particularly moral goodness). They attain the fullness of their act in resembling God in their existence and in their operations.[11] In so doing, they communicate God's goodness. After all, acting is fundamentally the communication of "that by which an agent is in act" (J. Wright 1957, 97; see also *De potentia* II, 1).

In summary, creatures do not possess goodness in the same mode and degree that God does (in an absolute manner as part of divine essence), but only do so in a participated manner according to the measure of their nature and their mode of operation (SCG III, 20, #2). For humans, the most distinctive and the highest powers they have are their rational faculties. Hence, one would expect human participation to be most apparent in free and intelligent action. Activity is not merely the manner by which humans imitate God's goodness, it is also reflective of their distinctive mode of operation.

Wide-ranging effects of activity

Creatures are meant not only to resemble God in their particular perfections but also to share these with others (J. Wright 1957, 190). All perfections come from God according to their participation by similitude in God. In this, special mention must be made of human beings' similitude to God in their created activity and how they can deliberately choose to share their perfections with others, just as God's goodness is self-diffusive.

The *telos* of existence is activity; the *telos* of activity is to move toward God as end. The perfective nature of created activity is manifested in manifold ways (such as communicating the goodness of God and bringing about accidental perfections and complete goodness) and works simultaneously at different levels—for the whole and its parts.

> It is in . . . created activity that the universe achieves the unity, intelligibility, and goodness which are proper to it. For when a being by its activity tends toward God as the common good of all, it necessarily shares its own goodness with all others, according to its capacity to give and theirs to receive. Hence the relations of all the parts of the universe to one another, which by reason of individual existence are only dispositions to act and be acted on, are made actual in the common tendency to God in created action. All the individual goods of particular beings are united into the supreme created common good of all, the good of the order of the universe. (J. Wright 1957, 189–90)

Creatures perfect other creatures in acting on them. After all, the individual and the common good, while distinct, are inseparable and are necessary conditions to each other. Thus, the twofold order of the universe is ultimately dependent on the particular activities of its individual parts. The greater the perfection of the parts, the more significant and extensive is the impact of their activity, as in the case of intelligent creatures.

The full actuality of human beings is in their resting in God and in the full approximation of their likeness in God, to the extent possible. Such actuality is attained only via activity. Since economic life is part of that activity it must operate in the context of the *telos* of the person's end in God. Like all other particular orders, the conduct of economic life must communicate the goodness of God and bring the person toward God.

Activity as transcending one's limitations

Operations highlight human finitude in two dimensions. First, as already mentioned, the need for operations implies composition. After all, potency is actualized only through activity. Secondly, operations are the only means by which creatures are able to reach out to other creatures.

> Why is it that for any creature 'being' differs from 'operating'? This difference has its basis in the finiteness of a creature's being. In every crea-

ture the being is enclosed within the limits of a determinate nature. But through its operation a creature extends to what lies outside the limits of its nature. (te Velde 1995, 42)

It is through their operations that substances interact with each other.[12] Activity is a unitive and ordering principle. The internal order of the universe is the proper effect of the activity of secondary causes. Indeed, one can even say that "the order uniting the universe is an order of activity" (J. Wright 1957, 96).

Operations are important not only for individual perfection but also for attaining the twofold order of the universe, which requires that parts (of the whole) assist each other to bring out their similitude to God's goodness. The internal order is constituted by operations, by such mutual assistance. Thus, in addition to reaching out to other substances, creatures change the environment around them through their activity. Commenting on ST I, 5, a.4 and I, 115, a.1 and a.2, Jean Porter remarks:

> [W]henever anything exercises efficient causality, it communicates something of its intelligible being by introducing a new quality, or a new ordering, into the configuration of events surrounding it. Hence, efficient causality can be spoken of as purposive, since any act of efficient causality is also necessarily an act of formal and final causality. (1990, 41)

Gilby, in describing causality, describes its impact as follows:

> A cause is thus a thing exerting *itself*, having its influence or imposing its character on the world. Ideally, the form it induces in things is its own form. (1969, vol. 3, appendix 2, 102; original emphasis)

Creaturely operations do change the milieu around them. The reverse is also true, as the environment in its own turn can either facilitate or impede individual operations.

Moral goodness

Reflexive quality to intellectual activity

Moral goodness is a participation in the excellence of God. Human beings communicate God's goodness to each other through their activity. However, what is equally significant is how they receive God's goodness through their own activity. Aquinas (SCG III, 22, #2) distinguishes three ways by which activity is related to ends. Since a thing can be a mover, be moved by others, or be both, activity perfects creatures either by being the cause of others, by being perfected within themselves, or both. Human beings are perfected as they move others or are moved themselves. Thus, human activity is both transitive (e.g., promoting others' good) and immanent (e.g., personal virtue) in the term of its perfective dynamics. Humans receive God's goodness not only through their existence but also through their operations. Activity is often viewed as being externally oriented in the term of its action, as it is in economic life. However, there is also a reflexive component that brings God's goodness to the agent; externally oriented activity is internally perfective.

Human secondary causality is different from God's or from nonrational beings' causality because of the reflexive nature of the human act. Effects reflect their causes. In the case of human acts, there is a feedback whereby effects precipitate changes in their causes. In particular, human beings are affected by their rational activities. Human acts shape and define their agents. After all, intellectual activity is perfective of their agents. The act proffered is perfective of the recipient (Wippel 1987, 146).

> As a thing realizes itself in its operation and the operation is the immediate end for the sake of which the thing exists, *a thing is called 'good' insofar as it is completed with regard to its operation.* (te Velde 1995, 41; emphasis added)

Metaphysical foundations

God's creative act is essentially a sharing of divine goodness according to creatures' capacity to receive and then communicate such goodness (J. Wright 1957, 191–92). Human beings are unique because they are created to know and love God, to the extent possible, as God knows and loves God (SCG III, 111; ST I, 65, a.2, reply). This is an "imitation of the divine essence in the intellect of God" (Kondoleon 1967, 714; SCG I, 54). It is the *telos* of human beings. The critical significance of this *telos* is delineated by J. Wright, who concludes that God "chose to communicate [to humans] what is formally divine, a share in the activity which immediately terminates to the divine essence as divine" (1957, 192). Thus, there is embedded within the human essence something that is formally divine, a form that accounts for the nature of human activity (including economic life) and for the beatific vision as the crown of moral goodness.

The form of the human person shapes the operational *telos* of the entire economic order. It also shapes the proper end of personal and collective economic behavior. Economic life is an important sphere through which the move from potency to act unfolds since there is a necessary material dimension to human flourishing. Thus, economic life becomes a venue for participation in that which is formally divine.

The ultimate perfection of each creature is its reflection of that dimension of God's goodness it is capable of receiving and communicating according to the mode of its being and operation. "The ultimate end of each thing is that which makes it most like God" (J. Wright 1957, 45). The most distinctive faculties of human beings are reason and will, and these are the primary modes by which their operation (and therefore perfection) is to be achieved.

God as Final Cause can be attained either by similitude or by intellectual activity, or both, as in the case of human beings (J. Wright 1957, 45–72). As natural beings, humans have an inclination toward God as good by virtue of their existence (first act, first perfection). This initial similitude (by existence) is completed through their operations, particularly through intellectual activity.

Activities bring about additional perfections which have been described in different ways: *virtus, vis* (power), accidental or secondary perfections completing the first perfection of existence, the completion of potency, that which "makes the substance good in the full sense," and the capacity to operate and achieve its "striving" and "act well according to its own nature" (te Velde 1995, 41). Aquinas claims that "whatever is found in anything by participation, must be caused in it by that to which it belongs essentially" (ST I, 44, a.1, reply). Justice, sacrificial love, temperance, prudence, and many other virtues are observed in some human beings. These qualities are accidental to humans, that is, they are not part of their essence because there are some human beings who do not possess these perfections. These virtues are additional, accidental perfections. Hence, they must be participated from God, who possesses these perfections in a supereminent and absolute manner as part of divine essence. Nevertheless, human virtues are a real, and not merely a logical, participation. Moreover, these powers are bestowed on humans by God since effects cannot initiate perfections of themselves when they do not have such excellence to begin with.

Communicating God's goodness

A proper effect of secondary causes is that of communicating God's goodness according to their nature and mode of operation. In fact, parts of the whole are able to bring the whole to God as end by receiving and communicating God's goodness to each other. Humans are rational, and thus an important part of their proper effect as secondary agents is intelligent activity that communicates their moral goodness as a reflection of God's goodness. Humans communicate such goodness by moving from ontological to moral goodness; the act of reaching toward the fullness of goodness is itself a communication of that goodness. After all, an agent communicates actuality only in the measure that the agent possesses such quality (J. Wright 1957, 69). And the more such excellence is communicated, the more profound is the agent's possession of such actuality. There is a self-reinforcing dynamic in moral goodness.

The human person is expected to actively participate in the communication of God's goodness (as a necessary condition of human happiness). We do not convey God's goodness solely in a passive way as do nonrational creatures, nor do we do so by necessity. Only the human person is able to do so deliberately because only the person is a moral agent capable of activity in a reasoned and free communication of God's goodness.

Human activity within the twofold order of the universe

Creatures receive and then communicate God's goodness within the larger context of the internal and external dynamic of the twofold order of the universe. Whether in receiving or in communicating God's goodness, creatures do so according to the nature of their being and the mode of their operations. And there is an immense variety in the nature of beings and modes of operation in the created order. Human beings, as parts of this whole, occupy a special place in the twofold order of the universe.

Aquinas's synthesis of the disparate Platonic and Aristotelean uses of forms in his metaphysics of participation (by similitude and by composition) accounts for how it is that the Many (creatures) are able to share in the One (God). By its nature, participation indicates an imperfect possession of the perfection of the *participatum*. Such a gap becomes even more pronounced when it comes to God and creatures. No single creature can adequately and fully capture by itself the goodness of God. Not even the universe as a single and entire ensemble of created beings is able to reflect the fullness of God's goodness, neither in its collective existence nor activity. Thus, there is a need for a wide variety of species and for a broad spectrum of differing degrees of perfection within creation itself in order to better mirror God's goodness, to the extent possible. The immeasurable and unique nature of God's goodness accounts for why there is the phenomenon of the *One and the Many* (ST I, 47, a.1, reply).

Human beings hold the highest degree of excellence within such a variety of creatures of differing grades of perfection. The capacity to know, to love, and to choose sets humans apart from the rest of creation; it is what gives them their closest likeness to God in all of the created order. Only humans attain God (as ultimate end) through knowledge and love (ST I, 65, a.2, reply; J. Wright 1957, 61).

All other corporeal creatures find their proximate *telos* in serving human flourishing. In the order of generation and the order of preservation, humans are at the top of the hierarchy with their needs filled by the fruits of the earth (SCG III, 22, #7–8; J. Wright 1957, 8). Given the twofold order of the universe, however, this also means that humans have obligations to all other beings of lesser perfection. After all, the internal order requires that parts of the whole assist each other to bring out the fullness of their respective similitude to God. Moreover, creatures of a higher perfection work to bring beings of a lower perfection to their highest possible good (J. Wright 1957, 44).[13] This is particularly true of humans since "the actions of intellectual substances are more intimately ordered to God in their end, than the actions of other things" (SCG III, 90, #5).

Creatures receive and then communicate the goodness of God according to the nature of their being and the mode of their operations. Given their essence and their capacity for intellectual activity, human beings, unlike all other corporeal creatures, have two modes by which they participate in the goodness of God: that which is by necessity and that which is free. Natural activity is predetermined according to how God created the world to operate. Thus, that humans breathe, eat, and grow in physique and strength are all manifestations of God's perfection; they are embedded within the nature given to humans and thus come about by necessity. On the other hand, the degree to which humans manifest their divine similitude through the act of knowing, loving, and willing is entirely voluntary in character. These are properly human acts, not foreordained but free; thus, they can even go against reason and not conform to the God-given twofold order of creation (Gilby 1969, vol. 22, appendix 7, 123).

As parts of God's created order, therefore, humans are free and reasoned in the manner by which they attain the goodness proper to themselves and by which they bring out the goodness in less perfect creatures. Since the two-fold order of the universe is entirely dependent on the activity of its constitu-ent parts and since humans are among its most important elements, the manner by which this dual order attains its common end comes about in two ways: that which is of necessity and that which comes about freely. In other words, as we see in chapter 3, humans play a pivotal role in bringing to fru-ition the twofold order of the universe.

ONTOLOGICAL MATERIAL SUFFICIENCY

Can we say anything a priori regarding the adequacy of material supplies to fill human needs? This appendix argues that a case can be made for sufficiency in human provisioning using God's threefold causality and Aquinas's twofold order of the universe.

The goods of the earth are meant to serve the needs of human beings (SCG III, 112). God could have designed the world in one of three possible ways. First, created material goods could have been deliberately set short of what is needed, thereby causing a condition of persistent deprivation. This is a state of permanent Malthusian scarcity. Second, material provisions could have been designed to be just adequate, with little surplus to compensate for unforeseen deleterious shocks to supplies of goods such as the vagaries of the weather and natural disasters. Third, the fruits of the earth could have been made to yield a great abundance that more than makes up for whatever material losses or destruction may result from human failures or physical evil. These three possibilities are mutually exclusive, and depending on which of these apply in reality, human provisioning can fall anywhere from chronic severe insufficiency (Malthusian scarcity) to bare sufficiency (frictional scarcity) to superfluity (unconditional material abundance).[1] The first and the third possibilities form the endpoints of a continuum of varying amounts of surplus as a cushion against whatever may cause a diminution of provisions to fill human needs.

In what follows, I first establish a priori whether there is material sufficiency or not by the nature of God's creation. If there is, the first possibility of a human condition of unremitting material exiguity by divine design could be eliminated from consideration. After establishing such adequacy in material provisions, the next step is to examine the degree of such sufficiency (second or third possibility).

METAPHYSICAL ARGUMENTS FOR MATERIAL SUFFICIENCY

The attributes of God furnish metaphysical arguments for why there is material sufficiency to fill human needs as part of the order of creation. The threefold divine causality—God as Formal, Efficient, and Final Cause—ensures the satisfaction of these necessities at a minimum, and possibly even with surplus to spare.

God As Formal Cause

God as Formal Cause is the exemplar for creation and its created order. While a multiplicity of created beings is needed to better reflect the goodness of God, the quantity of such species is not at all essential or relevant. J. Wright (1957, 6, 132–33, 189) observes that a mere numerical multiplication of creatures does not add to the intelligibility of the universe and therefore does not add to its intrinsic perfection. Thus, since scarcity pertains to adequacy in quantities available and not to the number of species of created goods, it might seem that material shortages do not take away from the perfection of the universe. A number of arguments can be presented against this view.

First, one must distinguish between perfection as intelligibility and perfection in operations. The variety of species (and not the quantity of each species) is important when referring to the former, in which perfection is measured according to how well the universe manifests and reflects the goodness of God. However, finitude in terms of the quantity of each species becomes a vital concern once we examine operational perfection. God's causality would be imperfect if privations (such as material shortages) embedded within the divine plan impede creaturely activities that are essential to the order of creation. In particular, cold, starving, and destitute human beings will not be able to function fully according to their intended nature and mode of operation. God's knowledge is perfect, and if God is the exemplar, there can be no flaws within the divine providence that undergirds all of creation.

Second, just as effects reflect back and say something about their causes (SCG III, 20, #5), creation mirrors the perfections of God, albeit in an incomplete and imperfect fashion. Beauty is one such perfection, and it necessarily includes an aesthetic of proper proportionality and integrity (ST I, 39, a.8, reply; II-II, 145, a.2). Thus, we expect creation to exhibit a likeness to divine beauty. At a minimum, such similitude in beauty must be manifested in the creaturely interactions within the internal order of the universe whereby parts act together to bring the whole to its external end. In other words, there has to be balance between humans and created goods (material provisions) as parts of the same whole. There would be neither due proportion nor integrity in the whole if there were material deficiencies by divine design in what is needed for some of the parts (human beings) to reach their *telos* (end). There has to be proportionality in creatures (both in terms of the number of species and quantity) to bring about a smooth functioning of the whole order. An insufficient supply of material sustenance for humans would mar creation as a participation of beauty in God.

Third, material sufficiency must follow from the view of creation as an outcome of the self-diffusiveness of goodness. After all, divine goodness is "the cause of the production of all things in existence" (ST I, 103, a.1). God communicates divine goodness through the order (both external and internal) of the universe. The good is that which is desirable and perfect—that which things aim for. Thus, there can be no intrinsic privation in goodness, and certainly not in God. The goodness reflected by creation is admittedly an imperfect and partial manifestation of God's goodness. In fact, there has to be not only a multiplicity in the number of species but also a wide range in degrees of perfection if creation is to reflect the goodness of God. However, imperfection in the manner by which created beings appropriate likeness unto God does not mean that there can be a privation in a particular aspect of goodness that is essential to the created order. In other words, the goodness received by the whole cannot be lacking in that which is vital to its continued existence, not to mention its activity. Thus, the goodness conveyed to creation as a whole must necessarily include the provision of species in quantities that are sufficient so as to preclude privation in that which is essential to the goodness of the whole. If overall want and destitution were embedded within the very nature of the existential order itself, then there would have been a deficiency in bringing about the intended existence and operation of beings according to their nature. Thus, there would be a privation intrinsic in the goodness proffered by God.

Fourth, perfections found in creatures must be in God in a supereminent way (SCG I, 28). Since human perfection is but a poor and imperfect reflection of that found in God, and since liberality is an accidental perfection found in some humans, munificence must be perfect in God. Such perfect liberality must at the very least furnish sufficiency, if not abundance, in human material provisioning. Moreover, humans anticipate and plan for the future, making sure there are adequate supplies to complete tasks and reach designated ends. We would expect God to be even more provident regarding creatures dependent on divine governance.

Fifth, God communicates divine goodness as a whole, as a single work in which each part of the universe receives a measure of that goodness according to its "own capacity and disposition, according to the place it occupies in the whole plan of God" (J. Wright 1957, 44). This means that the provision of the whole universe must be complete, including the means necessary to attain its external end in God.

Finally, a human condition of want and destitution by divine design in the order of creation would reflect flaws in divinity itself.

> [T]he perfection and form of an effect consist in a certain likeness to the agent, since every agent makes its like; and hence the agent itself is desirable and has the nature of good. For the very thing which is desirable in it is the participation of its likeness. (ST I, 6, a.1)

A permanent human state of tenuous subsistence living would indicate deficiencies in God.

God as Efficient Cause

God as Efficient Cause puts into effect the perfect "blueprint" that flows from God as Formal Cause. God as Creator wills the divine plan for creation flawlessly. In other words, material deficiency cannot arise because of failures in God's implementation of divine will.

First, the maintenance of creation falls under the purview of divine governance and divine providence. Existence is the highest perfection of creatures *qua* creatures. However, this is merely a participated perfection from God as *Ipsum Esse Subsistens* (SCG I, 22–23). Since only God has necessary existence, creaturely participation in God's *esse* has to be continuously sustained by divine will. The maintenance of human beings in such contingent existence, which includes material provisioning, falls under the divine activity of providence. Material sufficiency for human needs necessarily follows from God's simplicity. We can make this argument from Aquinas's description of God's providence:

> Now, since providence is concerned with directing to an end, it must take place with the end as its norm; and since the first provider is Himself the end of His providence, He has the norm of providence within Himself. Consequently, *it is impossible that any of the failures in those things for which He provides should be due to Him.* (*De veritate* q.5, a.5, reply; emphasis added)

Thus, the exiguous state of material goods observed in human affairs cannot be attributed to a divine deficit. God is Pure Act, and given such uncomposed nature, divine providence is flawless as it knows and effects perfectly the means necessary to attain the end. There can be no deficiencies in God's provisioning, for it is God who sets the norm for what is needed to sustain creation in continued existence.

Second, divine conservation pertains to a continuation of God's act of creation whereby God preserves creatures in existence directly while at the same time indirectly maintaining them according to their nature through intermediate causes. As corporeal beings, humans require material inputs (as intermediate causes) for their continued survival, growth, and development; thus, material sufficiency has to be part of divine conservation if human beings are to be maintained as beings with bodies and souls.

Third, the indefectibility of divine will means perfect justice on the part of God. God's justice brings into existence all that is necessary for the kind of universe God has created:

> God exercises justice toward the universe chiefly by creating those things which are required for the kind of universe He has determined to produce. Because He has infinite power and is without defect, and because

the whole universe is His principal effect, God produced by a single
act at one time the whole universe and all its essential parts. (J. Wright
1957, 78)

This observation on the proper operation of God's justice can be extended.
There has to be not only the creation of things, but also the provision of such
creatures in quantities that are proper and consistent with moving creation
to its ultimate end. In other words, the flawless nature of divine will necessarily leads to adequate provisions to satisfy the needs of creatures. It would
have been an act of malice to bring creatures into existence only to set them
up for physical extinction or vice and misery for want of material supplies as
in the case of Malthusian scarcity. Such would go against the perfect justice
of God.

Fourth, we can claim material sufficiency from the real causality given
to creatures. Gilby argues against Malebranche's occasionalism by noting
that creaturely activity is not merely an occasion for God's exercise of real
causality, but possesses real causality itself as part of its participation in divine perfections (1969, vol. 5, 99n.d.).[2] Material sufficiency has to follow
from such real creaturely causality because human beings would not otherwise be able to operate and discharge their true causality. In other words, in
sharing real causality with creatures, God would also have to provide the
necessary means to actualize such potencies. Otherwise, divine providence
would be flawed in not providing what is necessary for creatures' exercise of
their powers according to the mode of their being and operation. In fact, in
refuting one of the objections to God's direct and immediate provision for all
things, Aquinas observes:

[God's] dignity demands ministers [intermediaries] to execute its provisions, but *to lack a ruling policy for them to carry out would be inept. Any
practical science is so much better for attending to the details of its business.*
(ST I, 22, a.3, ad.1; emphasis added)

Economics is among the most important of the practical sciences as it pertains to the material foundations of human survival and flourishing, prereq-
uisites to their real causality.

Fifth, in appealing once again to the supereminent perfections found in
God, we note that since some human beings share goodness with others
using their will in deliberate action, how much more for God (ST I, 19, a.2,

reply). Thus, there has to be material sufficiency because it is part of the self-diffusive nature of goodness to share and then complete the goodness that it proffers to others, and to do so deliberately with an act of the will. If material shortages were intrinsic to creation, it would mean that God is defective either in will (God as Efficient Cause) or in the goodness that God shares (God as Formal Cause). Both go against the attributes of God.

God as Final Cause

Material sufficiency follows from the perfection and goodness of God as Final Cause. First, nothing escapes the causality of God. As efficient cause, God provides creatures with the necessary means to reach their end.

> [*Since*] *it belongs to the best to produce the best*, it is not fitting that the supreme goodness of God should produce things without giving them their perfection. Now a thing's ultimate perfection consists in the attainment of its end. Therefore it belongs to the Divine goodness, as it brought things into existence, so to lead them to their end. (ST I, 103, a.1, reply; original emphasis)[3]

> Since it belongs to the same cause to give a thing its being and to bring it to completeness, that is to govern it, the way God is the governor of things matches the way he is their cause. (ST I, 103, a.5, reply)

By deduction from the perfection of God as Formal and Efficient Cause, it is reasonable to expect God to create creatures, bring them to their proper perfection (end), and, therefore, provide the necessary means for them to exist and operate according to their nature.

Second, act and potency are proportioned to each other; perfection and the means to it are proportioned in like manner. Aquinas asserts that it does not make sense for God to give power that is not going to be exercised (ST I, 105, a.5, reply). A similar argument can be made for material provisioning because it does not make sense for God to imbue human beings with their signal rational faculties that either cannot be exercised or are poorly utilized for want of the requisite material means.

Perfection in God as Final End also means that the completion of God's plan will unfold according to the created order's mode of being and operation. The latter includes the necessary provisioning of human needs both in terms of the number of species and their quantity. The universe cannot reach its external end in God if its parts (humans, in this case) are unable to operate according to the nature of their being for want of material nourishment and the other means necessary for their full actualization. The twofold order of the universe would grind to a halt, with creation unable to reach its ultimate end in God. Thus, one can make the case for the adequacy of supplies of created goods for human needs based on the perfection of God's final causality. It is a contradiction to have a diffusion of God's goodness that is by design doomed to fail to reach its completion in the Final End.

In summary, God's attributes ensure that human beings, as parts of the whole, are adequately supplied with their material needs to enable them to continue in existence and to operate according to their nature. Such supplies are adequate both in terms of the number of species needed in the created order and in the quantities available for such created goods. We have thus eliminated the first of the three aforementioned possibilities (permanent state of Malthusian scarcity) in the way God could have created the world. However, given the extensive human experience of material want for most of economic history, this divine gift of material sufficiency must be merely provisional.

MATERIAL SUFFICIENCY FOR WHICH ORDER?

Does material sufficiency occur at the external order alone (that is, at the level of the universe as a whole), or does it go all the way down to the internal order (that is, at the level of individual parts)? In other words, is it the universe as a whole alone (e.g., humanity), or is it every individual part (e.g., every human being) in the universe that is offered such conditional material sufficiency? Is such conditional material sufficiency merely general or does it even go so far as to be person-specific? Is it applicable merely to general providence or even to particular providence?

As a consequence of the multiplicity of creatures and their grades of perfection, we would expect to find humans in an extensive variety of circumstances (ST I, 47, a.2; I, 47, a.1, reply), ranging from a superfluity of supplies to outright destitution and risk of physical death. Considered at the level of individual parts of the whole (internal order), human beings may indeed face material want given the expansive heterogeneity of social and personal circumstances in the order of creation, including contingency in economic processes. Thus, economic history is replete with countless instances of human want and poverty precipitated by physical evil such as blight, drought, climatic disorders, and other natural disasters. These are cases in which parts (nature) are unable to provide for other parts (humans) of the whole. In other words, there is no a priori metaphysical argument that precludes want at the level of individuals as parts of the whole. Thus, while there are a priori metaphysical arguments for why there is at least a state of conditional material sufficiency at the level of the universe as a single entity, it would seem that the same cannot be immediately said at the level of each individual part.[4] In fact, gradation as part of the order (Coffey 1949) and the necessary diversity of beings with different degrees of perfections unavoidably lead to scarcity of material goods for some at the level of individuals, a necessary imperfection in order to better reflect the goodness of God (SCG III, 71).

Against the preceding argument, one can still make a strong case for extending conditional material sufficiency down to the level of the individual parts. First, divine governance implies a divine plan, and since God is perfect, such plans must necessarily reach down to each individual part immediately (ST I, 19, a.6; I, 22, a.2; I, 103, aa.5–7; SCG III, 64; III, 94; III, 113).

Second, all the a priori metaphysical arguments for why there is material sufficiency in the order of creation by divine design would apply not only to the universe as a single entity, but to the individual parts as well. Whether argued from the flawless nature of God's providence, or from the necessary proportion of parts of the whole to each other (similitude in beauty), or from the perfection of the threefold causality of God's goodness, or from the indefectibility of God's justice, there is a need for these warrants to apply both at the level of the whole and of the individual parts. This should not come as a surprise because the internal and external orders of the universe are inextricably linked to each other and mutually reinforce one another. The a priori arguments for material sufficiency either applies to both halves of the twofold order of the universe or they apply to neither. After all, they are necessary conditions to each other's attainment of their respective proper orders. Thus, conditional material sufficiency has to apply both at the level of the whole and of the individual parts.

Third, the all-encompassing nature of God's causality also implies material sufficiency down to the level of individual parts within the universe.

The scope of anyone's governing corresponds to the scope of the end of that governing. As shown already, the end of God's government is God's own goodness. Since . . . nothing can exist that is not referred to the divine goodness as end, it is impossible that any single existent be removed from God's rule. (ST I, 103, a.5, reply)

Since nothing can fall outside the universality of God's providence and governance, every being is subject to divine providence and governance.[5] An insuperable material insufficiency as part of the order of creation would mean that some human beings are *by design* not meant to reach their fullness as corporeal-spiritual beings in God as Final Cause. Such determinism goes against authentic human freedom.

Fourth, immediacy in the nature of divine providence provides strong and direct justification for the claim that existential material sufficiency must apply not only at the level of the whole, but also at the level of every individual human being. God plans and provides for every creature; God knows things down to the level of their individuation in matter (ST I, 14, a.11) and "has the design of the government of all things, even of the very least" (ST I, 103, a.6, reply; see also ST I, 22, a.2; SCG III, 75–76). In response to the question if God provides for all things without intermediaries, Aquinas responds by distinguishing divine providence from divine governance. Secondary agents are used for the latter but not for the former.

God provides for all things immediately and directly. His mind holds the reason for each of them, even the very least, and whatsoever the causes he appoints for effects, he it is who gives them the power to produce these effects. *Consequently, the whole of their design down to every detail is anticipated in his mind.* (ST I, 22, a.3; emphasis added)

In not using intermediaries in formulating plans for creatures and their end, divine providence is immediate and direct for *every* creature and avoids the attendant limitations whenever created instrumental activity is employed. Thus, divine providence applies not merely at the level of the species but for every member of the species.

Fifth, humans are not merely any ordinary kind of species because they are the only creatures created by God for their own sake. Every being exists for its own proper act and its own proper end. In the case of humans, this entails knowing and loving God as their Final End (SCG III, 111–13). Thus, we are dealing not only with a Creator-creature relationship but with a special interpersonal relationship. It would be entirely fitting for God to will material sufficiency for every human being given their end and the nobility of their act. One would expect not merely a general providence, but a particular and special providence that flows from the Creator's personal solicitude for every human being, the highest of corporeal beings.

Finally, Aquinas observes that "God provides for all things according to the kind of things that they are" (ST I, 1, a.9) and that God's care "over all things matches the mode of their being" (ST I, 43, a.7). Human beings are corporeal and need material provisioning not only for their survival but also for their growth and development. It is appropriate, therefore, that if God truly provides for creatures according to their nature, every human being must be afforded the necessary means for material sufficiency.

In summary, there are a priori metaphysical warrants for the claim that God created a world characterized by material sufficiency. Material exiguity cannot be intrinsic to the design of the order of creation because of the perfection of divine exemplarism. And scarcity cannot arise because of a flawed implementation since such is the activity of a perfect Efficient Cause, nor can it be somehow a feature of the created order's nature because of the perfection of the Final Cause that draws creatures to their ultimate end according to their mode of being and operation. Such material sufficiency is intended not merely at the level of the whole, that is, for humanity as a single entity, but at the level of each human being as well.

There is no necessity to God creating a world of mere *conditional* material sufficiency. God could have easily chosen otherwise and provided for an even stronger form of material sufficiency—an unqualified plenitude not contingent on the free and intelligent, but defectible, activity of rational secondary causes. Thus, there are grounds for this study's speculative exercise in understanding why God as benevolent Creator chose not to do so.

NOTES

Chapter 1.   Malthusian Theodicy Revisited

1. See, for example, Godwin ([1793] 1992).

2. Waterman (1991a, 98) observes that Malthus uses "misery" as a shorthand for hardships that stem from the natural order and "vice" for moral failure.

3. Theodicy is the study of how we can reconcile the existence of God and evil in the world.

4. I limit my treatment of Malthus to the first edition of the *Essay* and do not consider revisions in his theory of population in the subsequent editions. Such is beyond the scope of this study and is not essential for my thesis.

5. See, for example, LeMahieu (1979), Pullen (1981), and Waterman (1983a, 1983b, 1991a).

6. Manichaeism, a third-century A.D. religious movement in Persia, held as core doctrines the beliefs that life is caught between two competing principles—goodness and evil—and that matter is evil. This heresy was subsequently revived by the Albigensians (Cathari) in twelfth-century southern France.

7. Evil does not have existence of its own because it is merely a posterior description of a perfection that has been damaged or lost.

8. This is the Pelagian heresy.

9. See appendix 3 for more on God as Final Cause.

10. God is Pure Act (SCG I, 22–23) with no tinge of potency to be further actualized.

11. Waterman (1983a, 201) points out an inconsistency here. Malthus dismisses the more traditional state-of-probation account of evil because it implies a defective foreknowledge on the part of God. And yet Malthus's explanation of sending "misshapen" vessels back to the original clump of clay is in itself reflective of a deficient foreknowledge on the part of the Creator.

12. *Ipsum Esse Subsistens* (SCG I, 22–23).

13. 1803, 1806, 1807, 1817, and 1826.

14. B. Gordon (1989) examines the phenomenon of scarcity from a biblical perspective but does not delve deeply enough to provide for a theodicy.

15. Economic history provides ample evidence that Malthus's theory of population is erroneous because it does not factor in technological change. Nevertheless, Malthus's basic theological question remains valid: Why does God permit a world characterized by material scarcity?

16. Human want may arise due to moral failure (e.g., avarice), the limitations of nature (e.g., finite goods of the earth and limited human capacity for work), or both. The former is called consequent scarcity, and the latter formal or existential scarcity. This study is only about consequent scarcity. Appendix 1 provides a fuller description of the different kinds of scarcity.

Chapter 2.   Communicating the Goodness of God

1. Economists will find "economic scarcity" a redundancy. Following Robbins ([1932] 1952), most economists view their discipline as the study of the allocation of scarce resources to their most valued uses. Thus, scarcity is already implicit in economics. Nevertheless, I use the two terms together to accommodate noneconomists who use *scarcity* in broad terms. For example, Gauthier (1986, 330) lists different kinds of scarcity: moral, scientific, erotic, emotional, and psychological. Thomas (1955, 162) even suggests a spiritual scarcity.

2. Metaphysics employs a language of its own that is unfamiliar to most readers. I have written the next two chapters to be as accessible as possible to a wide audience and have relegated any requisite technical discussion to the endnotes and appendices. Readers looking for a more thorough and rigorous exposition are referred to these.

3. God is a Subsistent Being, *Ipsum Esse Subsistens* (SCG I, 22–23). It is in the essence of God to exist.

4. Thus, we have the phenomenon of the *One and the Many*. See appendix 2.

5. God is Pure Act without any tinge of potency. Creatures, however, have yet to actualize their potency. Hence, one expects development, growth, and change in creatures.

6. See appendix 2 for a more technical discussion of the three components of complete created goodness.

7. Readers are reminded that I use the term *scarcity* to refer to the absence of unconditional material abundance.

8. God as Formal Cause. See appendix 3.

9. God as Efficient Cause. See appendix 3.

10. Appendix 3 is a more rigorous exposition on how the threefold causality of God (as Formal, Efficient, and Final Cause) provides ontological arguments for material sufficiency in human life.

Chapter 3.   Economic Agency as Perfective Secondary Cause

1. *Ipsum Esse Subsistens* (SCG I, 22–23).

2. Albertson observes: "God . . . is the proper cause of the effect's being simply, but the second cause is the proper cause of the effect's being *this,* such as being a man

or being white. The causality of 'being absolutely' is ultimately rooted in God, but the causality of those perfections which are added to and specify being pertains to the second causes. All perfections other than *esse* particularize and determine the *esse* of a being—a creature is not pure existence, but rather it exists in a certain limited way—and so St. Thomas says of second causes that, as particularizing and determining factors of the action of the First Cause, they have as their own proper effects those other perfections which determine *esse*" (1954, 433; original emphasis).

3. Only God has uncreated *esse,* and all other creatures merely have participated existence from *Ipsum Esse Subsistens.* Thus, nothing can be outside the scope of divine providence and governance (ST I, 19, a.6; I, 22, a.2; I, 103, a.5; I, 103, a.7; SCG III, 64, 94, and 113). Even as created beings can be a cause of *esse* in other beings (Wippel 2000), such causality can only be participated or created. To be more precise, they can only be secondary (particular, agent, created) causes to the First (primary, universal, uncreated) Cause of *esse* (SCG III, 66–67). Just as an instrument produces an ultimate effect greater than its own power by participating in the activity of the superior agent, so do created beings as secondary causes provide the occasion for the conferral of *esse* to other beings, a power innate to God alone. Like instrumental causes, secondary causes also have an effect proper to them. Albertson (1954, 431) notes that secondary causes are properly called instruments of God not only because their effects exceed their power but also because their activities go beyond the instruments' proximate goals and implement divine providence. Thus, effects exceed both the instruments' power and intentions.

4. *Esse simpliciter* (sheer existence) is the proper effect of the primary cause while *esse hoc* (matter taking form and existing in *this* particular, determinate form) is the secondary cause's proper effect (Johann 1947).

5. Primary-secondary causality is properly used only when juxtaposing uncreated and created causes (Albertson 1954; Johann 1947). In the absolute order of existence, *esse* as a perfection is properly attributed to the First Cause as a principal cause. However, all other limiting formal perfections in the ultimate effect can be attributed to the secondary causes since they can be properly considered as principal causes in the order of creaturely perfections (besides *esse*). Albertson argues that "since esse is the actuality or perfection of all perfections, God's activity is the most intimate and fundamental to the effect. But because the limiting formal perfections are the proper effect of the second cause, the effect is formally proportioned to it rather than to God" (1954, 434).

6. J. Wright observes: "It is not created goodness, but *divine goodness as shareable* that makes it fitting that the universe exist. The meaning and value of the universe is clear to us only when we see how *the internal order of the universe leads all creation to God,* to share in His goodness according to the plan of His wisdom and love. For, *in the last analysis, the order of the universe is nothing but the concrete embodiment of that plan*" (1957, 113; emphasis added).

7. Primary rank is accorded to rational beings in the order of preservation (SCG III, 22; III, 112).

8. After all, "an orderly relation toward the good has the formal character of a good thing" (SCG III, 21, #4).

9. Aquinas observes "[T]o the degree that one creature brings about good in another it imitates God as he is the cause of good in other beings" (ST I, 103, a.5, reply).

10. Note, for example, the Green Revolution of the twentieth century that increased agricultural production through the use of new technologies, such as hybrid strains of crops, chemical fertilizers and pesticides, and mechanization.

11. This is part of the phenomenon of the *One and the Many*. See appendix 2.

12. Economic transfers are only a partial accounting of human responsibility for ensuring material sufficiency for all because human defectibility is most likely also the major direct cause of Malthusian scarcity. Using the language of rights and freedom (Berlin 1958), one could view the role of human beings in providing material sufficiency in both a negative and positive sense. In a negative sense, human beings are supposed to restrain themselves and refrain from behaviors that impoverish others. In a positive sense, they are obligated to actively correct deficiencies that emerge from contingent processes and others' moral failings.

13. One can view scarcity for the personal powers and potencies it implies. The conditionality behind God's providence signifies powers accorded to human beings. In the order of divine plans, powers are always given to match the ends that are supposed to be achieved. Act and potency are proportioned to each other (ST I, 75, a.5, ad.1); moreover, the gift of power comes with the ordination to effect that power (SCG III, 78, #3). In other words, we cannot expect the secondary agent to produce an effect beyond its power. Thus, the overwhelming problems posed by material scarcity and the seemingly intractable economic task facing humans as secondary causes must surely imply comparably formidable human powers.

14. The act proffered by God is perfective of the recipient (Wippel 1987, 146).

15. Theirs is a real role in divine governance and not a mere front for God's direct, unmediated administration of the world (occasionalism).

Chapter 4.   Economic Agency in Covenant Election

1. Covenant election is the divine invitation extended to Israel to live a life of righteousness as part of the new order unleashed by God's entry into human history when the Chosen People were liberated from slavery.

2. "Poor" may refer either to the impoverished or to those who put their trust and hopes only in God (J. R. Porter 1990, 111, 114). I refer to the destitute in my usage of the term.

3. Land is an important issue regardless of source (J, E, D, and P). My thanks to J. David Pleins for this point. Scholars believe that the Torah came from four sources: J(Yahwist), E(Elohist), D(Deuteronomist), and P(Priestly). For a concise exposition on each of these, see Pleins (2001, 24–28).

4. Some scholars go so far as to argue that without land, there is no Israel. See C. Wright (1990, 7–9) for a review of the literature.

5. We have to distinguish three levels in this regard. The smallest unit is the "house of one's father" (*beth 'ab*) that "consists of those who are united by common

blood and common dwelling-place" and includes servants, aliens, widows, and orphans who live "under the protection of the head of the family." On a larger scale is the family-clan (*mishpahah*) that is founded on blood ties, shares "common interests and duties," and is "concentrated in one area, occupying one or more villages." The mutual obligation of redemption (*go'el*) from debt-slavery or of family land applies at the level of the family-clan. And, of course, the largest level of aggregation is the tribe. See de Vaux (1965, 1:20–21).

6. C. Wright (1990, 100–101) notes that belonging to a landholding family may indeed be one reason why a Hebrew slave would choose to forego freedom and simply remain as a member of his master's house. In the case of resident aliens, it is their attachment to a particular landowning Hebrew family that affords them the opportunity of being part of the cultic festivals.

7. See Pleins (2001, 67–70) for the priestly economic reform.

8. See Gottwald (1979) on egalitarian tribes.

9. This study is not an exhaustive examination of Old Testament teachings on economic life. For example, I will not be covering tort matters in the Law. This research is limited only to the care of the impoverished in the Hebrew law codes.

10. North (1954, 184–85) observes that there are multiple overlapping "seventh years" involved: (1) the sabbath of Lv 25:2, (2) the fallow of Ex 23:11, (3) the manumission of slaves in Ex 21:1 and Dt 15:12–18, and (4) the remission of debt in Dt 15:1–11. It is unclear if these overlap each other or not. What is clear, however, is that all these are either directly or indirectly related to the issue of debts.

11. North (1954, 185–86) examines the question of whether the seventh-year release pertains to the cancellation of the entire debt, to the suspension of the payment of interest, or to usufruct from the pledge for the seventh year. There is no consensus on this issue among scholars.

12. Neufeld's footnotes 16 to 22 provide bibliography of other scholars who also hold this view.

13. In economic terms, to charge interest is to impose an additional cost for the necessary liquidity in smoothing out consumption over time.

14. There are economic reasons for this. Grain prices are subject to fluctuations depending on supply conditions in the market. Grain is borrowed long after the harvest season when its price is high. On the other hand, grain is repaid during the harvest season when prices are likely to be low. Thus, there is a need for the premium to reflect the differential in grain prices at the time the loan is incurred and at the time it is repaid. See Neufeld (1953–54, 203–4) for a different economic explanation.

15. Moxnes (1988) examines in greater detail this phenomenon of "patron-client relationships" within a New Testament setting.

16. See Walzer (1983) for the notion of dominant goods.

17. I use "ideal" as a qualifier to describe the egalitarian ethos of Israel because the actual practice was far different from what the Law stipulates. The excesses and the resultant inequalities of the monarchial period are well-recorded.

18. Lohfink (1986, 224–25) observes that Leviticus 25 is akin to and falls within the "limited goods" phenomenon in peasant economies. See Foster (1967) and Gregory (1975) for an exposition on the features of a limited-goods society.

19. These are two different functions. Land return to ensure a source of livelihood for the family is restorative in nature. It reestablishes the family as a landholding household and wipes the slate clean from whatever economic misfortunes or mistakes may have impoverished the family in the past. Thus, this restorative function takes on greater potency when land return occurs simultaneously with the release of all debts and slaves. On the other hand, the practical goal of restricting inequalities through land return is redistributive in nature and is meant to "level the playing field" for all. The redistributive and restorative functions of the Jubilee Law are not mutually exclusive; they can be operative at the same time.

20. See also Lowery (2000, 38–39) for numerous examples of the various releases of an economic nature practiced by Israel's neighbors.

21. For example, one similarity is the role of divinity in relation to land. Canaanites ascribe the fertility of their land to Baal. Israel simply replaces Baal with YHWH as the owner of the land responsible for its fruits. Just like the Canaanites, whom they displace from the land, Hebrews adopt the practice of directly attributing land ownership and fertility to divinity (von Waldow 1974, 494).

22. This is not to say that Israel is completely immune from this phenomenon. After all, one must remember that the Law is being refined, expanded, and rewritten within a monarchic setting. Pleins (2001, 517–36) acknowledges that the hierarchical underpinnings of Hebrew society are partly responsible for the diversity of social visions in the Hebrew canon.

23. Of course, YHWH is Israel's "monarch."

24. Nevertheless, the focal point of every individual action is still the common, social endeavor of living up to their election to responsibility as the Chosen People of God.

25. Cf. Lv 20:26.

26. Doron (1978, 76) suggests that the whole point of didactic motive clauses is to underscore the role of Law in providing direction to the path that leads to life.

27. The importance of such willing compliance is illustrated in the difficulty of public enforcement for many of these economic ordinances. For example, Kahan (1972, 1274) notes that many farmers, heavily burdened by so many state exactions, simply give up tithing.

28. Ex 32:13; Lv 20:24; Nm 26:53, 33–36; Dt 29:8, 31:7. See also Joshua. Von Waldow (1974, 496) notes that the phrase "the land which Yahweh your God gives you for an inheritance" is not used until Deuteronomy (4:21, 4:38, 12:9, 15:4, 19:10, 20:16, 21:23, 24:4, 25:19, 26:1). Thus, Israel is able to justify displacing people who had occupied the land before her.

29. Cf. Ogletree (1983, 80).

Chapter 5.   Law, Scarcity, and Striving

1. An alternative approach to employing the Old Testament in grappling with the question of scarcity is the flood story in Genesis. After all, Ancient Near Eastern thinking uses flood narratives to deal with the issue of overpopulation. The Old Tes-

tament is aware of this (Gn 6:1) but subsequently diverges from these flood stories and focuses instead on human violence rather than scarcity as the main problem. For more on the flood stories, see Moran (2002). My thanks to Norbert Lohfink (personal correspondence) for bringing up this point.

2. This phrase is from the *Kiddushin* 4:14. See Danby (1933, 329).

3. The shift in Old Testament scholarship toward creation theology lends itself well to viewing divine creation as God's way of provisioning human needs. See Brueggemann (1996) for these developments in the literature.

4. Von Waldow (1974, 499) cautions against unduly magnifying prosperity in the Promised Land beyond all proportions because the constant refrain and reference to a "land flowing with milk and honey" may be reflective of a people getting carried away in their enthusiastic gratitude. Whether it was due to intense appreciation or not is unimportant for this study. What is critical to note is that even the people themselves perceive that they have abundant material provisions and that these came from God as a gift.

5. Lohfink (1991, 42; 1987) views the use of such "mythic language" as indicative of God's inauguration of a new and just society for Israel.

6. In particular, see Dt 8, 28, and 30; Lv 26. See also Dt 6:3, 14:28–29, 15:10–11, 16:15, 23:19–20, 26:1–15; Lv 25:18–22; Ex 23:25.

7. See, for example, Ezekiel 34 and Amos 9:13–14.

8. Habel (1995) notes that there are six distinct land ideologies in the Hebrew scriptures, to wit: royal (I Kings, Psalms), theocratic (Deuteronomy), ancestral household (Joshua), prophetic (Jeremiah), agrarian (Leviticus), and immigrant (Abraham narratives). It is beyond the scope of this study to evaluate each of these views of land. It is sufficient for our purposes to observe that the foregoing claim that land is a conditional gift from God subject to people's fidelity to the Covenant falls along the lines of what Habel describes as the theocratic ideology of Deuteronomy.

9. Unconditional abundance would be immune to failures in human response. An example is the manna in the desert, where people always had enough regardless of whether they had followed God's instructions or not (Ex 16:17–30).

10. See also Pleins (2001, 452–83).

11. Gamoran (1971) cautions that just because Jews are charging each other interest in Egypt does not necessarily mean that Jews in Israel are also violating the laws against usury.

12. The Ifugaos are a mountain tribal people in the northern Philippines.

13. There are several law collections in Babylonia named after kings who promulgated them. These include the code of Ur-Nammu of Ur (2050 B.C.), the code of Lipit-Ishtar of Isin (1850 B.C.), the code of Hammurabi of Babylon (1700 B.C.), and the laws of the city of Eshnunna (pre-dating Hammurabi and perhaps even Lipit-Ishtar). See de Vaux (1965, 144–46). These ancient Near Eastern laws are significant because they provide insights to the provenance of Hebrew Law.

14. In losing the element of surprise, such regular debt releases could potentially give rise to moral hazard problems or to credit simply drying up in anticipation of a forthcoming scheduled debt release. Thus, it is understandable why the

Deuteronomist has to explicitly remind people of their moral obligation to lend to their needy brethren even as the year of remission approached (Dt 15:7–10). North (1954, 224) speculates on how demoralizing such recurring universal releases must have been to the thrifty and hardworking segments of the population, besides not being workable at all.

15. C. Wright (1990, 249–57) disagrees that Leviticus 25 does away with the practice of slavery since the Jubilee Law refers to landholders that had fallen into economic distress. This contrasts with the slave-release laws of Exodus and Deuteronomy that pertain to the Hebrew landless classes who are forced to sell themselves for unpaid debts. This will be discussed further in a later section on the development of law.

16. The Code of Hammurabi can be found at the website of the Avalon Project at Yale Law School: http://www.yale.edu/lawweb/avalon/medieval/hammenu.htm

17. Note that this is only an imputed wage since slaves do not receive any actual monetary compensation (Cohn 1972, col. 1655).

18. Of course, some differential should be factored in to cover the living expenses of the slave. As it is, however, we have a 100 percent differential. Feldman (1972, 41) records the average annual wage rate of a free laborer at six to eight shekels, and the purchase price of a slave at thirty shekels. Cf. Ex 21:32.

19. De Vaux (1965, 72–74, 166–67); Mays (1987, 148–49); Chirichigno (1993, 113–30, 139–42); Neufeld (1955, 376–78); J. R. Porter (1990, 103); Lowery (2000, 13–15); Kahan (1972, 1270); Ogletree (1983, 67–69).

20. As we see in the next section, some scholars do not believe that Leviticus 25 abolishes the practice of debt-slavery.

21. Kahan (1972, 1269) notes that the purchase price of a slave later rises to fifty shekels or more.

22. Feldman (1972, 40) notes that Italy, the center of the Roman Empire, has a 30 percent slave population. By Ezra's and Nehemiah's figures, this means that Israel has nearly half the rate.

23. Feldman (1972, 40) himself notes this. There would have been more war-captive slaves at the time of Israel's expansion during the reigns of David and Solomon. The decline of Israel and Judah in the centuries that followed can only mean a diminution of such kind of slaves in Israel. Kahan (1972, 1269, 1275) also concludes similarly.

24. Rasor (1993–94, 185) interprets the six-year service of debt-slaves as the presumption that debt would have been paid by then.

25. Of course, one would have to deduct from this the living expenses of the slave.

26. Recall that the Jubilee Law from Leviticus 25 is the radical socioeconomic reform every fifty years when ancestral lands are returned to their original owners, slaves are freed, and debts are forgiven.

27. Soss's (1973, 340–42) economic analysis of the Jubilee Law leads him to conclude that it is so anti-buyer in its provisions because of the risks and the unfavorable terms imposed on the buyer. If land sales were truly governed by the Jubilee Law, there would have been no buyers to begin with. That there are still land sales going on

at that time despite the provisions of the Jubilee Law suggests that the law is never truly enforced.

28. To get an idea of ancient tax burdens, note that under Roman taxation the state's share in the farmer's produce is 25 percent (Kahan 1972, 1274). See Oakman (1986) for calculations on the heavy fiscal impositions on peasants at the time of Jesus.

29. Even in a modern economy of growth and surplus, interest rates in the upper teens are considered to be a burden. How much more burdensome must interest rates have been in ancient economies that are low growth to begin with and where the rates are relatively much higher.

30. Total debt is most likely even more, given the limit on loan recovery due to the Sabbath slave-release.

31. The period of the monarchy and exile runs from 1020–539 B.C. See Brown, Fitzmeyer and Murphy (1990, 1229–37).

32. Lang (1985) disputes this and uses social scientific criticism to argue that early Israel is not an egalitarian, classless society as is commonly believed. There are deeply rooted tensions between peasants and landlords stemming from the inherently uneven distribution of power in the working arrangements of an agrarian economy.

33. Gottwald (1979, 257–94) describes the nature of clan mutual assistance in Israel.

34. Albright (1948); Noth (1960); Mendenhall (1962); Gottwald (1979).

35. See Pleins (2001, 26) for the dating of the Deuteronomic Code.

36. Some scholars disagree and point to disparities in the language of Proverbs and Deuteronomy. See, for example, Pleins (2001, 452–83).

37. Pleins (2001, 75–81) disputes this and notes that the prophets have their own distinctive critique.

38. Mercantile exchange blossoms because of the centralization of power and because of Israel's access to and control of port facilities on the Red Sea (Kahan 1972, 1269).

39. C. Wright (1990, 106) observes that even as this forced levy applies only to the Canaanite population, the Hebrews are nevertheless deprived of much-needed agricultural labor that could have otherwise worked on family landholdings. However, Kahan (1972, 1269) argues that because Solomon requires much more labor for his building projects than is available from war-captive slaves, hundreds of thousands of free Israelites are pressed into service as corvée labor. In either case, ordinary landholding families suffer from these royal impositions.

40. De Vaux (1965, 72–74, 166–67); Mays (1987, 148–49); Chirichigno (1993, 113–30, 139–42); Neufeld (1955, 376–78); J. R. Porter (1990, 103); Lowery (2000, 13–15); Kahan (1972, 1270); Ogletree (1983, 67–69).

41. See also Pleins (2001, 58–61).

42. Soss (1973, 329–32) observes that early Hebrew legislation is not designed to affect the pre-tax distribution of income. Note, for example, the proportional nature of the poor tithe in which a constant proportion is contributed regardless of one's income level.

43. Moreover, Gamoran (1971) argues that such interest-free loans are instituted because the loans are predominantly subsistence, not commercial, loans.

44. Gamoran (1971) distinguishes between resident and nonresident aliens and claims that the former have the same protection as the poor. Gnuse (1985, 20) argues that the explicit specification that it is alright to charge foreigners interest reflects the development of the Israelite economy toward more commercial activities with her neighbors.

45. Even the modern economy mandates certain kinds of loans. Because of their higher risk and the higher cost of managing their loans, farmers and small-scale businesses generally are unable to compete for credit relative to the industrial, capital-intensive sector. Thus, governments have on occasion required banks to set aside a certain portion of their portfolios for agricultural and small business loans.

46. See, for example, Pleins (2001, 88n.63); C. Wright (1990, 58); Chirichigno (1993, 17–29); Schenker (1998, 40n.32); Gamoran (1971, 132n.45); von Waldow (1970, 182–83).

47. He believes that Exodus 21:2–6 pertains to debt-slaves.

48. Even if the Jubilee is early legislation, one could still not ignore the improvement in the treatment of debt-slaves in moving from Exodus to Deuteronomy. Of course, scholars who read Leviticus 25 as the abolition of debt-slavery would not accept it as an early legislation; but it would be out of character for Exodus and especially Deuteronomy to move toward a harsher treatment of slaves when the moral sensibilities of Israel are self-evidently improving between the Covenant and Deuteronomic Codes.

49. For example, note the simultaneous humane and discriminatory treatment of slaves. See Hanson (1977, 116–17).

50. See Pleins (2001, 517–36) for an excellent discussion of the diversity of social visions in the Hebrew canon.

51. In scholastic language, note that humans are not only instrumental but secondary causes as well since final effects can be properly attributed to them (see chapter 3).

52. This phrase is taken from *Kiddushin* 4:14. See Danby (1933, 329).

53. Lowery (2000, 85–86) sees a double entendre in the use of the word *bara'* in Genesis to describe God's act of creation. Besides meaning "to create," *bara'* can also signify "to fatten oneself" and to separate fats from liquids as in the case of oils, including those that are used for ceremonial royal anointing. The anointing of the monarch, besides manifesting God's favor on the king, is also meant to invoke a period of prosperity and stability in the new reign of the king. Moreover, *bara'* has been used to refer to that which is fat (as in the case of the cows in Pharaoh's dream in Gn 41:2–20), rich and lavish (as in the case of Hb 1:16) and healthy (as in the case of Dn 1:15). Given all these associations, Lowery argues that *bara'* is used in Genesis 1 to refer both to God's act of creating and to describe the resulting creation as "fat," prosperous, and overflowing with goodness and abundance.

54. It is in this sense that one is to read B. Gordon's (1989, 11–20) exposition on the biblical solution to the problem of scarcity via "observance of the law."

Chapter 6.   Participated Righteousness: Incarnational and Instrumental

1. Pneumatology is the branch of theology on the study of the Holy Spirit.

2. Byrne (1981, 570–76) cites Romans 8:9–11 as an example.

3. Piper (1980) cites Romans 3:25–26 as an example of such subjective genitive use of righteousness. In contrast to Romans 3:21–22, verses 25–26 describe "conditions of the will" in God's nature: "faithfulness, allegiance, commitment, devotion, loyalty, . . . inclination or will . . . inexorably committed always to preserve and display his glory" (Piper 1980, 31).

4. Byrne (1981, 558n.3) and Piper (1980) provide bibliography on the literature on this question. See also Nebe (1992) and Denney (1908–26).

5. Byrne (1981, 576) cites literature that suggests a narrowing of the gap, if not outright convergence, between the Catholic and Protestant positions on this issue.

6. See also Verhey (1984, 104–5).

7. See also 1 Cor 1:30; Phil 3:9. Ziesler (1972, 164–65) summarizes the commonalities of these passages.

8. See also Dahl (1977, 95–120).

9. This threefold dimension of "community-cross–new creation" is examined in greater depth in the next chapter.

10. See, for example, Käsemann (1971, 66–70) and Dahl (1977, 110).

11. Cf. Vatican Council II (1965).

12. Thus, Paul is so adept at shifting gears in his letters from lofty theological discourses to resolving practical, down-to-earth problems of living together as a community.

13. Rom 3:21, 5:12–21; Phil 3:9; 1 Cor 1:30.

14. See Sacred Congregation for the Doctrine of the Faith (1986).

15. Augustine, in the opening paragraph of his *Confessions,* writes: "[Y]ou have made us for yourself, and our heart is restless until it rests in you" (1960, 43).

Chapter 7.   Economic Agency in Kingdom Discipleship

1. Q is the hypothetical additional source that both Matthew and Luke are believed to have used for material common to their respective gospels that is not found in Mark.

2. As does Hengel (1973, 24).

3. Wheeler (1995, 71). See B. Gordon (1989, 46n.6) for other authors who take the same position.

4. Cf. Verhey (1984, 16).

5. Even one's relationship to God is affected by such economic exchanges. Perkins observes that there is a "biblical perception that one's religious status is a function of how the exchanges of such limited goods as wealth and honor are distributed in the community" (1994, 59).

6. Satisfying economic rights (basic needs, food, health care, clothing, shelter, employment, etc.) require real resources that can only come from others in the community.

7. A zero-sum phenomenon arises when a person's consumption of a particular good leaves that much less for everybody else. Most commodities cannot be used or consumed by more than one person at the same time. There is rivalry in consumption.

8. See also Schrage (1988, 13–39).

9. See appendix 3 for a lengthier discussion of God's threefold causality.

10. Scholastic distinctions will be helpful at this point. As we have seen in part I, God is Pure Act (no potency at all in God). Thus, God is righteousness in its fullest sense, encompassing all, but not limited to, the manifold senses of the term in Hebrew Scripture: as power, fidelity, uprightness, and right relations (Achtemeier 1962b).

11. Humans have both potency and act. Since they are finite and defectible, humans will not be able to fully actualize their participation in God's righteousness.

12. It is akin to the *exitus-reditus* schema of Thomas Aquinas in his *Summa Theologiae* in which God's self-donation (*exitus*) is followed by a return of the creature to God (*reditus*).

13. Not "unitive" because, properly speaking, only God has that kind of power to bring about a union, as in the case of the Body of Christ. A "welcoming inclusiveness" is a better description when speaking of humans relative to each other.

14. Readers are reminded of the difference that we have already seen in chapter 3 between a secondary cause and a mere instrument. A final effect can be properly ascribed to a secondary cause because the latter's contribution is distinctive and proper to itself. A mere instrument does not have such a similar proper effect. Thus, in talking of a sculptor (principal cause) and his chisel (instrument), the statue (final effect) is properly the sculptor's and not the chisel's effect because of the form of the statue that the sculptor has in his mind. Relative to God, however, God is the First Cause of the statue, while the sculptor is only a secondary, albeit principal, cause.

Chapter 8.   Nature and Impact of Scarcity

1. Note the distinction between needs (vital for human flourishing) and mere wants (nonessential demand).

2. Scarcity, after all, applies not merely to tangible commodities but also to social positions. See, for example, Hirsch (1976).

3. S. Gordon's (1980, 213–14) "The Economics of the Afterlife" examines the implications of the absence of scarcity in paradise by distinguishing world time from heaven time. The former has duration, but not "width" of experience, while the latter has "width" and intensity of experience, which renders duration redundant. I disagree with his characterization of "width" in heaven time. While the breadth of human heavenly experience will be much greater than that in world time, nevertheless, such "width" will not come close to approximating the perfect fullness of God's

vision. Moreover, duration becomes an irrelevant consideration in the face of an eternal life that is devoid of any instrumental activity.

4. Limiting formal perfections are the powers and characteristics embedded within creatures that define them to be what they are in their mode of being and operation (including their deficiencies) which is also known as their *form*.

5. Recall the difference between secondary and instrumental causes outlined in chapter 3.

6. Economists describe this as externalities in consumption.

7. J. Wright (1957, 6–7) enumerates these as the multiplicity of species and their essential perfections, the order following both accidental and essential perfections, and the order of the whole to the end flowing from the goodness of its parts and their internal order. See also ST I, 25, a.6.

8. After all, there are no chance events to God, who is all-perfect and, thus, omniscient (ST I, 103, a.7).

9. However, what "I have" does not capture the totality of who "I am"; my body does not present the fullness of who I am.

10. Note, in particular, Malthus ([1798] 1960, 138–39).

11. This is not to say that there is temporality in God or that God is mutable. I use "response" in the sense of God acting in a single sweeping vision in which the past, present, and future converge in a single instant.

Chapter 9. Malthusian and Participative Theodicies: A Comparison

1. See Waterman (1983a, 197-98) for a brief assessment of the sources of Malthus's epistemology in relying solely on natural theology.

2. See also Malthus ([1798] 1960, 132).

3. This is a movement from potency to act (see appendix 2).

4. See Waterman (1991a, 58-82) for the larger intellectual backdrop of the era.

5. Quoted in Waterman (1983a, 201).

6. See James (1979) for a more extended discussion on the development of and the broader historical backdrop behind Malthus's position on poor relief.

7. See Waterman (1983b, 1991a) for an in-depth examination of the impact of philosophical and theological premises on economic policy among nineteenth-century British Christian political economists.

8. This would certainly be one way of accounting for the disconcerting claim of Deuteronomy 15:11 that there will always be poor in our midst.

9. Recall that Malthus writes his *Essay* in reaction to views on human perfectibility such as Godwin's. Participative theodicy is not an apology for Godwin's ([1793] 1992) social agenda or his views on private property ownership. This study merely claims that material sufficiency for all falls within the effect that is proper to human beings' operation as free and intelligent secondary causes. This includes the social assistance programs of collective secondary causality.

10. See, for example, Musgrave (1959), Ver Eecke (1998), Head (1974), and Brennan and Walsh (1990).

11. See, for example, the position of Hegel on the economy (Maker 1987).

12. My thanks to the anonymous referee for alerting me to the similarities between my conclusion on activist social ameliorative policies and the merit-goods literature. Both affirm (1) the need to provide certain goods to every member of the community, to the extent possible, and (2) the use of economic transfers to effect such entitlements. However, I go beyond current notions of merit goods in economic scholarship in a number of significant ways.

First, merit goods are justified in economic literature on utilitarian grounds, through their improvement of allocative efficiency. Merit goods are insufficiently provided because the private benefits appropriated by economic agents fall short of these goods' social benefits. Thus, economic theory justifies policy intervention in supplying merit goods because of the resulting improvement in economic efficiency. In contrast, I call for the provision of these merit goods for their *intrinsic value* in effecting human flourishing (rather than enhancing allocative efficiency). This is a deeper noneconomic warrant for the provision of merit goods.

Second, merit goods in economics are limited to a clearly defined set of goods and services, such as subsidized housing, free school lunches, and medical care. The problem here is the justification of additional, noneconomic criteria that determine what gets to be included in the basket of merit goods. There is no consensus on this question. This study partially fills this lacuna by suggesting a foundational standard: the instrumental value of goods in effecting human flourishing. Moreover, this suggested yardstick dovetails A. K. Sen's (1999) emerging "capabilities and functionings" alternative to the much-touted utility function of neoclassical economics.

Third, the provision of merit goods in economics is generally seen as a governmental responsibility. I broaden the obligation to a wider circle of providers. This study's metaphysical and scriptural arguments independently arrive at the same conclusion: as individuals and as a community, we are responsible for each other's well-being. Thus, the duty of provisioning those who are in want goes beyond state institutions to include a wide spectrum of private human associations based on their ability to provide assistance. This opens the door to a new understanding of merit-goods provision in terms of the principle of subsidiarity.

13. Cf. Lohfink (1987, 5–15).

14. Irenaean theodicy focuses on the growth and development that follow in the wake of evil, while Augustinian theodicy sees evil as an attendant punishment for sin. See Hick (1981).

15. Moreover, in not casting earthly life as one of probation, participative theodicy avoids the problem of divine foreknowledge in Malthus's formulation. See Pullen (1981, 41–42).

16. See, for example, Verhey (1984).

Chapter 10.   Toward a Theology of Economic Agency

1. This is from the phenomenon of the *One and the Many*. See appendix 2.

2. These include finitude and defectibility in human nature and chance and contingency in economic processes.

3. We are responsible for one another's well-being and must attend to each other's economic distress. See Barrera (2005) for a fuller examination of the notion of economic security as a threefold divine gift of (1) God providing for our material needs (2) through our own efforts and (3) with the nurturing support of the community.

4. See, for example, Monaghan (2003).

5. Note, for example, Maki's (2001) collection of essays that examine the metaphysical premises of modern economic analysis.

Appendix 1.   Typology of Scarcity

1. Aristotle (1941a). The Aristotelean categories are substance and its nine accidents. Predicaments derived from within the subject are quantity, quality, and relation. Those external to the subject are *habitus,* time, place, and position. Those that are both external and internal to the subject are action and receptivity (being acted upon).

2. Danner (1995) examines scarcity in the context of personalism and holds that the longings of the human spirit far exceed the material means to satisfy them. After all, people use "material goods not only to benefit physically, but also to transcend in thought and action matter's limitations" (28).

3. The word "economics" comes from *oikos* (household) and *nomos* (law). Aristotle (1941b, 1941c) uses *oikonomia* to refer to the management of the household. If economic life is to social activities as species is to genus, then the distinctive character of economic life as a species is the need to allocate. Aristotle's definition presupposes Robbins's because there is always a need to allocate in any household management. "Economics" is used in both senses in this study. Aristotle's notion is especially apt whenever we refer to the economic sphere as a particular realm within the twofold order of the universe since it can be effectively adapted to refer to the management of the larger community's material affairs. On the other hand, Robbins's usage is a more precise technical description of the task. The context should indicate to readers whether I am using the broader Aristotelean sense or Robbins's much narrower definition.

4. Davenport (1913) is credited with the original use of the expression "opportunity cost," although von Wieser ([1889] 1988) is believed to have formulated the concept (Ohrenstein and Gordon 1992, 57–58).

5. Thus, S. Gordon (1980) even goes so far as to claim that there is an economics of the afterlife, since human nature's limitations circumscribe the enjoyment of that beatitude.

6. In contrast to the neoclassical school of thought, heterodox economists distinguish between needs and wants. Social economists have long grappled with this issue. See, for example, Danner (1994) and O'Boyle (1994).

7. Note, for example, the disequilibria caused by business cycles.

8. Waterman (1991b, 469) notes the further distinction that some scholars make between poverty and indigence. Poverty is a condition of subsistence income; indigence is a step below this socially conditioned subsistence income.

Appendix 2.   Goodness Received, Goodness Communicated

1. This is also known as existential, substantial, or transcendental goodness.

2. See also Gilby (1969, vol. 10, appendix 2, 180).

3. In looking at created goods in relation to God, we move from the form to the efficient cause and then to the end. This is the order from the perspective of the thing caused. When viewed from the perspective of causing, the order is from the end to the efficient cause and then to the form (ST I, 5, a.4; Dewan 1978, 298).

4. J. Wright (1957) states: "[In] the twofold order in the universe, ... [the external order is] directed to God, the other [the internal order] between creatures that they may assist one another in arriving at a divine likeness" (8). Later, he adds, "The order to one another . . . is to assist one another in achieving the end, in becoming like God" (17).

5. We examine this in greater depth in chapter 3 when we delineate how scarcity provides a critical occasion for moving from ontological goodness to moral goodness.

6. These arise either from variations in degrees of participation, as in the different degrees of hotness, or from the forms themselves being different in degrees of perfection, as in the colors' varying shades relative to the "luminosity of white" (te Velde 1995, 39).

7. Examples of other kinds of accidental goodness are personal skills and talents.

8. Aquinas writes, "[T]hings are ordered to God as an end, not merely according to their substantial act of being, but also according to those items which are added as pertinent to perfection, *and even according to the proper operation which also belongs to the thing's perfection*" (SCG III, 20, #8; emphasis added).

9. The former, being-in-act, is also called first act or first perfection; the latter, being-in-operation, is called second act or second perfection (te Velde 1995, 42).

10. Thus, the use of the phrase "God's activity" is analogical because there is no potency in God.

11. Included under operations are the activities necessary for survival and the communication of their existence to others (J. Wright 1957, 97n.108).

12. Two points must be made. First, essence, existence, and operations are identical in God, who is Pure Act. Second, operations occur not only because of the limitations of one's nature. In fact, operations may be a part of the creature's nature itself as in the case of the social nature of human beings. They reach out to each other not only because of their need for one another but because of the relational nature of human beings themselves.

13. Thus, the claim that created goods are meant to serve human needs cannot be used as a license for wanton ecological abuse. Created material goods serve human needs only in the measure that both parts and the whole move toward revealing that dimension of God's goodness they bear within their being and activity.

Appendix 3.   Ontological Material Sufficiency

1. Refer to appendix 1 for an explanation of the different kinds of scarcity.

2. See also ST I, 105, a.5; SCG III, 69; *De potentia* III, 7.

3. See also SCG III, 69, #16.

4. In this study, I deal only with human beings and not with the adequacy of provisioning for other living creatures.

5. ST I, 19, a.6; I, 22, a.2; I, 103, aa.5–7; SCG III, 64; III, 94; III, 113.

REFERENCES

Achtemeier, P. J. 1962a. "Righteousness in the NT." In *The Interpreter's Dictionary of the Bible,* edited by George Arthur Buttrick. 4 vols. New York: Abingdon Press.

———. 1962b. "Righteousness in the OT." In *The Interpreter's Dictionary of the Bible,* edited by George Arthur Buttrick. 4 vols. New York: Abingdon Press.

Albertson, James. 1954. "Instrumental Causality in St. Thomas." *New Scholasticism* 28:409–35.

Albright, William. 1948. *From the Stone Age to Christianity: Monotheism and the Historical Process.* Second edition. Baltimore, MD: Johns Hopkins Press.

Aquinas, Thomas. 1923. *Summa Contra Gentiles.* Translated by the English Dominican Fathers. London: Burns, Oates & Washbourne.

———. 1934. *On the Power of God (Quaestiones disputatae de potentia dei).* 3 vols. London: Burns, Oates & Washbourne.

———. 1947/8. *Summa Theologica.* Translated by the Fathers of the English Dominican Province. 3 vols. New York: Benzinger Brothers.

———. 1952–54. *Truth (De veritate).* 3 vols. Translated by R. W. Mulligan, J. V. McGlynn, and R. W. Schmidt. Chicago: H. Regnery.

Aristotle. 1941a. *Categories.* In *The Basic Works of Aristotle,* edited by Richard McKeon. New York: Random House

———. 1941b. *Nicomachean Ethics.* In *The Basic Works of Aristotle,* edited by Richard McKeon. New York: Random House.

———. 1941c. *Politics.* In *The Basic Works of Aristotle,* edited by Richard McKeon. New York: Random House.

Augustine. 1953. *Enchiridion (Manual to Laurentius Concerning Faith, Hope, and Charity).* Translated by Ernest Evans. London: S.P.C.K.

———. 1960. *The Confessions of Saint Augustine.* Translated by John Ryan. New York: Image Books.

Barker, Ernest. 1980. *Social Contract: Essays by Locke, Hume, and Rousseau.* Westport, CT: Greenwood Press.

Barrera, Albino. 2005. *Economic Compulsion and Christian Ethics.* Cambridge: Cambridge University Press.

Barth, Markus. 1968. "Jews and Gentiles: The Social Character of Justification in Paul." *Journal of Ecumenical Studies* 5:241–67.

Beasley-Murray, G. R. 1976. "The Righteousness of God in the History of Israel and the Nations: Romans 9–11." *Review and Expositor* 73:437–50.

Berlin, Isaiah. 1958. *Two Concepts of Liberty*. Oxford: Clarendon.

Betz, Hans. 1979. *Galatians: A Commentary on Paul's Letter to the Churches in Galatia*. Philadelphia: Fortress Press.

Birch, Bruce. 1991. *Let Justice Roll Down: The Old Testament, Ethics, and Christian Life*. Louisville, KY: Westminster John Knox Press.

Blackman, E. C. 1962. "Justification, Justify." In *The Interpreter's Dictionary of the Bible*, edited by George Arthur Buttrick. 4 vols. New York: Abingdon Press.

Blaug, Mark. 1985. *Economic Theory in Retrospect*. Fourth edition. Cambridge: Cambridge University Press.

Boecker, Hans Jochen. 1980. *Law and the Administration of Justice in the Old Testament and Ancient East*. Translated by Jeremy Moiser. Minneapolis: Augsburg Publishing.

Bottorff, J. F. 1973. "The Relation of Justification and Ethics in the Pauline Epistles." *Scottish Journal of Theology* 26:421–30.

Brennan, Geoffrey, and Cliff Walsh, eds. 1990. *Rationality, Individualism and Public Policy*. Canberra: Australian National University.

Brown, Raymond, Joseph Fitzmyer, and Roland Murphy, eds. 1990. *The New Jerome Biblical Commentary*. Englewood Cliffs, NJ: Prentice-Hall.

Brueggemann, Walter. 1977. *The Land*. Philadelphia: Fortress.

———. 1985. "Theodicy in a Social Dimension." *Journal for the Study of the Old Testament* 33:3–25.

———. 1994. "Justice: The Earthly Form of God's Holiness." *Reformed World* 44:13–27.

———. 1996. "The Loss and Recovery of Creation in Old Testament Theology." *Theology Today* 53:177–90.

Byrne, Brendan. 1981. "Living out the Righteousness of God: The Contribution of Rom 6:1–8:13 to an Understanding of Paul's Ethical Presuppositions." *Catholic Biblical Quarterly* 43:557–81.

Carlyle, Thomas. 1888–89. *Works*. 30 vols. London: Chapman & Hall.

Chirichigno, Gregory. 1993. *Debt-Slavery in Israel and the Ancient Near East*. Sheffield: JSOT Press.

Coffey, Brian. 1949. "The Notion of Order According to St. Thomas Aquinas." *Modern Schoolman* 27:1–18.

Cohn, Haim Hermann. 1972. "Slavery." *Encyclopaedia Judaica* 14:1655–58.

Culpepper, R. Alan. 1976. "God's Righteousness in the Life of His People: Romans 12–15." *Review and Expositor* 73:451–63.

Dahl, Nils Alstrup. 1977. *Studies in Paul: Theology for the Early Christian Mission*. Minneapolis: Augsburg Publishing.

Danby, Herbert, trans. 1933. *The Mishnah*. London: Oxford University Press.

Danner, Peter. 1994. "The Person and the Social Economy: Needs, Values, and Principles." In *The Social Economics of Human Material Need*, edited by John Davis and Edward O'Boyle. Carbondale: Southern Illinois University Press.

————. 1995. "Personalism and Scarcity." *Forum for Social Economics* 25:21–32.

Davenport, Herbert Joseph. 1913. *The Economics of Enterprise.* New York: Macmillan.

Dearman, John Andrew. 1984. "Prophecy, Property and Politics." *Society of Biblical Literature Seminar Papers* 23:385–97.

Denney, James. 1908–26. "Righteousness (in St. Paul's teaching)." In *Encyclopædia of Religion and Ethics,* edited by James Hastings. New York: Charles Scribner's Sons.

de Vaux, Roland. 1965. *Ancient Israel.* Two vols. New York: McGraw-Hill.

Dewan, Lawrence. 1978. "St. Thomas and the Causality of God's Goodness." *Laval Theologique et Philosophique* 34:291–304.

Dodd, C. 1936. *The Parables of the Kingdom.* New York: Charles Scribner's Sons.

Donahue, John. 1977. "Biblical Perspectives on Justice." In *The Faith That Does Justice: Examining the Christian Sources for Social Change,* edited by John Haughey. New York: Paulist Press.

Doron, Pinchas. 1978. "Motive Clauses in the Laws of Deuteronomy: Their Forms, Functions and Contents." *Hebrew Annual Review* 2:61–77.

Eichrodt, Walther. 1961. *Theology of the Old Testament.* Vol. 1. Translated by J. A. Baker. Philadelphia: Westminster Press.

Fager, Jeffrey. 1993. *Land Tenure and the Biblical Jubilee: Uncovering Hebrew Ethics Through the Sociology of Knowledge.* Journal for the Study of the Old Testament Supplement Series 155. Sheffield: JSOT Press.

Feldman, Leon, ed. 1972. *Ancient and Medieval Jewish History.* New Brunswick, NJ: Rutgers.

Forbes, Dalton. 1960. "Temporal Goods in the Christian Economy: A Thomist Synthesis, Part I." *Revue de L'Universite D'Ottawa* 30:185–206.

————. 1961. "Temporal Goods in the Christian Economy: A Thomist Synthesis, Part II: Temporal Values in the Christian Economy: Positive Attitudes." *Revue de L'Universite D'Ottawa* 31:39–71.

Foster, George. 1967. "Peasant Society and the Image of Limited Good." In *Peasant Society: A Reader,* edited by Jack Potter, May Diaz, and George Foster. Boston: Little & Brown.

Furnish, Victor Paul. 1968. *Theology and Ethics in Paul.* Nashville, TN: Abingdon Press.

Gallagher, David M. 1994. "Aquinas on Goodness and Moral Goodness." In *Thomas Aquinas and His Legacy,* edited by David M. Gallagher. Washington, DC: Catholic University of America Press.

Gamoran, Hillel. 1971. "The Biblical Law Against Loans on Interest." *Journal of the Near Eastern Studies* 30:127–34.

Gauthier, David. 1986. *Morals by Agreement.* Oxford: Clarendon Press.

Gemser, B. 1953. "The Importance of the Motive Clause in Old Testament Law." In *Congress Volume, Copenhagen,* Vetus Testatmentum Supplements, vol. 1. Leiden: E. J. Brill.

Gilby, Thomas, ed. 1969. *Summa Theologiae.* 61 vols. Garden City, NY: Image Books.

Ginzberg, Eli. 1932. *Studies in the Economics of the Bible.* Philadelphia: Jewish Publication Society of America.

Gnuse, Robert. 1985. *You Shall Not Steal: Community and Property in the Biblical Tradition.* Maryknoll, NY: Orbis.

Godwin, William. [1793] 1992. *Political Justice* (Enquiry Concerning Political Justice and Its Influence on Morals and Happiness). 2 vols. Facsimile reprint. New York: Woodstock Books.

Gordon, Barry. 1982. "Lending at Interest: Some Jewish, Greek, and Christian Approaches, 800 BC–AD 100." *History of Political Economy* 14:406–26.

———. 1989. *The Economic Problem in Biblical and Patristic Thought.* New York: E. J. Brill.

Gordon, Scott. 1980. "The Economics of the Afterlife." *Journal of Political Economy* 88:213–14.

Gottwald, Norman. 1979. *The Tribes of Yahweh: A Sociology of the Religion of Liberated Israel, 1250–1050 B.C.E.* Maryknoll, NY: Orbis.

Greenberg, M. 1972. "Sabbatical Year and Jubilee." *Encyclopedia Judaica* 14:577–78.

Gregory, James. 1975. "Image of Limited Good, or Expectation of Reciprocity?" *Current Anthropology* 16:73–92.

Gustafson, James. 1977. "Interdependence, Finitude, and Sin: Reflections on Scarcity." *Journal of Religion* 57:156–68.

Habel, Norman. 1995. *The Land Is Mine: Six Biblical Land Ideologies.* Minneapolis: Fortress Press.

Hanson, Paul. 1977. "Theological Significance of Contradiction Within the Book of the Covenant." In *Canon and Authority: Essays in Old Testament Religion and Theology,* edited by George W. Coats and Burke O. Long. Philadelphia: Fortress Press.

Harvey-Phillips, M. B. 1984. "Malthus' Theodicy: The Intellectual Background of His Contribution to Political Economy." *History of Political Economy* 16:591–608.

Haughey, John. 1977. "Jesus as the Justice of God." In *The Faith That Does Justice: Examining the Christian Sources for Social Change,* edited by John Haughey. New York: Paulist Press.

Hays, Richard. 1987. "Christology and Ethics in Galatians: The Law of Christ." *Catholic Biblical Quarterly* 49:268–90.

———. 1996. *The Moral Vision of the New Testament: Community, Cross, New Creation; A Contemporary Introduction to New Testament Ethics.* San Francisco: Harper.

Head, John. 1974. *Public Goods and Public Welfare.* Durham, NC: Duke University Press.

Hengel, Martin. 1974. *Property and Riches in the Early Church: Aspects of a Social History of Early Christianity.* Translated by John Bowden. Philadelphia: Fortress Press.

Hick, John. 1981. "An Irenaean Theodicy." In *Encountering Evil: Live Options in Theodicy,* edited by Stephen Davis. Atlanta: John Knox Press.

Hirsch, Fred. 1976. *Social Limits to Growth.* Cambridge, MA: Harvard University Press.

Hoenig, Sidney. 1969. "Sabbatical Years and the Year of Jubilee." *Jewish Quarterly Review* 59:222–36.

Hume, David. [1739] 1978. *A Treatise of Human Nature.* Oxford: Clarendon.

Jackson, Bernard. 1988. "Biblical Laws of Slavery: A Comparative Approach." In *Slavery and Other Forms of Unfree Labor,* edited by Leonie Archer. New York: Routledge.

James, Patricia. 1979. *Population Malthus: His Life and Times.* London: Routledge & Kegan Paul.

Johann, Robert. 1947. "A Comment on Secondary Causality." *Modern Schoolman* 25:19–25.

Johnson, Luke Timothy. 1981. *Sharing Possessions: Mandate and Symbol of Faith*. Philadelphia: Fortress Press.

Kahan, A. 1972. "Economic History." *Encyclopaedia Judaica* 16:1266–1324.

Käsemann, Ernst. 1969. "'The Righteousness of God' in Paul." In *New Testament Questions of Today*. Philadelphia: Fortress Press.

———. 1971. "Justification and Salvation History in the Epistle to the Romans." In *Perspectives on Paul*. Translated by Margaret Kohl. Philadelphia: Fortress Press.

Keck, Leander. 1984. "Ethics in the Gospel According to Matthew." *Iliff Review* 41:39–56.

Klubertanz, George. 1967. "Analogy." *New Catholic Encyclopedia* 1:461–65.

Kondoleon, Theodore. 1967. "Exemplarism." *New Catholic Encyclopedia* 5:712–15.

Lang, Bernhard. 1985. "The Social Organization of Peasant Poverty in Biblical Israel." In *Anthropological Approaches to the Old Testament*, edited by Bernhard Lang. Philadelphia: Fortress Press.

Leibniz, Gottfried Wilhelm. [1710] 1966. *Theodicy*. Edited and abridged by Diogenes Allen. Translated by E. M. Huggard. Indianapolis: Bobbs-Merrill.

LeMahieu, D. L. 1979. "Malthus and the Theology of Scarcity." *Journal of the History of Ideas* 40:467–74.

Locke, John. [1690] 1952. *The Second Treatise of Government*. Edited by Thomas Peardon. New York: Bobbs-Merrill.

Lohfink, Norbert. 1982. *Great Themes from the Old Testament*. Translated by Ronald Walls. Chicago: Franciscan Herald Press.

———. 1986. "The Kingdom of God and the Economy in the Bible." *Communio: International Catholic Review* 13:216–31.

———. 1987. *Option for the Poor: The Basic Principle of Liberation Theology in Light of the Bible*. Berkeley, CA: Bibal Press.

———. 1991. "Poverty in the Laws of the Ancient Near East and of the Bible." *Theological Studies* 52:34–50.

Lohse, Eduard. 1991. *Theological Ethics of the New Testament*. Translated by M. Eugene Boring. Minneapolis: Fortress Press.

Long, D. Stephen. 2000. *Divine Economy: Theology and the Market*. New York: Routledge.

Lowery, Richard. 2000. *Sabbath and Jubilee*. St. Louis: Chalice Press.

Maker, William, ed. 1987. *Hegel on Economics and Freedom*. Macon, GA: Mercer University Press.

Maki, Uskali, ed. 2001. *The Economic World View: Studies in the Ontology of Economics*. Cambridge: Cambridge University Press.

Maloney, Robert. 1974. "Usury and Restrictions on Interest-Taking in the Ancient Near East." *Catholic Biblical Quarterly* 36:1–20.

Malthus, Thomas Robert. [1798] 1960. *On Population (An Essay on the Principle of Population, as It affects the Future Improvement of Society. With Remarks on the speculations of Mr. Godwin, M. Condorcet, and other writers)*. Edited and introduced by Gertrude Himmelfarb. New York: Modern Library.

Masterson, Reginald. 1967. "Instrumental Causality." *New Catholic Encyclopedia* 7:549–51.

Matera, Frank. 1996. *New Testament Ethics: The Legacies of Jesus and Paul.* Louisville, KY: Westminster John Knox Press.

Mays, James. 1987. "Justice: Perspectives from the Prophetic Tradition." In *Prophecy in Israel: Search for an Identity,* edited by David L. Petersen. Philadelphia: Fortress Press.

McCarthy, Dennis. 1965. "Notes on the Love of God in Deuteronomy and the Father-son Relationship between Yahweh and Israel." *Catholic Biblical Quarterly* 27:144–47.

Meeks, Douglas. 1995. "Comment—Personalism and Scarcity." *Forum for Social Economics* 25:33–36.

Meislin, Bernard, and Morris Cohen. 1964. "Backgrounds of the Biblical Law Against Usury." *Comparative Studies in Society and History* 6:250–67.

Mendenhall, George. 1954. "Ancient and Biblical Law." *Biblical Archaeologist* 17:26–46.

Miller, Patrick. 1985. "The Human Sabbath: A Study in Deuteronomic Theology." *Princeton Seminary Bulletin* 6:81–97.

———. 1990. *Deuteronomy.* Louisville, KY: John Knox Press.

Monaghan, Peter. 2003. "Taking on 'Rational Man': Dissident Economists Fight for a Niche in the Discipline." *Chronicle of Higher Education* 49(20):12–15.

Moran, William. 2002. *The Most Magic Word: Essays on Babylonian and Biblical Literature.* Catholic Biblical Quarterly Monograph Series 35. Edited by Ronald Hendel. Washington, DC: Catholic Biblical Association of America.

Moxnes, Halvor. 1988. *The Economy of the Kingdom: Social Conflict and Economic Relations in Luke's Gospel.* Philadelphia: Fortress Press.

Musgrave, Richard. 1959. *Theory of Public Finance.* New York: McGraw-Hill.

Nebe, Gottfried. 1992. "Righteousness in Paul." In *Justice and Righteousness: Biblical Themes and Their Influence,* edited by Henning Graf Reventlow and Yair Hoffman. Journal for the Study of the Old Testament Supplement Series 137. Sheffield: JSOT Press.

Neufeld, Edward. 1953–54. "The Rate of Interest and the Text of Nehemiah 5:11." *Jewish Quarterly Review* 44:194–204.

———. 1955. "The Prohibitions Against Loans at Interest in Ancient Hebrew Laws." *Hebrew Union College Annual* 26:355–412.

———. 1960. "The Emergence of a Royal-Urban Society in Ancient Israel." *Hebrew Union College Annual* 31:31–53.

North, Robert. 1954. *Sociology of the Biblical Jubilee.* Rome: Pontifical Biblical Institute.

Noth, Martin. 1960. *The History of Israel.* Second edition. New York: Harper & Row.

Nozick, Robert. 1974. *Anarchy, State, and Utopia.* Oxford: Oxford University Press.

Oakman, Douglas. 1986. *Jesus and the Economic Questions of His Day.* Lewiston, NY: E. Mellen Press.

O'Boyle, Edward J. 1994. "Human Physical Need: A Concept That Is Both Absolute and Relative." In *The Social Economics of Human Material Need,* edited by John Davis and Edward O'Boyle. Carbondale: Southern Illinois University Press.

Ogletree, Thomas. 1983. *The Use of the Bible in Christian Ethics: A Constructive Essay.* Philadelphia: Fortress Press.

Ohrenstein, Roman, and Barry Gordon. 1992. *Economic Analysis in Talmudic Literature: Rabbinic Thought in the Light of Modern Economics.* New York: E. J. Brill.

Paley, William. [1802] 1972. *Natural Theology.* Houston: St. Thomas Press.

Patrick, Dale. 1985. *Old Testament Law.* Atlanta: John Knox.

Pemberton, Prentiss, and Daniel Rush Finn. 1985. *Toward a Christian Economic Ethic: Stewardship and Social Power.* Minneapolis: Winston Press.

Perkins, Pheme. 1994. "Does the New Testament Have an Economic Message?" In *Wealth in Western Thought: The Case for and Against Riches,* edited by Paul G. Schervish. Westport, CT: Praeger.

Phillips, Anthony. 1984. "The Laws of Slavery: Exodus 21:2–11." *Journal for the Study of the Old Testament* 30:51–66.

Piper, John. 1980. "The Demonstration of the Righteousness of God in Romans 3:25, 26." *Journal for the Study of the New Testament* 7:2–32.

Pleins, J. David. 2001. *The Social Visions of the Hebrew Bible.* Louisville, KY: Westminster John Knox Press.

Porter, J. R. 1990. "Wealth and Poverty in the Bible." In *Christianity and Conservatism,* edited by Michael Alison and David L. Edwards. London: Hodder & Stoughton.

Porter, Jean. 1990. *The Recovery of Virtue: The Relevance of Aquinas for Christian Ethics.* Louisville, KY: Westminster John Knox Press.

Pullen, J. M. 1981. "Malthus' Theological Ideas and Their Influence on His Principle of Population." *History of Political Economy* 13:39–54.

Rasor, Paul. 1993–94. "Biblical Roots of Modern Consumer Credit Law." *Journal of Law and Religion* 10:157–92.

Robbins, Lionel. [1932] 1952. *An Essay on the Nature and Significance of Economic Science.* London: Macmillan.

Sacred Congregation for the Doctrine of the Faith. 1986. *Instruction on Christian Freedom and Liberation.* Boston: Daughters of St. Paul.

Samuelson, Paul Anthony. 1955. *Economics: An Introductory Analysis.* Third edition. New York: McGraw-Hill.

Sanders, E. P. 1977. *Paul and Palestinian Judaism: A Comparison of Patterns of Religion.* Philadelphia: Fortress Press.

Schenker, Adrian. 1998. "The Biblical Legislation on the Release of Slaves: The Road from Exodus to Leviticus." *Journal for the Study of the Old Testament* 78:23–41.

Schnackenburg, Rudolf. 1965. *The Moral Teaching of the New Testament.* Translated by J. Holland-Smith and W. J. O'Hara. Freiburg: Herder.

Schrage, Wolfgang. 1988. *The Ethics of the New Testament.* Translated by David E. Green. Philadelphia: Fortress Press.

Schweitzer, Albert. 1910. *The Quest of the Historical Jesus: A Critical Study of Its Progress from Reimarus to Wrede.* Translated by W. Montgomery. London: Adam and Charles Black.

Sen, Amartya K. 1982. *Poverty and Famines: An Essay on Entitlement and Deprivation.* New York: Oxford University Press.

———. 1999. *Development as Freedom.* New York: Random House.

Smith, Adam. [1776] 1937. *The Wealth of Nations*. Edited by Edwin Canaan. New York: Modern Library.

Soss, Neal. 1973. "Old Testament Law and Economic Society." *Journal of the History of Ideas* 34:323–44.

Spengler, Joseph. 1980. *Origins of Economic Thought and Justice*. Carbondale: Southern Illinois University Press.

Stein, S. 1953. "The Laws on Interest in the Old Testament." *Journal of Theological Studies* 4:161–70.

Stump, Eleonore, and Norman Kretzmann. 1988. "Being and Goodness." In *Divine and Human Action: Essays in the Metaphysics of Theism,* edited by Thomas V. Morris. Ithaca, NY: Cornell University Press.

Suits, Bernard. 1978. *The Grasshopper: Games, Life and Utopia*. Toronto: University of Toronto Press.

Sumner, John Bird. [1816] 1850. *A Treatise on the Records of the Creation and on the Moral Attributes of the Creator*. Sixth edition. London: J. Hatchard.

Synod of Bishops. 1971. *Justice in the World*. Boston: Daughters of St. Paul.

te Velde, Rudi A. 1995. *Participation and Substantiality in Thomas Aquinas*. Leiden and New York: E. J. Brill.

Thomas, Jean. 1955. "The Love of Our Neighbour and the Economics of Giving." In *Love of Our Neighbour,* edited by Albert Plé. Translated by Donald Attwater and R. F. Trevett. London: Blackfriars Publications.

Vatican Council II. 1965. *Gaudium et Spes*. Boston: Daughters of St. Paul.

Ver Eecke, Wilfried. 1998. "The Concept of a 'Merit Good': The Ethical Dimension in Economic Theory and the History of Economic Thought or the Transformation of Economics into Socio-economics." *Journal of Socio-economics* 27:133–53.

Verhey, Allen. 1984. *The Great Reversal: Ethics and the New Testament*. Grand Rapids, MI: Eerdmans.

von Rad, Gerhard. 1966a. "The Promised Land and Yahweh's Land in the Hexateuch." In *The Problem of the Hexateuch and Other Essays*. Translated by E. W. Trueman Dicken. New York: McGraw-Hill.

———. 1966b. "There Remains Still a Rest for the People of God: An Investigation of a Biblical Conception." In *The Problem of the Hexateuch and Other Essays*. Translated by E. W. Trueman Dicken. New York: McGraw-Hill.

von Waldow, H. Eberhard. 1970. "Social Responsibility and Social Structure in Early Israel." *Catholic Biblical Quarterly* 32:182–204.

———. 1974. "Israel and Her Land: Some Theological Considerations." In *A Light Unto My Path: Old Testament Studies in Honor of Jacob M. Myers,* edited by Howard N. Bream, Ralph D. Heim, and Carey A. Moore. Philadelphia: Temple University Press.

von Wieser, Friedrich. [1889] 1988. *Natural Value*. Edited by William Smart. Fairfield, NJ: A. M. Kelley.

Walzer, Michael. 1983. *Spheres of Justice: A Defense of Pluralism and Equality*. New York: Basic Books.

Waterman, A.M.C. 1983a. "Malthus as a Theologian: The *First Essay* and the Relation between Political Economy and Christian Theology." In *Malthus, Past and Present,* edited by J. Dupâquier, A. Fauve-Chamoux, and E. Grebenik. New York: Academic Press.

———. 1983b. "The Ideological Alliance of Political Economy and Christian Theology, 1798–1833." *Journal of Ecclesiastical History* 34:231–44.

———. 1991a. *Revolution, Economics, and Religion: Christian Political Economy, 1798–1833*. New York: Cambridge University Press.

———. 1991b. "The Intellectual Context of *Rerum Novarum*." *Review of Social Economy* 49:465–82.

Weinfeld, M. 1961. "The Origin of the Humanism in Deuteronomy." *Journal of Biblical Literature* 80:241–47.

Wheeler, Sondra Ely. 1995. *Wealth as Peril and Obligation: The New Testament on Possessions*. Grand Rapids, MI: Eerdmans.

Wippel, John. 1987. "Thomas Aquinas and Participation." In *Studies in Medieval Philosophy*. Washington, DC: Catholic University of America Press.

———. 2000. "Thomas Aquinas on Creatures." *International Philosophical Quarterly* 40:197–213.

Wolff, Hans Walter. 1973. "Masters and Slaves: On Overcoming Class-Struggle in the Old Testament." *Interpretation* 27:259–72.

World Bank. 2000. *World Development Report 2000/2001: Attacking Poverty*. New York: Oxford University Press.

Wright, Christopher. 1990. *God's People in God's Land: Family, Land, and Property in the Old Testament*. Grand Rapids, MI: Eerdmans.

Wright, John. 1957. *The Order of the Universe in the Theology of St. Thomas Aquinas*. Analecta Gregoriana 89. Rome: Apud Aedes Universitatis Gregorianae.

———. 1967. "Universe, Order of." *New Catholic Encyclopedia* 14:457–61.

Ziesler, J. A. 1972. *The Meaning of Righteousness in Paul: A Linguistic and Theological Enquiry*. Cambridge: Cambridge University Press.

INDEX

widows, orphans, and strangers in,
47, 50, 63, 69, 71
law of unintended consequences,
189–90
Leibniz, Gottfried Wilhelm, 157
LeMahieu, D. L., on Malthus, 4, 5–6, 10,
185, 189, 239n.5
Leviticus, 245n.8
18:1–5, 62
18:24–30, 49
19:2, 62, 104, 144
19:9–10, 50
19:33, 63
19:35–37, 63
20:7–8, 62
20:22, 49, 62
20:24, 62, 74, 244n.28
20:26, 62, 244n.25
21:8, 62
21:15, 62
21:23, 62
22:9, 62
22:16, 62
22:31, 62
22:32, 62
23:22, 50
25, 50, 53, 84, 87, 88–91, 92, 100,
243n.18, 246nn.15, 20, 26,
248n.48
25:1–7, 50, 51
25:2, 243n.10
25:18–22, 52, 88–90, 245n.6
25:18–24, 50, 51
25:23, 47, 54, 67, 68
25:35–37, 50
25:35–38, 63, 97
25:36–37, 50
25:39–43, 51, 63, 83
25:47–55, 51, 83
26, 245n.6
26:1–13, 63
26:40–45, 63
Code of Holiness (17–26), 50, 61, 70,
85, 99–102, 173, 248n.48
vs. Deuteronomy, 80, 84, 85, 87,
99–102, 246n.15,
248n.48

vs. Exodus, 87, 99–102, 246n.15,
248n.48
Lipit-Ishtar of Isin, code of, 245n.13
loans
among Assyrians, 78–79, 80
among Babylonians, 78–79, 245n.13
debt remission, 15, 50–51, 53, 54, 55,
58, 63, 76–82, 80, 84, 91, 92, 97,
100, 137, 174, 177, 242n.5,
243nn.10, 11, 244n.19, 245n.14,
246nn.15, 26
to foreigners, 81, 97, 98, 248n.44
grain loans vs. money loans, 51, 79,
91–92, 243n.14
with high interest rates, 76, 78–82,
91–92, 247n.29
and Hillel, 77, 81
among Ifugaos, 78, 245n.12
interest-free loans, 15, 50, 63, 79–82,
84, 93, 96–97, 98–99, 177, 248n.43
in modern economy, 248n.45
moral suasion regarding, 81–82
to the needy, 50, 77, 81–82, 84,
95–96, 97–98, 245n.14
and opportunity costs, 78–82
in Persian empire, 79
pledges for, 50, 63, 78, 81, 84, 87,
95–96
prosbul, 76–77, 81
in Ptolemaic Egypt, 79, 80
in Roman Egypt, 80
usury, 60, 78, 92, 245n.11
Locke, John, 166, 170
Lohfink, Norbert, 71, 74, 75, 81, 122,
172, 243n.18, 244n.1, 245n.5,
252n.13
on Covenant Code, 93
on Deuteronomy 15:1–11, 176
on equality, 53
on the Exodus, 48, 55, 57, 59, 103
on God's concern for the poor, 49
on God's sovereignty, 52
on Israel as contrast-society, 62, 66,
94
on land ownership, 46
on poverty, 49, 55, 56, 70, 80, 176,
185, 194

Albino Barrera, O.P., is professor of humanities at Providence College, where he teaches theology and economics.